# DREAM JOB

## MY WILD RIDE ON THE CORPORATE SIDE, WITH THE LEAFS, THE RAPTORS AND TFC

## RICHARD PEDDIE

### WITH LAWRENCE SCANLAN

HarperCollins*Publishers*Ltd

*Dream Job*
Copyright © 2013 by Richard Peddie.
All rights reserved.

Published by HarperCollins Publishers Ltd

Originally published in Canada by HarperCollins Publishers Ltd in a hardcover edition: 2013
This trade paperback edition: 2014

HarperCollins books may be purchased for educational, business,
or sales promotional use through our Special Markets Department.

HarperCollins Publishers Ltd
2 Bloor Street East, 20th Floor
Toronto, Ontario, Canada
M4W 1A8

www.harpercollins.ca

Library and Archives Canada Cataloguing in Publication
information is available upon request

ISBN 978-1-44341-877-5

Printed and bound in the United States of America
RRD 9 8 7 6 5 4 3 2 1

**"LEADERSHIP DEVELOPS DAILY, NOT IN A DAY."**
—John Maxwell, *The 21 Irrefutable Laws of Leadership*

# CONTENTS

# CONTENTS

# CHAPTER 1

# "A HUNDRED THOUSAND PEOPLE WANT MY JOB..."

The popcorn at Maple Leaf Gardens was stale. Really, really stale. And it had been stale for a long, long time without anyone apparently noticing. I noticed.

I was telling this to Lawrence Scanlan as we toured the Air Canada Centre—which I am proud to say I was instrumental in building and whose cornerstone bears my name. Lawrence is the writer who was going to help me write my memoir, and we were just days into the project. He is also a long-standing Leaf fan from southeastern Ontario and had expressed an interest in seeing the ACC, the dressing rooms, the boardrooms, the works. The Leafs, I told him as I played tour guide, played their last game at the Gardens on February 13, 1999, and their first game at the Air Canada Centre a week later. Much connects the old barn on Carlton Street that Conn Smythe famously built in 1931 and the still-slick and constantly being reinvented hockey/basketball palace by Union Station, but much separates them too.

The only food you could get at the Gardens, I told Lawrence as we paused by the gleaming copper kettles of the microbrewery inside the ACC, was pizza and hot dogs—that and stale popcorn. The reason it was stale was this: they had far too few popcorn makers to make it fresh, so it was produced in batches weeks and months ahead of time. The whole operation was *archaic*.

I was appalled, and I'm still appalled—a decade and a half later. My first forays as a young entrepreneur and CEO were in the world of potato chips and crescent rolls, with Hostess and Pillsbury, and I well knew how freshness and customer service counted. Two words capture my lifelong approach to business: "vision" and "values"— two seemingly simple words that have long guided me on where I wanted to go with my dreams and precisely how I planned to get there. I had dreamed since I was twenty years old of being the president of an NBA basketball team, and every move I had made in my career was meant to inch me closer to that goal. One of the values we would adopt at the Air Canada Centre was "Excite every fan," so the notion of peddling old popcorn to fans was for me at best an insult and at worst a form of heresy.

Maple Leaf Gardens was the company that time forgot. It was an historic hole—with the sex scandal hanging over the place, horrid food, bad washrooms. I have always believed that management gets the workforce it deserves, and the relationship between management and the hourly staff at the Gardens was absolutely toxic. By *sex scandal* I am referring to the tragic case, brought to light only in 1997, of how some ninety children—most of them boys—were sexually abused by several Gardens employees between the 1960s and the 1980s. Red Kelly, who played for the Leafs in the '60s and coached them in the '70s, would observe a decline at the Gardens that coincided with the arrival on the scene of the late

Harold Ballard. The Gardens, Kelly said, had been run with military precision, but when Ballard came, "it was as if a bunch of pirates had taken over."

Management-staff relations at Maple Leaf Gardens were poisoned as a result. Not so at the ACC. On one of my last days on the job there, I spent the entire day giving to each of 600 employees a fine bottle of wine encased in a wooden box bearing an inscription by American novelist Brian Andrews: "Someday, the light will shine like a sun through my skin and they will say, 'What have you done with your life?' And though there are many moments, I think I will remember in the end that I will be proud to say, 'I was one of us.'"

It was a good bottle of wine from Sterling Vineyards in California's Napa Valley and supplied by Diageo, one of Maple Leaf Sports and Entertainment's corporate sponsors. I footed the bill.

When I gave a bottle to Dwane Casey, along with the other Raptor coaches, he said he would read to the players the quotation inscribed on the box before an important future playoff game. Every single employee, whether at BMO Field or Ricoh Coliseum, at our broadcast centre or on the floors and in the offices of ACC and Maple Leaf Square, got a bottle in a box. My favourite handout of the day was to each of the unionized hourly workers (ice crew, cleaners, maintenance). I had had a rough start with them fourteen years previously: I was seen as an outsider with all kinds of new ideas. They called my approach "Raptor land." In the end, we developed an authentic respect and affection for one another. This confirmed my belief that for employees as for customers, the rule is this: Respect first, affection second.

In addition to the formal retirement party put on by the Board of Directors at Maple Leaf Sports and Entertainment, there was also a part-time and full-time employees party held for me in the arena. I ended my speech by reciting the same Brian Andrews quotation that was inscribed on the wine box. I was so emotional that it took me about a minute to get it out. This was a rare showing of feeling, one that most of my employees had never seen before.

* * *

As Lawrence and I stood at Gate 1, the canyonesque entryway to the Air Canada Centre, I spotted a tall (like, really tall) man in a matching brown overcoat and fedora. I am a former Boston marathoner who used to be a rail-thin five feet, eleven inches and 140 pounds, though these days I'm closer to 185. The man clad in brown seemed to get bigger and bigger the closer we got to him: he turned out to be Jamaal Magloire, six feet, eleven inches and 265 pounds.

The Toronto Raptors centreman recognized me right away. "Hey," said the gentle giant, and a big paw reached out to envelop first my hand and then Lawrence's. Magloire, the first Canadian-born player to suit up for the Raptors, was, at age thirty-four, in the final stretch of a twelve-year career with the NBA. The team would release him in October 2012, but a month later he would be hired back as a basketball development consultant and community ambassador.

"What are you doing now, my friend?" he asked me. It was early in March 2012—exactly sixty-five days after I had stepped down as president and CEO of MLSE, a hockey/basketball/soccer/broadcasting/real estate/restaurant/rock music empire now worth $2 billion and one that I played a pivotal role in building and shaping. In my time there, not only did the Leaf franchise expand mightily but the entire MLSE corporation increased in value almost sixfold.

As we entered the ACC, I said to Lawrence, "I wonder if we've left this security pass active." He laughed and pointed out that I'd used "we," as if I were still at the helm of MLSE.

During the tour of the bowl, I pointed out what I refer to as the most expensive real estate in Toronto: the elegant suites behind the best seats down low, where the chosen of a law firm or corporation can retreat between periods. The suites are well appointed but small: it wouldn't take too many people to give them that crowded party feel. What $500,000 a year gets you is this: great seats for all hockey and basketball games and concerts, your own private suite with bench and bar seating, round tables and a TV, and a well-stocked bar. (Sometimes the suits linger in the private suites when the next period is already under way, which makes for bad optics: it looks to TV viewers that the ACC has few fans at a Leaf game. Compounding that impression is the fact that ushers allow the suits to take their seats only when there's a break in the action.)

A woman cleaning one of the suites spotted me and we hugged as she shared sad tidings.

"Did you hear the news?" she asked me. "Burt passed." Burt Riley was a twenty-one-year veteran employee.

At one point in my career, I was CEO of SkyDome—as the home of the Toronto Blue Jays was then called. I made a point of knowing the names of all 125 full-time employees. I have been the president of six large companies, and I'm strong on financials, but I actually started off in marketing. I was one of those marketing weenies. We were young and thought we knew everything. At Colgate, we wanted to make the packages bigger to accommodate promotional items such as three-dimensional plastic heads of hockey players (Brad Park, Phil Esposito, Bobby Clarke); we wanted changes to the labels and graphics. We made life hell for the plant workers. Later, as part of my training, I spent three months working in the plant, and I came to realize how important those men and women were. Knowing a person's name matters—a lot.

That day on the tour, I walked through the wide doors leading from the private suites and up the stairs into the bowl of the ACC.

I showed Lawrence the hockey seats I had had for all those years—section 119, row 9, seats 13 and 14, behind the Leaf bench at centre ice. The Raptors had played the night before, so the wooden court was still in place, the red T. Rex claw print shining at the centre of the polished parquet floor. The only human in sight was a man in uniform with a sniffer dog in a training session, going up and down the rows looking for explosives.

Then we ducked back down through the passageway, this time into the Chairman's Suite—an opulent 4,000-square-foot private restaurant with a long marble bar. During the recession of 2008, fifteen of the ACC's corporate suites were vacant. No takers. My bold idea was to remove ten suites and replace them with a restaurant. Why not, I asked at the time, create a premium experience? Why not, in other words, combine fine dining with a Leaf or Raptor game? The well-heeled can lease one of the 200 seats in the Chairman's Suite—for an annual fee of $50,000. The seats are all taken.

It's more than just about the game now for those seat holders. It's about the experience. The team isn't always going to win. But at least they can say, "I had a great steak," or "I had a great bottle of wine." The only fly in the ointment is that folks from the regular seats want to wander in when their ticket doesn't entitle them to. If you go to the Chairman's Suite page on the Air Canada Centre website, here's what you'll find it says: "The Chairman's Suite is an exclusive suite for a select few." I call it "our section 108 problem."

\* \* \*

Why, Lawrence wanted to know, did I leave MLSE when I did? We were sitting in my old Leaf seats, staring into the bowl.

I sat quiet for a moment before saying anything, then I started to talk, about winning and losing. In everything—from playing pickup basketball to launching a microwave pizza line to acquiring a soccer franchise—I was in it to win. I hated, loathed, despised losing. My success in the boardroom was rarely matched on the ice or court or soccer pitch. The stinging reproach from bitter fans was that my cohorts and I on the fifteenth floor of MLSE didn't care who won or lost as long as the profits kept rolling in. That is absolutely not the case, and I'll come back to this point later.

I do have regrets about some of the general managers I hired, and there's no escaping all the toxic email and telephone messages—even death threats—I received over the fifteen years I was connected with the Raptors of the NBA, then the Leafs of the NHL and the Marlies of the AHL (American Hockey League), and finally Toronto Football Club of Major League Soccer. I might have stayed on longer at MLSE (I'm sixty-six as I write this, yet do not lack for energy), but I just got tired of losing.

* * *

Two days after I took Lawrence through the Air Canada Centre, the *Globe and Mail* ran a piece by the eminent sports writer Roy Mac-Gregor. The subject: Brian Burke (who was famously fired in January 2013, and I have lots to say on that subject too). What "Burkie" said about his job as general manager of the Leafs equally applied to me and my job at MLSE. "The place that hockey occupies in the universe that is Toronto, the place that the Leafs occupy," Burke told MacGregor, "is that it's No. 1. And there are no analogies for it in other sports. I was talking to Theo Epstein one time when he was still running the Boston Red Sox and he said, 'Is your job like mine?' and I said, 'Theo, the GM of the Toronto Maple Leafs is like the GM of the Patriots, Celtics, Red Sox and Bruins combined. There are five million Leaf fans in Toronto and millions all over Canada. Wherever we go, we see blue. And they all know more about running this hockey team than I do.'"

Brian Burke had been GM of the Vancouver Canucks and of the Anaheim Ducks when the latter team won the Stanley Cup. Neither of those jobs had prepared him for the roller-coaster ride he had in Toronto.

"I have the best job in hockey," Burke told MacGregor, "and it's the worst job in hockey. But I wouldn't trade places with anybody."

I could say the same thing about myself. Steve Stavro, a former Leaf owner, clashed mightily and often with me. I once left a board meeting so enraged at him that I threw a thick binder twenty feet across the hallway. The binder jacked open and the papers were sent flying. In those days, Stavro and I sometimes sat side by side to watch the Leafs. In the heat of a game, especially a playoff game, the veins on Stavro's neck would bulge and he'd hammer his fist into my shoulder. Stavro once told me, "Richard, a hundred people want your job." To which I replied, "Steve, a hundred thousand people want my job." Or at least they think they do.

# CHAPTER 2

# "YOU'RE DEAD"

The death threat came at five in the morning and was left on my voice mail. Was the caller a security guard? A maintenance worker? An employee of one of the stores? I never did find out.

The caller had uttered a stream of obscenities, followed by "You're dead," before hanging up. I already knew how important it was to fans for their team to win—and how hard it is to win; what I was about to learn was how losing could have potentially dire consequences.

This was in 2004 during what was undoubtedly the worst stretch in my fourteen years as president and CEO of Maple Leaf Sports and Entertainment. The word "fan" comes from "fanatic," and Toronto fans of hockey, basketball and football (the proper name for soccer) take winning and losing very, very seriously. Counting radio, TV, newspapers, websites and recognized bloggers, some fifty journalists cover MLSE in the city. And they love to throw oil on the fire. I remember the day (November 29, 2008)

I introduced Brian Burke as the new general manager of the Leafs. I counted the TV cameras: there were seventeen.

Looking back on that dark time in 2004, I can see that I was terribly naive. I thought I had the media figured out. My theory was that if I returned a reporter's calls, if I always talked on the record, I was amassing goodwill—like cash in a bank account. I thought I had all this equity, which I could call on later when I might really need it. How wrong I was.

On April 1, 2004, I had fired the GM of the Toronto Raptors, Glen Grunwald, along with coach Kevin O'Neill and his four assistant coaches. We had narrowly missed making the playoffs and it was time for a change. That's when the dominoes began to fall. I remember a TSN interview. It was a scrum, an awful ambush. I had said yes to a media request for an interview at halftime, assuming it would be a brief one-on-one exchange. But when I walked into the room, waiting for me were thirty reporters, who immediately encircled me. One reporter's tape recorder kept hitting my ear. At that moment I looked in that goodwill equity account of mine and saw that it was empty. Insufficient funds. I thought I had friends, but a different truth had asserted itself: the media like to see a little blood on the floor. Fans too. And that year, there was blood on the floor. Mine.

When I let Grunwald go, I didn't have a logical successor, so I brought in on an interim basis Jack McCloskey, a former long-time GM with the Detroit Pistons. He was a good man, but time had passed him by. Meanwhile, I was looking at other possible candidates, and I got approval from one owner to talk to his general manager.

In any case, I did talk to this fellow—someone I knew well—and we agreed to have another meeting once his team was out of the playoffs. So the positions of new coach and new general manager for the Raptors were both on hold, and fans and media were growing restless. Then the owner changed his mind about me speaking to his GM. Meanwhile, I had already confidently told the media that I would be announcing a new GM in a few weeks. I had even named a date on which I would be making this announcement: April 30. This was a big mistake, for it set in motion a countdown.

The draft and free agency were approaching, and there was no one in a position to make the decisions on whom to select and make trades. The team was rudderless. Our star player, Vince Carter, was agitating for Julius Erving—a legendary NBA player with no GM experience. Jack McCloskey was suggesting an assistant manager in Minnesota. My boss, Larry Tanenbaum, the chairman and long-time part owner of Maple Leaf Sports and Entertainment, was none too pleased with how I was handling all this.

I was overwhelmed. I wasn't sleeping. The media coverage was scathing and very personal. Sometimes, and foolishly, I went online to see readers' comments on these pieces. They were unsigned and unspeakably horrible.

I am, of course, just one of many public figures subjected to such withering attacks. Mike Murphy, senior vice-president of operations with the NHL, is called upon to make a decision, after viewing videotape replays, on whether a certain goal is to be counted. His office is at the ACC in what the NHL calls "the Situation Room," though it's also known as "the War Room." Fans don't forget when the call goes against the home team. Mike told me that several years ago, when he let it be known that he was in remission after being treated for cancer, someone wrote in anonymously, saying, "I hope your cancer comes back."

Colin Campbell, director of hockey operations for the NHL and formerly the league disciplinarian on questionable hits, told me about an anonymous missive that expressed this morbid wish for his son, Gregory, who plays for the Boston Bruins: "I hope your kid gets paralyzed."

Most fans, 95 per cent of them, are wonderful. They are polite, and even when they have critical comments to make, they are respectful. I enjoyed talking to them in the concourses and in the seats at the Air Canada Centre.

My contract at MLSE meant that I received tickets (in the seventh and ninth rows for basketball and hockey respectively). These tickets cost more than $200 a seat and are tough for the average fan to get. Some nights I chose to stay only for the first period of a Leaf game or the first half of a Raptor game—I wanted to wander the arena during the rest of the game or maybe spend some time in the Directors' Lounge but didn't want the seats to go empty. So one thing that gave me special joy was giving away the tickets to these seats in the lower bowl, close to the action.

This is what I would do: shortly after the gates opened, when the arena was still virtually empty, I climbed up as far as I could get in the upper bowl and searched out a certain type of fan. I was looking for an adult with a child wearing a Leaf or Raptor jersey. Invariably, I discovered that they had come a long way for the game and that this was a special occasion—and often their very first game.

I went up and stood in the aisle right in front of them, introducing myself. "What are your names?" I asked both the child and adult. Not only is this question polite, but it establishes an immediate connection. Was this their first time at the Air Canada Centre? Was this their first Leaf (or Raptor) game? Were they celebrating a special occasion, a birthday perhaps? Initially, they were a little reserved, wondering why this guy in a suit was coming up to talk to them. But that all changed when they found out that I was offering them my seats. In almost every case there was something special about these fans being at the game, and my giving them my seats made the night, some of them later told me, "priceless." I gave them my card, suggesting they could show it to the usher should their right to occupy my seats be challenged. I almost always got an email the next day or a letter in the mail a few days later. For a ten-year-old child seeing his or her first Leaf game, ninth-row seats at centre ice becomes part of a truly memorable experience. Moments such as this served to remind me that I had a special job, one I needed to enjoy more.

One survey I have seen suggests that some 60 per cent of Canadians have not been inside an NHL arena in the past five years. Whereas I've been to so many games, it's easy to forget just how special seeing a Leaf or Raptor game is.

When I used to walk the concourses of SkyDome in the early 1990s with Blue Jay president Paul Beeston, he happily greeted fans, always asked their names and then used their names during the conversation. I did that too. I also learned that wearing a big smile usually got a like response from fans. During the bad games, I had to learn how to wear a big, phony smile.

There were times, though, when I lost that smile. The annual meeting of the Ontario Teachers' Pension Plan brings together the CEOs of all the companies it has investments in to share learning and best practices. One year, an outside speaker started off his presentation with a Leaf joke. But I sure didn't laugh—in fact, I fumed all morning long. In the afternoon session I was on a panel, and right after the introductions I spoke up. I could not help myself. I told the audience that as the CEO of Maple Leaf Sports and Entertainment, I was not amused by Leaf jokes; in fact, they made me grit my teeth in anger.

I had a rule at the Air Canada Centre: if someone held up a "Fire Richard Peddie" sign, that was fine. (Though I wish in hindsight I had offered to buy some of the clever or misspelled ones: they would have made wonderfully comic props for speeches.) Fine too was the old gambit of putting a paper bag over your head to convey embarrassment over the home team's performance or to protest a losing streak. But the moment fans started to swear or disturb others nearby, they were ejected.

During those awful moments in 2004, the sentiment "Fire Peddie" was in the air. Literally. Someone hired a plane to fly past the Air Canada Centre trailing a long banner that read: "Fire Peddie." Three "Fire Peddie" websites were also up and running—two to do with the Raptors, the other with the Leafs. One day at 6 a.m. I went into a Starbucks for a coffee and the barista asked, "Have you hired a GM yet?" I wanted to scream.

Of course, the last thing I needed was late-night obscene phone calls. Like many people, I associate calls that come in the middle of the night with painful events. For one, I learned about my father's fatal heart attack through a late-night phone call from my younger brother, Tom.

I was just twenty-one when my father died. He had become overweight and had been, like my mother, a smoker most of his life (Camels, two packs a day). Looking back, I think he was a victim of the work he did and the lifestyle that went with it. A decade later, I would be running marathons, partly as a reaction to his early death. For the obvious reasons, none of the Peddie offspring ever smoked a cigarette, and Tom and I took a lifelong interest in fitness.

We were all heart-broken by my father's sudden death, but we had to get on with our lives—me as a university student and my mother in her new role now as breadwinner. She went back to school, earned a bookkeeping diploma and worked first in a retail store and then in a hotel. She eventually sold the house, for $17,000, and later died at the age of seventy from emphysema. I answered a 2 a.m. call in Winnipeg to learn that news. Calls in the small hours rarely bring good tidings.

In 2004, the vile calls to my house came in batches. The first one, full of obscenities and threats, was a rude awakening for me.

Until that time, I never once thought that I needed an unlisted telephone number. I had always believed I should be accessible to the media and to Leaf and Raptor fans. If I was comfortable sitting in the stands and walking the Air Canada Centre's concourses, why not have my number listed?

The first call at 5 a.m., laced as it was with obscenities and vague threats, was unpleasant and unsettling, but I tried to put it out of my mind. It was, I believed, a one-off. A young man had evidently come in late from a night out and decided to vent.

When I went to bed the next night, I tried to put the call out of my mind, but as I tossed and turned, I realized I was waiting for the phone to ring. And when it finally did, in the early morning at about the same time as the previous day, I wasn't really surprised. Deep down I knew that it was the same character calling, but I still felt compelled to answer the phone—maybe my brother or sister had been hurt, or something had happened at the Air Canada Centre. Though the caller let fly once again with his disturbing tirade, I did nothing—surely, I thought, he would grow weary of this.

The next morning the phone rang once more, but this time I did let it go to voice mail. Same voice, same person, but in addition to the now-familiar string of obscenities came one more chilling statement: "You're dead."

MLSE has an excellent relationship with the Toronto Police Service. So I had our head of security give the police a call and explain the situation. A young detective came to my office that morning and took my statement. Because I had the message on voice mail and because I had call display, he had information to go on. He also advised me in no uncertain terms to get an unlisted telephone number, which I did that afternoon.

Since that day, I have had numerous unlisted numbers but no late-night calls. In fact, I guard my home and mobile numbers very carefully. In all my years at MLSE, nothing—not the websites dedicated to my dismissal, not the signs held aloft at the ACC, not the cruel and negative press—were as personally violating as late-night calls to my home. I realized then that there is a very dark side to what many assume is one of the best jobs in Canada.

* * *

I believe in luck, fortune, providence—whatever it is that arranges for two people who would make a good pairing to actually become paired. Some people have the misfortune of looking all their lives and never meeting "the one." At the time of those late-night calls, I was living with Colleen McAnoy, so she had to endure them too. But I had her support, and I was glad of that.

I had met Colleen on January 17, 2002, on a blind date. I had recently divorced and was looking for a new partner—someone who was a sports fan. Ideally, this new partner would share certain values, certain liberal political leanings, a love of nature, an interest in fitness, business acumen. Colleen and I had a list of what constituted the ideal partner, and we were soon both going check, check, check.

Colleen is a sports fan through and through. In their youth, she and her brothers thought nothing of driving from Toronto to Minnesota for a baseball game. She was a season seat holder for the Toronto Raptors from day one. Colleen is a partner and CFO at Bensimon Byrne, the largest independently owned Canadian ad agency in Canada, with 150 employees. In her office, the wall behind her desk is one long stretch of framed-behind-glass basketball and football jerseys signed by the likes of Steve Nash and Jay Triano (Chris Bosh's sweater once graced the wall but now sits pointedly parked on the floor under another framed sweater—like a naughty child at a daycare given a time out). The opposite wall of shelves is home to a rich, multi-coloured gallery of sports knickknacks and trinkets, bobbleheads and souvenirs—and a shoe once worn by Chris Bosh.

I marvel at how grounded Colleen is, how kind and thoughtful. I also admire her athleticism and technical savvy, her thoroughness before a significant purchase. And she admires much about me, especially my resilience. "There are times that many would not have made it through what he has been through," she has told friends. "His job was to get beat up every day, mostly by the public, who have no clue. There were times when it got to him, but he just separated himself from it. He could go out and have a good time."

When the obscene phone calls started, Colleen tracked the source: a pay phone in the Manulife Centre at Bay and Bloor in downtown Toronto.

\* \* \*

Jeannie Ferreira has been the switchboard operator at MLSE and at Maple Leaf Gardens before that for almost forty years. MLSE has four important annual corporate awards for its employees: Rookie of the Year, Coach of the Year, (an eight-person) All-Star Team and Most Valuable Player (MVP). Jeannie won MVP a few years back. I have always judged the legitimacy of the MLSE awards by the reaction of the staff and the recipient. In Jeannie's case, she received a lengthy standing ovation from hundreds of employees, and she cried. Perfect.

If I had been away and didn't know the score of the Leaf game the previous night, I could either check online or I could call Jeannie and listen to her tone when she answered the phone. I could always hear it in her voice when the home team lost.

For some Leaf fans, winning is everything. Or is it the *only* thing?

Debra Watkinson then worked in the "people" department (what most companies call the human resources department) at

Maple Leaf Sports and Entertainment. She described having her lunch at a small park near the ACC late in the summer of 2012. Just before heading back to the office, she checked her phone for emails—a move that brought up several local Wi-Fi networks. One was called "Leafs Suck."

Debra was gobsmacked. "Really?" she said in a note to me. "Someone feels that personally connected to a sports team's performance that they label their home Internet connection that way?" What Debra had encountered was something I had known a long time: in Toronto and for many fans, sports is not entertainment. It's personal, tantamount to religion.

I had this morbid fascination with fan rage, and I kept a file. One clipping, from 2011, reported that two men were shot in the parking lot at Candlestick Park after a San Francisco 49ers preseason football game. One of the victims was apparently wearing a T-shirt that read, "Fuck the Niners." Earlier that year, a San Francisco Giants baseball fan was beaten in the parking lot at Dodger Stadium. That man, a young paramedic named Bryan Stow, suffered brain damage and is permanently disabled.

Finally, from the annals of American college football, how's this for fan anger? A sixty-three-year-old University of Alabama fan, former state trooper Harvey Updyke, was charged with criminal mischief for dumping herbicide in 2010 on two century-old oak trees at historic Toomer's Corner in Auburn, Alabama, where Auburn Tiger fans have traditionally celebrated victories by decorating the trees with toilet paper. The case was mind-boggling, and sad: Updyke had named his daughter Crimson Tide (the Alabama team's nickname) and his son Bear (after former Alabama coach "Bear" Bryant). He wanted to name another child Ally 'Bama, but his third wife vetoed it. Even his dog, Nick, was named after Alabama's coach, Nick Saban. Broadcaster Paul Finebaum wrote a piece for SportsIllustrated.com in which he described a regular caller to his Birmingham-based radio show, a man who called himself "Al from Dadeville" (though it was likely Updyke) boasting about the crime and then later expressing deep remorse amid fears he would go to prison and there die a violent death. This obsessed football fan admitted to Finebaum that, in hindsight, he had been "just too full of 'Bama." Updyke was sentenced to six months in jail and credited with 104 days for time already served. He was released in June 2013.

A fan once wrote in to tell me that the hot dogs at the Air Canada Centre didn't taste very good. I would get such letters—about lousy hot dogs, unfriendly staff, people smoking, too-loud music—when the team was losing, but seldom when the team was winning. The fans are heavily invested in the fate of their team, and the more they pay for tickets, the more they are invested and the more winning and losing come to mean for them. The same is true of Toronto's football and basketball fans.

When we announced our decision to draft Charlie Villanueva at a 2005 Raptor party, I overheard one fan say, "This is the worst day of my life." Charlie didn't turn out all that well—for us and especially for the Detroit Pistons, who eventually signed him to a really bad deal (a five-year contract worth $35 million). But an errant draft choice makes this the worst day of your life?

I was leaving BMO Field one day after the Toronto Football Club had lost a game. Behind me I heard someone say, "I think that's Richard Peddie. I've always said, 'If I ever saw him, I'd take a swing at him.'" With me was my wife, Colleen, a fine and fit athlete. She and I have run together for years, and although I used to be faster than her, that was no longer true. Colleen had done some boxing and lost a split decision the previous spring in a charity boxing match. She was keen to defend me.

"You want to hit him," she told the guy, "you have to hit me first." In any case, the situation was defused. No punches thrown.

But there was always that risk. At the Air Canada Centre, I would sit in my usual seat nine rows behind the Leaf bench and I would walk the concourses. In 2010 I started carrying a little clicker I could press to bring security running. That same year, a security guard named Bill Mooney was posted in the passageway near our seats to keep an eye on Larry Tanenbaum and me. He'd escort us to the parking garage. Never once did I have to use the clicker. Although I never felt threatened, I *could* feel the hostility in the air and so took Colleen's advice to never ride the subway home after a game. Looking back, I believe that MLSE should have suites set aside for owners and executives so they are spared the umbrage of fans—especially when things are going sour on the ice, the court or the football pitch.

I'm retired now, and I don't miss the anger of fans. I certainly don't miss losing, which sometimes made me nauseous. I remember being at a Leaf game in November 2011; we were in first place, yet fans booed the players off the ice at the end of the second period. When I was in the food business, our product was always the same. Customers didn't boo me. But with sports teams, you can't guarantee the "product." It changes minute to minute.

In time, I'll be able to go to a Raptor game, say, and not worry about hot dog sales or ticket renewals. In the months after I left MLSE, I worried about then Leaf general manager Brian Burke and how he was being treated in the press, and now I worry about his replacement, Dave Nonis. I'll continue to worry for a while about missed opportunities (will a Real Sports Bar & Grill, modelled on the one at the Air Canada Centre, go into Vancouver—or not?) If I were still in the president's and CEO's chairs, I'd be on the phone and in the thick of it. As every month passes, I know less and less about what's really going on at Maple Leaf Sports and Entertainment. And that suits me fine. I don't mind the silence.

In my twenty-two years of working in sports and entertainment, I saw a dramatic change in the attitude and virtual behaviour of fans. Two things happened. The world of media become much more competitive—with radio, TV, newspapers, websites and bloggers competing for eyes and ears. Often this competition manifests itself in who can be the most negative about the city's sports teams. The other big change was the advent of social media vehicles such as Twitter and Facebook. Fans became their own media outlets.

I laugh when I read some fans' comments on published reports, the comments that start with "As I predicted back in . . ." In many digital vehicles, fans can hide behind ridiculous handles and phony names. Without the accountability that comes with writing under your own name, some people have lost their civility and say the most awful things. Just read the responses to articles in the *Toronto Sun* sometime. They are often illiterate but also racist, homophobic and sexist. Other areas of society are not immune to this hateful stuff. Politicians, entrepreneurs, ordinary individuals and columnists get this type of treatment too. I like what the *Windsor Star* and the *New York Times*, among other publications, do to encourage readers responding to articles to be more civil: to comment, you must first identify yourself.

Today, well-run companies monitor social media and interact with it. MLSE has a manager of social media who keeps up a steady dialogue with many of its fans. Interestingly, many fans who respond to a newspaper article or tweet that they don't like what's going on and are going to cancel their season seats are not even seat holders. If fans gave their names in an article, we looked them up in our files and then contacted them. Often they didn't exist in our records. Likewise, a recent article in the *Harvard Business Review* pointed out that many of the people complaining about this or that company are not even customers.

Much of the time, fans have it wrong. They're extremely knowledgeable, many of them, but they're not in possession of all the facts—what a junior hockey coach or college basketball coach truly felt about this or that player, say. Or what the confidential psychological and medical testing revealed. Or what our scouts were saying. Or what the police checks revealed.

Let's look, for example, at the hiring of coaches and general managers. In 2007, I was trying to save the job of John Ferguson Jr., then the floundering general manager of the Leafs. Should we bring in Scotty Bowman, who had enjoyed a sparkling career as a coach in the NHL, to help Ferguson? Or should we sack Ferguson and bring in Bowman as GM?

I didn't want it getting out that we were having these discussions, so I arranged a cloak-and-dagger meeting at my condominium. To avoid being seen by the concierge (a long-time Leaf fan), I met Scotty in the garage and spirited him up to my place. I remember him animatedly waving a newspaper—an anonymous source had let it be known that he was being interviewed for the Leaf job.

"That's me," he said, pointing to the article.

Yeah, I sighed. That's you all right, Scotty. I was convinced that he himself was often the anonymous source. Bowman had certainly proven his mettle as a coach, and the media were convinced he'd make a great GM. I was not. He was asking for a lot of money (much over the going rate) to general manage the Leafs—much of the time from a home in Florida. An academic I had hired to do a statistical analysis of prospective GMs liked him based on the statistical model, but my contacts in Detroit and Montreal, where Bowman had worked previously, advised against hiring him. They were senior people and while they acknowledged his great success as a coach, they did not believe that he possessed the skills to be successful in a GM role. Bowman and I met twice and talked for a total of five hours before I introduced him to Larry Tanenbaum. But in the end, I decided against hiring him.

Today, MLSE relies heavily on psychological testing as part of the hiring process. Hire slowly, fire quickly was my mantra. Such testing, had it been firmly in place from the beginning of my tenure, might have spared me some grief. Kevin O'Neill, Raptor coach in 2003, drove all night to get to the interview, arriving with a binder full of notes to show how prepared he was as coach. But he was hot-tempered. I liked Sam Mitchell, Raptor coach from 2004 to 2009 and coach of the year in 2006. He was hired in mid-June. By July he was fighting with the GM, Rob Babcock, who soon wanted to fire Sam. Jay Triano, the Canadian-born coach of the Raptors from 2008 to 2011, was a wonderful guy, but he wasn't edgy or aggressive enough. Psychological testing would have shown that—and maybe spared us Kevin O'Neill.

Like the fans, the media too are not generally enlightened by all the facts. Most reporters have only a flimsy grip on the financial side of sports (Dave Shoalts at the *Globe and Mail*, Theresa Tedesco at the *National Post* and Michael Grange at Sportsnet are exceptions), and many reporters delight in stirring the pot. Ron Wilson's firing as the coach of the Toronto Maple Leafs on March 2, 2012, followed a two-month "watch" in the *Toronto Sun*, as that paper seemed to take delight in waiting for the axe to fall.

But the most egregious error that both fans and the media typically make is to assume that owners and CEOs—and especially those connected with profitable teams such as the Toronto Maple Leafs—don't care whether the team wins or loses. That only the bottom line matters.

I have enormous respect for Larry Tanenbaum. But he and I once tangled over Vince Carter when that player was being relied upon to take the Raptors to the next level. After that, Larry and I were very cool to each other for about a year. Steve Stavro, another part owner of the Leafs, likewise almost came to blows with me: he was so angry on one occasion that I worried he would have a heart attack. When I was in charge at SkyDome, then Toronto Argonauts owner Harry Ornest—in his late sixties and twenty-four years my senior—and I were pretty close to fisticuffs. I detail these encounters in later chapters, but the point I want to make here is that if you think the fans are alone in their passion and their anger, you're wrong. Boardrooms in Toronto and all over North America can get hot too. Very hot.

Sometimes disgruntled fans find amusing and creative ways to vent their frustration. Before one Toronto Football Club (TFC) game, some fans handed out "money-hungry" (or so it said on the fake currency) $200 bills, with an image of my head superimposed on an image of a naked man. A very fit naked man. Tom Anselmi, the COO at the time, had taken on the TFC file—the thinking being that once I retired he would be promoted to my position (which happened—more or less—in 2012. Tom was made president and COO, one rung below CEO). We had thought to give him a taste of running a professional team.

I showed Tom one of these ersatz bills and jokingly said, "You deserve this recognition, not me."

Almost all owners and team managers get the same rough treatment when their teams run afoul of the fans. I remember talking to my friend Tom Wilson, then president of Palace Sports and Entertainment (which owns the Detroit Pistons of the NBA and, formerly, the Tampa Bay Lightning), and now president of the Detroit Red Wings. I was complaining about the first "Fire Peddie" website, launched by a disgruntled Raptor fan. "You *just* got your first one?" he asked. "About time you joined the club."

I was the guy whom Toronto fans loved to hate. That wasn't always the case. In my early days at MLSE, the Leafs were making the playoffs every year and we were competing for a Stanley Cup. Ken Dryden, the former Hab goaltender who had joined the Leafs as president in 1997, said to me around that time, "You're the Teflon man—nothing sticks to you."

If that were true, it didn't last long. The NHL lockout that cancelled the 2004–2005 season, a new collective bargaining agreement that restricted player spending, the John Ferguson years on the Leaf side, the Vince Carter drama and the Rob Babcock mistake on the Raptor side: all these things stoked the flames. In hindsight, I can see how I made my situation worse by making myself available to reporters and broadcasters. I *liked* being on TV and being quoted in the press. I simply talked too much—especially about the successful business side of MLSE and its profitability. Fans and media don't want to hear from suits. They just want their team to win.

Presidents and owners who have a say about their teams are seen as meddlers. In my time with MLSE, I never once told a GM whom to draft, trade, sign as a free agent or play more—or less. My mistake was that I knew too much because I always knew the details behind our decisions. And when I talked to a broadcaster or reporter, I could explain the rationale behind the move. Fans and the media confused my knowledge with meddling. After a while I just shut up.

But if the fans sometimes made me crazy, reporters made me crazier. Writers and broadcasters speculate, gossip, invent and sometimes even lie. One time I called out a newspaper writer about a blatant error in his article. His reply? "It doesn't matter—I just need to be correct 80 per cent of the time." (Wouldn't he have made a fine surgeon?)

A radio personality similarly told me that the accuracy of his sports reporting counts for little. "I am really just in the entertainment business," he said. I call the talking heads on the sports channels SYWGs—Some Young White Guys who read from prompters and who generally don't know much more than the average fan. Then there are the commentators on draft night or between periods: ex-GMs and coaches who often had lousy records running their teams but who are now "experts." The networks give these individuals multiple TV, weblog and Twitter platforms, all of which give them even more credibility. My advice to fans? Look up the stats on the performance of these guys and decide for yourself whether you should believe them.

As the CEO, all I could do was hire the GM to do the job and hope he did it well. I now understand how hard it is to win, how the odds are stacked against you. Thirty to one, to be precise.

Then there was the business side of my life, and that side I could better control. I was the kind of CEO who picked up even the smallest bit of garbage from the floor at the Air Canada Centre. An employee recounts the time I was with him in the garage and spotted a Tri-Sorter (a wide container that allows for three options: waste deposit, plastic recycling and paper recycling) that lacked the three stickers showing what went where. I wanted to know how it happened that the stickers were missing. But, really, my style was to leave the issue for a few days and wait for it to be addressed. If it wasn't dealt with, the person responsible would catch it. Such attention to detail I considered part of my job.

On a ramp leading down to parking below the Air Canada Centre, a football-sized rock that should not have been there in the first place was left way too long. For me, the rock was a form of garbage and symbolic of a much wider problem involving the manager responsible. I took that one-pound rock, wrote "Think Like a Fan" on it and plunked it down on the desk of his replacement—who still has it.

At one Raptor game, I was up as usual in section 119, and I could see that a cameraman on the floor was wearing a blue T-shirt under his jacket. A Blue Jay shirt. I sent an email to the staff on the floor: "Can we make sure the camera guy walking on our floor isn't wearing someone else's gear?" I'm a very competitive guy, and I wanted as many sports dollars as possible going to my teams—the

Leafs, Marlies, Raptors and TFC. The Blue Jays and the Argos were the competition, and what I saw was a guy whose salary I was paying shilling for the enemy.

When the Air Canada Centre was built, the old Canada Post building was taken down to make way for it, though the south and east walls were retained and several art deco bas-relief pieces were incorporated into the new structure. I was amazed to discover that someone had installed peepholes in the walls to keep an eye on workers. ACC management never did that, of course, but we did want to know how our customers were being treated. We did send faux fans through the centre, asking them to report back to us on their experience. Were staff invariably courteous and helpful? Were the washrooms clean? Was the food up to standard?

I was never content to tune the engine at MLSE; I wanted to keep building new and better machines. I was always, as one of my staffers once put it, "swinging for the fences."

# CHAPTER 3

# THE EARLY YEARS

I was not an adventurous child. When I was six years old, my mother walked me the kilometre or so to school on my first day, then turned back for home. What she did not realize is that I followed her. She had to walk me back.

On the other hand, there is this memory from that first year in school: Our grade one teacher had cut out the profile of a train, with windows in each passenger car behind the engine. We were to bring in a picture of ourselves and place the photo where we wanted to be in the train. Which window did I choose? None. I wanted to be in the locomotive, *at the head* of the train. I didn't always want to be the one to try things first, and yet . . . I was bossy with my brother, Tom (who was one year and ten days younger than me), and I was bossy with my friends. "Let's do *this*," I'd say, and they would follow my lead. I gathered friends and organized baseball games—we preferred hardball to softball—and invariably I made myself coach.

Smell is the gateway to memory, and for me one of the most powerful smells of my childhood is the sharp tang of oil and metal that my father brought home on his hands from his job at Colonial Tool—a Windsor firm that made precision parts for the auto industry. My uncle and cousins all worked on the line at Chrysler or Ford. With overtime, a man in his early twenties could soon make as much money as a university graduate did: enough in the 1960s to purchase a muscle car that you cleaned and polished and then showed off on a Saturday night at the local A&W. Some of us worked summers at National Radiator—"the finger factory," as it was called. Maybe no one had actually lost digits in that plant, but urban myth suggested they had.

My father was a skilled tradesman and a union man who knew that the union ensured a fair wage. But he also realized that unions can protect bad workers and limit productivity.

Lawrence Edward Peddie (or Lee, as friends and relations called him) believed in fairness, teamwork, hard work—and telling the truth. One day, the police showed up at the house. Along with a friend, my brother, Tom, and I had indulged in a little mischief behind the high school, burning our notebooks at the end of the school year. No drugs or alcohol were involved; it was nothing more than a little rebelliousness. The problem was that the charred spines of some of my notebooks had drifted on the wind, landing on the properties of numerous neighbours who lived near the school, one of whom spotted my name and called the police.

"What were you guys doing last night?" the officer asked me. I could tell by his demeanour that the jig was up.

"We burnt our notebooks."

"Yes, you did," he said, and I was marched over to the house of the neighbour who had called the police, to apologize and clean up the mess.

My mother, June Peddie, was a stay-at-home mother, looking after Tom and me and our older sister, Carol. My mother could sometimes be abrupt or dismissive, and I can sometimes be that way too.

The five of us lived in a tiny two-storey, postwar house at 479 Roseland Drive East in Windsor. There were no curbs on the street, just little drainage ditches, with two large boulders marking the end of our driveway. Defining our half-acre property was an eight-foot-high prickly hedge whose rosehips drew brown thrashers and cardinals. Even as a boy, I was keen on birds. I was in grade four when my parents gave me an Audubon book that must have weighed ten pounds.

During spring, when the birds were migrating north, my father would take Tom and me out of school—writing a note to our teachers to explain why—and drive us to nearby Point Pelee National Park to bird watch. I remember the joy of seeing my first indigo bunting. We'd stop at a creamery in Leamington on the way home. I have vivid memories of my father driving our 1956 Dodge, holding out an extra ice cream cone to the family dog in the back seat. Tornado was a mixed-breed cocker spaniel who would live to the ripe old age of seventeen.

My father had served in the army during the Second World War, teaching soldiers how to shoot before they were sent overseas. He likewise taught Tom and me to shoot—starlings and crows. My father was intensely interested in birds, but in his eyes there were good birds and bad birds, and starlings and crows fell into the latter category. When I was sixteen years old, I shot a starling. That act simply did not feel right, and it marked the last time I picked up a gun.

We were a working-class family. My parents were careful with money, and we ate liver, lower-quality cuts of meat, and eggs if they happened to be on sale. I never felt poor, but I recognized that there were others who had more. Still, every few years my father bought a new car. I remember one yellow Impala, and a Rambler we called the Green Pig. Vacation meant renting a simple cabin with an ice-block fridge on Manitoulin Island. One year in the late 1950s, we all piled into the car and drove to Florida—that was special. What stuck with me was how blacks in the Deep South had to use separate washrooms and drinking fountains. I was ten years old and it was my first brush with racism. I remember my father giving an especially generous tip to the black bus boy in our hotel. There wasn't a racist bone in my father's body.

In our house, books and sports mattered. My father stood six feet, two inches tall and was a talented athlete (including baseball player) who thought nothing of swimming the two-and-a-half-kilometre span of the Detroit River. A voracious reader who loved crossword puzzles, he would read aloud to us Thornton Burgess books (*The Adventures of Sammy Jay, The Adventures of Reddy Fox*) and the Peter Rabbit series by Beatrix Potter. My love of books and of nature started here. In the backyard, Dad built large cages—home over the years to two sets of rescued baby raccoons, a pet duck, a crow, baby rabbits and a baby screech owl. When we first got the owl, we kept it in the house to let it fly around, but its habit of soiling the drapes ended that experiment.

Although my father had only a high school education, he was smart and well-read and interested in the world. He was active in the community, volunteered with the Rotary Club and coached the baseball teams that Tom and I played on—with ice cream cones all around and the honking of horns when we won. Tom was a fine catcher, and Dad built a backstop in the backyard for us. In winter, my father created a floodlit ice rink at the side of the house, and I can see him yet, in the cold dark with the garden hose making fresh ice. During the winter, Tom and I played shinny in the basement, and when the weather allowed it we shot hoops at nearby Ivor Chandler Public School (since torn down). Tom was by far the better athlete—indeed, he was Athlete of the Year in high school, and a star football and basketball player. Even now, at the age of sixty-five, he does Ironman competitions. We never fought and remain the best of friends. Every summer we go away on what we call the "brothers bonding weekend," spent canoeing, biking or golfing somewhere.

But as a child I was actually closer to my sister, Carol, who was six years my elder. She took me to concerts and art galleries. The Miss Manners of the family, she taught me to eat with my mouth closed, to keep my fingernails clean and to send handwritten thank-you notes when called for. All useful lessons that I retain to this day. Every year, on Mother's Day (though I call it Sister's Day), I send her flowers.

My father installed a chin-up bar in the backyard, which Tom and I used a lot. I weighed 129 pounds, but I was strong and wiry. One year I set a record for my high school with thirty consecutive pull-ups. But it wasn't all play on Roseland Drive: Tom, Carol and I were all expected to do chores around the house, to do the dishes, cut the lawn and shovel the snow. In our early high school years, Tom and I had a lawn-cutting business. We literally ran with the lawn mowers; we ran because we were both kinetic types, and the faster we got the job done, the more time there was for play. Yet we were (and remain) meticulous, and we took great pride that a proper trim with hedge clippers was part of the Peddie brothers' service. Later, I worked in a Jack Fraser clothing store. I remember my Christmas cheque: $51 for fifty-one hours worked.

I was an amiable enough child, but I was never a joiner—of Cubs or Scouts or running clubs. I wasn't big on rules. The irony is that later in life I would run companies where the rules were all of my creation. My first leadership moment, if one could call it that, came in grade eight when I was made a captain of the safety patrol. I wore a white sash and a polished badge as I guided pupils across the street or took attendance in class. This was a responsibility I took very seriously.

My mother, June Peddie (née Martin), kept house and made meals—in the 1950s tradition. She was, I regret to say, a generally lousy cook who turned roast beef into shoe leather. We ate a lot of hot dogs and beans. The chief recreations for her and my father were bridge, cribbage and bowling with friends and neighbours. Strange to say, since I read history with a passion, I have no interest in the Peddie or Martin genealogy. My own family history is a kind of black hole.

\* \* \*

Our house backed onto the Roseland Golf Club. We lived a seven-iron shot from the eleventh hole, the same one that would be my undoing during a two-county golf tournament. With 400 other young golfers competing to get there, I had earned a place in the top sixteen. During the championship flight, I was in match play—with my opponent and me tied after eighteen holes. We were now in sudden death. Win the next hole and you move on; lose that hole and you're out.

I was poised over the ball. "Be careful," advised my brother, who was caddying for me. "You'll hit the ball with a practice swing." That's exactly what I did.

The headline in the sports section of the *Windsor Star*? "Dick Peddie Loses Heartbreaker."

\* \* \*

All my life to that point I had had a brush cut, but now—influenced by The Beatles, who had come on the scene—I started letting my hair grow. My father did not approve.

When I finished grade twelve at Vincent Massey Collegiate, I was a year away from making a choice: the University of Windsor or the university of Chrysler. No one in my family had ever gone to college or university. Tom and I would be pioneers.

First, though, I had to get out of high school. In those days, classes were ranked alphabetically. If you were in 9A, you were deemed to rank at the top; I was in 9H. My marks were poor and remained poor throughout high school. Going on to college or university looked like remote options for me. I lacked motivation, my work habits were poor. Biology, history and geography were okay, but math was a bridge too far. My math teacher, Mr. Morgan, told me I would never pass grade nine.

On the other hand, I had tasted factory life and I knew it wasn't for me. One summer I spent all of one day working at National Radiator for $2 an hour. I can still smell that factory floor, with its residues of oil and burnt metal. Next day I quit.

One option was to press on and take grade thirteen, but in those years all students had to pass "departmentals"—province-wide exams that all Ontario students took at precisely the same time and with anonymity, so that teachers didn't know which students they were marking. That thought terrified me. One other window would have allowed me entry into the University of Windsor, but it was a tiny one. The university was then offering something called Preliminary Year—meant to attract American students (especially ones with a talent for basketball). On that score, the program was eminently successful, as the University of Windsor won five national men's championships in the 1960s.

The problems with Prelim (for me, at least) were twofold: the tuition was $500, and you needed a mark of at least 65 per cent. I was a shade below that. My father made only $10,000 a year in those days but (bless him) he came to the aid of his middle child. As for the missing marks, my high school principal, Mr.

Whetstone, on hearing of my ambition to go to the University of Windsor, did a very kind thing. He grabbed a pencil, erased the marks on my report card and replaced them so that the average was 65.2 per cent.

"Will that do?" he asked me.

"I think so," I replied.

Many years later, I thought of Mr. Whetstone. I had thanked him at the time, of course, but not properly and not the way I should have—something I still regret.

* * *

In the 1960s, Tom and I successfully ran for student council at the University of Windsor. These were the days of sit-ins, Vietnam War protests, long hair, tie-dyed shirts and left-leaning politics. Tom and I—in our cord jackets and ties—didn't fit that mould. We were both commerce students who kept an eye on the student council budget, earning the moniker "the penny-pinching Peddies."

In the classroom, I struggled. Lots of Cs and Bs, even an F during my first year. I failed statistics and had to take the course again. Enrolled in a bachelor of commerce program, I was hard pressed to handle accounting and finance. In my business career, numbers would play a huge role, but I was thirty years old before I got comfortable with them.

In my third year, I met my first love—a nurse named Lynne who was eighteen months older than me. We'd spend weekends hunting for antiques. At one point, she gave me a burlap-covered blank journal in which I articulated my dream of one day running an NBA franchise.

By the fourth year of university, I was connecting with both my professors and the programs. The banks in those days were sending young employees—many of them married and in their mid- to late twenties—back to university. Mingling with mature and ambitious older men (only two of my eighty classmates were female) had a huge impact on me. They raised my sights. We all wanted to help one another, so we studied and played together. (And we *still* play together: even now, more than forty years later, we gather for reunions and golf weekends. I also stayed in touch with certain professors, and when some of them died I made a point of attending their funerals. "Weddings are optional," the saying goes, "but funerals are mandatory.")

My degree was in marketing, and I seemed to have a knack for it. In my final year, I was getting pretty well straight As and made the Dean's List.

Three straight years of summer jobs with Air Canada—two at the Windsor airport and one in sales promotion at company headquarters in Montreal—taught me a great deal about customer service. I learned the truth of the old saw "You catch more bees with honey than with vinegar." I was checking luggage and handwriting tickets, making boarding announcements, helping elderly passengers onto planes—prop planes such as Vanguards and Viscounts and the new DC-9s. The hours were perfect for me then: 11 a.m. to 7 p.m. I could sleep in every morning, and shoot hoops or go out with friends after work. Playing Ping-Pong with stewardesses in one of the storerooms at the airport, chatting with passengers such as Gordie Howe and members of the Ford family—this wasn't work, this was fun.

During Christmas break 1968, about twenty-five of us young university sales reps from across Canada were flown to Montreal for a course to upgrade our skills. We were essentially on-campus Air Canada sales reps, encouraging our varsity teams and fellow students to fly Air Canada. I even created my own ad campaign. This being the '60s, almost every student agent attending the Montreal course signed a manifesto demanding more pay. I was among the few dissenters. I thought the whole thing was naive. (That stance would help me get a summer job later on in the North American sales promotion department at the Air Canada offices in Montreal.)

My entire experience at the University of Windsor—the friends I made, the professors who taught me and who sometimes joined us on social occasions, the heady success of the Windsor Lancers on the basketball court—marked a turning point in my life. When I graduated, I was ready.

# CHAPTER 4

# ON A (CRESCENT) ROLL

In the spring of 1970 as I neared my last year of studying commerce at the University of Windsor, some of the big corporations—Bell, Sunoco, Colgate-Palmolive (as it was then known; now it is just Colgate), Procter & Gamble—came to the campus to hire candidates for jobs. These were opportunities for students to leap directly from school to work. The day Colgate was to come, I forgot and thus neglected to wear a suit—negating any chance of an interview. A time had been set aside for me, and now that opportunity was lost.

I immediately wrote a handwritten note apologizing for my inexcusable behaviour, a lapse, I said, that reflected badly on the school and wasted an executive's valuable time. I added that I would truly welcome another chance at an interview. That note went into my file at Colgate and when, by sheer good luck, the firm came to the campus a second time, I was granted an interview. And hired.

I look back on my career and have to concede that I had a lot of luck. A TSN commentator once observed: "When a nuclear bomb goes off, I want to be beside Richard Peddie." But I also firmly believe that luck is best defined as when preparation crosses paths with opportunity.

Here are two examples of luck that came my way.

In the summer of 1969, I worked at the Air Canada headquarters in Montreal with its North American sales promotion department. Before that, as I mentioned, I had worked summers at the airport in Windsor as a passenger agent. Flash forward almost three decades: I am the Raptors' CEO and in final negotiations with Air Canada CEO Lamar Durrett, and what helped smooth the waters between us was the swapping of stories about working at the airline.

In the spring of 1970, fresh out of university, a marketing degree in my pocket, I received several job offers (from both Bell and Sunoco) but ultimately chose a job in sales and marketing with Colgate-Palmolive. Procter & Gamble did consider me, but its psychological testing showed that I was an entrepreneurial cowboy. The phrasing is mine, but that's what I took the test results to mean. I believed that P&G was the better company, but it had a particular way of doing things and you had to fit that mould. Colgate offered employees greater freedom, and I was drawn to that. In the end, I benefited hugely from making that choice.

I started on June 1, 1970, and, as part of a training program for all new recruits, I was immediately put in sales. A week of training. Here are the keys to the car (an old green Chev). Go! That's how it was. I went into Loblaws, A&P and Dominion stores—nine calls a day. Over the course of the first six months, I missed only one day. It was more about service than selling. Still, some managers didn't want to see me, others were rude. You had to build up your confidence and accept rejection, and I had no difficulty with that. Despite my reputation as a marketer, I'm actually a better salesman.

I was living in a furnished one-bedroom apartment in Hamilton, Ontario, and ranging over a territory that included the Niagara Peninsula and the Kitchener-Waterloo area. My ambition then was to become a brand manager—and getting there meant time in sales. Purgatory to some, but not to me. Looking back, it wasn't so tough (at least not compared with the boardroom wars that came later in my career). Selling is about forcing yourself, about overcoming a "no." Selling starts with the utterance of that word.

Sales is not for everyone, but it's excellent training: no matter what work you do, at some point you have to sell ideas—or yourself—whether to a skeptical prospective employer, to someone who may want the skills or mindset you have to offer, to a banker, to your colleagues or to your superior.

By January I was back in the head office at 64 Colgate Avenue in what was then an unsavoury part of east-end Toronto (the building has since been demolished and condominiums are going up there now). Erected in 1918, the building must have been handsome in its day, with bands of red and white brick framing small square panels of glass. Inside, the hierarchy was plain to see. The building's top floor was occupied by the president and several vice-presidents, with the brand managers on the floor beneath them, and the sales force below them. I worked out of a cubicle, separated from my peers by decorative glass. The dress code forbade sports jackets, so I simply rotated through the three suits I owned and which my thin frame struggled to fill.

After sales, the next step in my training program and my first job in head office was a three-month position in the market research department. In my time there, I got hooked on market research, and what I learned—how to conduct market research, how to analyze it and the importance of it—would have a profound impact on my entire corporate career. I was doing phone interviews, leading focus groups and knocking on doors. It was a different world then: women would answer the door and let someone like me inside their homes. Asked which laundry detergent they were using, they'd often say "Tide," but after asking to see their laundry facilities, I could see that they were, in fact, using a bargain brand. I was fascinated by the psychology of all this.

At Colgate, and unlike Procter & Gamble, we often researched the impact that certain formula changes had on consumer preferences. Instead of focusing on superior quality, we looked for cost savings every year. In a liquid dishwashing soap, for example, we'd lower the amount of active ingredient (which determines cleaning efficiency) from, say, 37 to 36 per cent. Next year we'd try 35 per cent. We wondered, would customers notice? It was death by a thousand cuts and all so clear looking back. Too many changes, too many people—including green employees such as me—with their fingers in the Colgate pie.

From market research, the usual next step for trainees was to become an assistant brand manager. Much to my surprise and disappointment, the company decided to put me in the industrial engineering department for another three months. I was what the grizzled veterans in the plant called "a market weenie." Young people like me made their lives difficult by coming up with formula or package changes that, although often creative, were always more expensive and very often difficult to execute. During my time in industrial engineering, I can't say that I learned a lot about making detergent, but I did learn a lot about the people who worked in the plant. What was important to them. How they wanted to be treated and what made them tick. At the time I did not understand the importance of working effectively with a unionized workforce, but as my career progressed, it became much clearer to me. However, I was getting tired of the months of training and also a little worried. One of the recent commerce grads had already been fired. Now I was sure I ranked last among the rookies, and though I was working hard, I felt like I was struggling.

Finally I was moved to the marketing department and promoted to assistant brand manager. I worked on such forgettable brands as Wildroot Cream-Oil, Colgate Tooth Powder and Cashmere Bouquet bar soap. I also worked on more important brands, such as Colgate toothpaste. Ironically, while working on Colgate (since my future with an NHL team was still a ways off), I worked with the NHL on two separate hockey in-pack promotions. One involved small plastic heads depicting current NHL stars (the roster of the famous 1972 team that played the Russians), and the other, hockey stamps. The giveaways were real headaches for the plant people, as they had to be manually inserted into the toothpaste cartons, which then had to be individually taped shut to prevent theft. When the hockey stamps were delivered to the plant, we learned that there was no glue on them. "You want glue?" the supplier asked. "Glue is extra." Our inexperience cost the company.

Tom Knowlton—who would go on to become dean of the Faculty of Business at Ryerson University—was another University of Windsor grad (he had an MBA), hired by Colgate-Palmolive the same day I was. We weren't pals at school but at Colgate we were. Both of us remember our first early disappointment there. I was twenty-five years old and had been at Colgate for a few years by then. And I was consumed with the idea that I would be promoted to brand manager, where I could control or influence the marketing of a particular product. Indeed, all six of us new recruits who had been hired expected to become product managers within one to three years. After three years, three of the remaining five were promoted. The two who were not? Tom Knowlton and Richard Peddie. We felt absolutely gutted. I thought my career was over. Six months later, however, we were both made brand managers. I had in the meantime thankfully turned down a job to be a brand manager with Bristol-Myers. That would have been a career mistake—to show impatience.

Tom went on to enjoy a sterling career with the Kellogg Company, General Foods and the advertising agency Leo Burnett. He understands full well why he and I were held back in the beginning. We had the technical skills, but we lacked the softer skills, such as strategy and leadership. Those skills don't bloom until later. As for those three guys who became brand managers before us, all became mired in middle management.

Colgate-Palmolive placed a huge emphasis on tactical action: this meant that as a young man of twenty-six, I got a lot of hands-on experience with advertising, packaging, pricing and promotion. I was soon writing ads for Fab detergent, changing the design on the box from the colour blue to a sunburst pattern in hopes that shoppers would more easily spot it, and, in the case of Ajax detergent, putting everything from towels to silverware to dishes inside the box to entice buyers. In fact, I was creating lots of new marketing initiatives but continuing to make lots of rookie mistakes too.

The brand manager concept had started with Procter & Gamble back in the late 1940s. As brand manager (in my case, of Ajax and Fab), even though you don't truly have total control of the brand, you behave like you're the hub of that particular wheel. But you also have to work with all the other departments and brands within the company. Whatever my brands, I was their champion within the company. To this day, I still love walking through grocery stores, noting which brand has prized position on the shelf. I still use Colgate toothpaste and Palmolive liquid soap (though I eventually quit using Fab—out of pique—when it stopped using my design).

The atmosphere at Colgate was at once collegial and unrelentingly competitive. "I just got a call from a headhunter," one colleague would boast, sending the rest of us into a tailspin. "How many brands do you have?" we would ask one another. It was all very macho, and very like the contemporary television series *Mad Men*, depicting a 1960s New York ad agency. Ad agencies would hold seminars at the Royal York Hotel during Advertising Week, with the company men hitting on agency women.

I smoked a pipe in those days (though I never inhaled). Everyone smoked. I thought the Brigham pipe and cherry-flavoured tobacco lent a certain air. I remember how thick the smoke was in the office as we watched the 1972 Russia-Canada hockey series.

By 1973, my career was starting to roll. General Foods came calling and offered me a job managing Jell-O, a big and important brand. I turned it down; I liked my colleagues at Colgate. But at the same time, I was seeing flaws in the company's so-called long-range strategic plans. I remember asking why our detergent share was forecast to grow three points in three years. Because of a new brand of detergent, I was told. Which brand? They didn't know, but they knew there would be one! Phony strategic plans would be the norm for most of my consumer products career. The bad taste I got from those largely fictitious plans led me to create solid, buttoned-down plans when I later landed on the (then far) shores of Maple Leaf Sports and Entertainment.

In 1974, General Foods called once more—this time offering me Tang flavour crystals. That product has now mostly faded because more affordable and much better-quality real juices arrived on the scene. But in those days, frozen juice concentrate was seen as pricey, inconvenient and uneven in quality (given the frost and hurricanes that repeatedly ravaged Florida orange groves). Tang was a bag of chemicals; on the other hand, it offered vitamin C, it was affordable, it always tasted the same—and I believed in it (as I did all the products that came under my purview. A four-year-old could mix up a pitcher of the stuff. Tang even went to the moon with the astronauts that year. A fast-growing, major brand, the product cost so little to make that it offered almost pure profit. Tang was a feather in my cap, General Foods was a hot shop and I was now one of its new young stars.

We sold ersatz products: Jell-O, Dream Whip, Cool Whip, Minute Rice. Remember, this was the 1970s, when women were starting to move into the workforce en masse (while still being expected to cook for the family). Convenience was queen. I would spend twelve years at General Foods, rising up through the ranks. General Foods sold big brands such as Maxwell House and Sanka. I'm not sure who called it "a coffee company with hobbies," but it's a good way to describe the company. At General Foods, I worked on virtually all of its hobbies: the aforementioned Jell-O, Dream Whip, Cool Whip, and Minute Rice, as well as Kool-Aid and Post cereals (Sugar Crisp, Alpha-Bits, Honeycomb). I went from brand manager to senior brand manager to product group manager and then to marketing manager of all General Foods products with the exception of coffee. An incredible climb up the ladder in only a few years. At twenty-nine years of age, I was a company vice-president.

One very good aspect of this period in my career was that I spent a lot of time in the plants working with both managers and workers. At General Foods, a market weenie such as me was anathema to the guys running the plants, most of them with engineering degrees. The two types usually mix like oil and water. That wasn't the case with me. I continued to learn about respect, communication, getting along with people, mentoring and coaching. I did all that by getting my hands dirty.

Take, for example, my time as president of Hostess—from 1983 to 1985, my final years with General Foods. One plant and head office were in Cambridge, in southwestern Ontario. The office had a '50s feel to it, with ample oak desks, worn sofas and orange-brown curtains. It felt like my old homestead in Windsor, with this exception: the smell of cooking oil was pervasive.

The potato chip is a fresh, fragile product. In those days, I was running marathons and weight gain was not an issue for me. I *loved* potato chips. For me, there was no such thing as junk food— only junk diets. Sometimes I'd take a big bag of chips hot off the line and eat the entire package. The trick with transporting potato chips is to not ship them too far lest they lose their freshness. Hostess had four plants manufacturing chips across Canada and more than thirty feeder warehouses to deliver the product, with up to twenty trucks fanning out from each of them.

I would get in my Audi (which raised an eyebrow or two at Hostess, where the dull but reliable Dodge K car was the car of choice) and drive out to visit those warehouses, staying in cheap motels along the way. Early in the morning, I bought coffee and doughnuts for the driver-salesmen and helped load the trucks, and when riding shotgun, said I didn't mind if the driver smoked (I lied). A measure of my desire to pitch in (and my clumsiness) was when I badly scored my hand with a case cutter during an unloading operation. The potato fields supplying the Ontario Hostess plant were north of Barrie, and I walked those fields with the farmers who tilled them. I worked on the assembly line with the Portuguese women who had been working there for years. They loved it when I blew my assignment (reminiscent of the *I Love Lucy* episode when Lucy and Ethel get work on a candy assembly line). Plant managers had some fun with the president being there, and I'd often hear an announcement on the loudspeaker about a quality-control problem on the very line where I was working. My being there was both strategic and a learning opportunity for me, and it paid huge dividends. I took the custom with me: just as some people always keep a Swiss army knife in a jean pocket, I didn't leave for work without it.

When I took the job at Hostess Potato Chips, I told myself it was a two-year gig. I knew I wasn't a long-term fit with the parent company, General Foods. After only three months on the job, I had lunch with the Canadian company's CEO, Bob Hurlbut, and I said, "I've been president for only a few months—what advice would you give me?" Bob said, "Oh, there is no advice I can give you." A year later, I asked Bob's replacement for feedback. He said, "You marketing guys are always asking for feedback." Needless to say, I received no counsel from him either. I learned then that presidents rarely get real evaluations. And I decided right then that whenever and wherever I landed in the president's chair, I would give well-thought-out verbal and written evaluations to my staff.

\* \* \*

One day, my boss at General Foods, Don Loadman, shared with me some words of wisdom. "You will be a president," he said, "when others *see* you as a president." So I doubled my efforts to earn the respect of people in other areas of the company. I also decided to face the fact that I was a lousy public speaker.

"Should I take lessons?" I asked Loadman.

"You don't need to," was his reply. But Don Loadman himself was just an average speaker, and I wanted to be much better than that. I went to a Toronto voice coach named Robert Vallée. He put me on camera and had me deliver one of my old speeches. After watching me for only a couple of minutes, he stopped me and said, "What can I tell you? You suck."

Robert completely reworked my approach to public speaking, an approach I have refined over time. The key is slowing down to let the words land with your listener, and pausing at critical junctures for effect.

I have kept every speech I have given since 1983. I don't commit to making a speech when the topic has no personal appeal or when I'm not given enough time to prepare. Winston Churchill once said, "If you want me to speak for an hour—give me a moment's notice; if you want me to speak for half an hour, give me a day's notice; if you want me to speak for five minutes—give me a week." Today when I accept a speaking engagement, I open a file (a digital file now but for most of my life it was a file folder) and, over the weeks leading up to the date, jot down my thoughts, and quotes that might prove useful. Then, when I write the speech, the basics of the structure are there. To write one minute of a new speech takes me an hour, and that includes gathering ideas, researching quotes, drafting, rewriting and practising. I have found that seventeen to twenty minutes is long enough for someone to listen to me.

In 1983, after I had spent five years as a vice-president at General Foods, there occurred a major shake-up at the top. Jack Scott, the president of Hostess was being promoted to run the grocery division. I was offered his position and immediately jumped at it—without even asking what my salary would be. (Only when I got my first cheque a few weeks later did I realize that General Foods had got me on the cheap—and I didn't forget that.) I believe I was chosen because my leadership style and approach to business were well suited to Hostess, a wheeling and dealing company very unlike its parent firm.

When my promotion was announced, the first call I received was from the manager of the plant that produced the beverage and cereal products for which I was ultimately responsible. Bob Olsen was a tough nut for marketing weenies to crack. He said, "Richard, you earned this. You were our favourite for the next president, for sure." Don Loadman was right after all.

* * *

Hostess was a wonderful place to be a young president, in no small part because I had almost complete autonomy. We had the Maple

Leaf Gardens chips account, though I remember meeting the Leafs' majority owner Harold Ballard only once. I overheard him saying to King Clancy, a legendary player and by then his sidekick, "He looks like a young kid."

What a rough-and-tumble, up-and-down-the-street business was potato chips. Direct sales in those days involved a lot of off-invoice discounts. Too many, in fact, and quite out of control. After watching my Calgary sales rep try to open some new accounts, I offered to do the next one on my own. So I went into the drugstore and sold the owner on carrying Hostess products because of our quality marketing and service. I went back out to meet my rep at his truck to tell him the good news.

"What discount did you give the store?" he asked me.

"No discount," I said. "I just sold him on everything else."

"We can't do that," he said. "We give *all* stores a discount off the price." Then he went into the store to give the owner a lower, discounted price—one the owner had not requested. The problem at Hostess was this: the retail sales force fought constantly with the national sales force over discounts, with each side upping discounts to the trade and bringing truth to Pogo's saying, "We have met the enemy and he is us." Ultimately, an American company competing for the Canadian market, Frito-Lay, embarked on a campaign—not merely to match Hostess's discounts but to dramatically increase them while outspending Hostess for retail space and sales. Frito-Lay discounted Hostess to death, depressing both Hostess's profits and General Food's enthusiasm for the business. In the end, Frito-Lay bought a 50 per cent share of Hostess and, later, 100 per cent. When I was its president, Hostess held a commanding position in the Canadian marketplace. Today, it's only a very small brand.

In 1985, after twelve years, I left the General Foods family (or Kraft Foods, as it's known today). I had gone from product manager in 1974 to vice-president to president of the Hostess division in 1983. I was lucky in that the baby boom generation was just coming into the workforce and senior managers were reaching retirement age. The demographics worked in my favour.

It had been a great run and I learned much about how to operate, and how not to operate, a company. Years later I would learn the term "best practices," or as Jack Welch called them, "legitimate plagiarism." What I often learned at General Foods was what I now call "worst practices."

One was "analysis paralysis." We joked that the coffee division did only one financial analysis a year. It started on January 1 and finished December 31. General Foods analyzed new products and strategies to death. Afraid to take risks, the company was constantly being pre-empted by competitors, forcing General Foods to scramble to catch up. From that experience I vowed to be more aggressive and take risks.

Driven home to me even more was the importance of selling and getting to know the trade. I realized that I did not deal with the big issues facing me in the sales area at Hostess—and I should have. I realized that our approach to the hourly workforce was reactive and poor. We took pride in saying we fought off union drives, instead of proactively fixing the problems. (The plant was unionized a year after I left.)

I did not stay long enough; nor, frankly, was I an experienced enough president to really address important issues with the competition or to make the company more strategic or sophisticated. Before I left, my strong vice-president of operations, the late Stu Cairns, gave me an important piece of advice that I would take with me. "You should have made changes at the senior level," he said. "You didn't surround yourself with the best people."

I did, though, try a few things. Here's one example. By this stage in my career, I was coming to realize the importance of what I called "authentic recognition." General Foods was then in the habit of giving an annual president's award to every division. At Hostess, that prize went one year to a salesman who had written his own recommendation and who was widely recognized as completely undeserving. It became clear to me that poorly executed corporate awards were worse than no awards at all. If you were going to have a corporate recognition plan, it had to be credible and it had to be clear to all that the winner had earned the award.

My best recognition idea at Hostess cost less than a dollar each.

The animated spokesmen for Hostess potato chips were three little characters called The Munchies. They were on our trucks, our packages and in our advertising, and they were the very personification of craving. A few people complained that The Munchies had a marijuana connotation. As far as I was concerned, if they did, all the better. We created a huge sales contest to ensure that we made our annual profit target. All who met their target were to get a little Munchies pin with the number "1" on it. The sales force loved it, and our sales went through the roof. For months after that, everyone proudly wore the pins, which reinforced the notion that every salesman was part of the larger Hostess family.

My regrets about the promotion? For one, once you put the number "1" on a pin, where do you go from there? And two, I should have involved the entire company, including the office workers and plant people. I still have one of the pins in my personal collection. And I later used such pins successfully at both Pillsbury and SkyDome.

* * *

One day in 1985 I got a call from George Enns, a Toronto headhunter I respected. He said, "I have a great job opportunity for you at Pillsbury/Green Giant."

"How big is the company?" was my first question. At Colgate we had all believed that the next job should be a bigger job.

"Its sales are $125 million," George replied.

"I already run a $200 million company," I told him, explaining why I was declining. "I now want to run a much larger one."

"Don't turn down an opportunity until it has been offered to you" was George's advice. After countless interviews at the Pillsbury head office in Minneapolis, I definitely wanted the job. And it certainly helped me get a good compensation package when the international president said to me at the end of the interview process, "Richard, we want you to be the Canadian president and CEO. What will it take to get you"? I had learned from my mistake when I took on the Hostess job; I took the Pillsbury job, but I did not come cheap.

Back at General Foods, CEO Jack Scott could not understand why I was going to a smaller company. So he had the international president, Erv Shames, come and try to talk me out of it. He said something that really got me worried. "Never," he told me, "have I seen someone make such a huge career mistake."

Was I doing the right thing?

Years later, I was talking to John Cassaday, president and CEO of Corus Entertainment. John once worked for me at General Foods, where he was a true star, but his style did not fit that firm any more than mine did. When he announced that he was leaving to go to Campbell Soup, Erv Shames told him exactly the same thing. John and I had a laugh over that.

* * *

At Pillsbury/Green Giant, I was finally president and CEO of my own company. The offices were located in a tall tower in north Toronto off the Don Valley Parkway, and my corner office faced east. Around this time, I had pitched to Dave Nichol, then the head of Loblaw's successful President's Choice line of products. I noted that one entire wall of his office was a whiteboard; I liked the idea so much that I had a similar wall installed in my own office. Of all the offices I had worked in to this point, this was the nicest.

Pillsbury had quality products and an iconic brand spokesman in the Pillsbury Doughboy (or, as one of my marketing guys, Paul Clark, referred to him, "the little naked white guy"), the Jolly Green Giant and even the Little Green Sprout. The only problem? The company was completely asleep at the switch. The only new product was a new flavour of pizza. Consumer promotions failed to leverage our unique brand spokesmen. We thought we had a good trade reputation, but research that I immediately commissioned upon coming onboard proved that we ranked a lousy eighth out of ten food companies. And relations with our unionized workforce were at best below what they should have been.

In the weeks before taking the Pillsbury job, I was reading *In Search of Excellence*, by Tom Peters and Robert H. Waterman Jr., for ideas that could apply to my potential new company. I was pleased to learn that the parent company had launched a vision and values statement only a month before. The vision was to be "the best food company," with three core values: "People make the difference." "Quality is essential." And "Excellence must be a way of life." Great, I thought. I can work with these, and I wanted to try out the vision and values theory anyhow. So I asked how the company was rolling out the new statement. Every office employee (but none in the plants) had received an attractive pocket-size calculator with the statement on it and embossed vision-and-values plaques went up on walls across the company. That was it.

Within a month on the job, I wrote and delivered a speech that everyone in the company—including those at the company's four plants—would eventually hear. In that speech, I outlined a clear vision of what we were about to do. I listed our goals:

- Consistently live our vision and practise our three core values
- Aggressively launch new products
- Create only those consumer promotions that link to our brand spokesmen
- Acquire new companies
- Significantly improve our trade reputation
- Be a great place to work
- Become one of Canada's hot food companies

A recording of Bob Dylan's song "The Times They Are a-Changin'" played a prominent role in that speech. I needed to shake things up. Pillsbury employees thought the company was far better than it was. They had a thinly disguised contempt for accounts such as Loblaws, which they saw as an aggressive and demanding client. Their creativity was virtually non-existent. Many of the staff, including the senior management team, were simply not good enough if we wanted to be daring, different and first. Those at head office were skeptical and initially resisted the changes. The plant people were even more skeptical. When I spoke to the hourly staff at our Midland, Ontario, plant, I was openly challenged by the union steward. He said he didn't believe what I said—but gave me marks for coming out to talk to the plant people.

Three years later when the *Globe and Mail* wrote a glowing story on Pillsbury's turnaround, that same shop steward was quoted. He graciously conceded that I had done precisely what I had promised to do. Four years later, I reread the speech and was amazed by how much of it had come to pass. The action plan used a lot of the lessons learned in my fifteen years at Colgate, General

Foods and Hostess. I can remember saying after a year in that I hoped my action plan worked because head office was letting me do almost anything I wanted.

In sales, for example, our trade approach was unique. The vice-president of sales, the late Eric Hellstrom, was a giant of a man at six feet, seven inches. He was well regarded in the trade but was never given the support or the tools to do the job well. In the week before starting at Pillsbury, I called him up and asked him to meet me at an A&P store. He did not know me, and I am sure he was apprehensive about meeting his new, much younger boss. We walked the store and talked about products and trade plans. I promised to be a president who would actively help sales.

Eric and I went on to have a great relationship. When I left to go to SkyDome four years later, in 1989, he inducted me into the Pillsbury Sales Hall of Fame. We introduced two initiatives that completely reshaped our reputation in the trade. Every year we created a major sales presentation that Eric and I took to the presidents of major accounts across Canada. We had several annual themes, including "Grow with the Giant" and "Popping fresh ideas from Pillsbury." In those days, most trade presentations by consumer product companies focused on how much money the company was spending with the account. Instead, we talked about quality and creative ideas that would grow both our company and theirs. We left the numbers to the last page. Each call was intended to be a productive business meeting. We shied away from entertaining—taking buyers for dinner or Leaf games. We thought that was lazy, even phony. We believed in respect first, affection second.

Our second tactic was called "preferred supplier." Introduced by Pillsbury USA, this concept had by then been in the trade for several years. We just took it up a notch by branding it. We combined a number of departments into one preferred sales department and moved one of our young marketing stars, Allan Oberman, into the newly created position of director of preferred supplier. This program became an important piece of our annual coast-to-coast sales presentations. Results were terrific. Sales went up. Spending as a percentage went down. And our ranking among the ten food companies went from eighth to second.

One promotion was meant to underline the freshness of our products. We picked early corn from our fields one morning and had it in a creatively designed burlap bag on the buyers' desk by noon that day.

We went on a tear, from having no new products to launching fifty-four products over the course of four years. One was an important acquisition. I was wandering through a Safeway store in Winnipeg one day and decided to introduce myself to the store's grocery manager. I was young, I was feeling confident and I was looking to buy companies.

"Hi," I said. "I'm the president of Pillsbury. What's your hot seller?" He took me over to the freezer section and showed me a product called Pizza Pops. This was basically cheese and sausage enveloped in pizza dough, a calzone—though they were known as "gut bombs" by local teenagers who ate them in enormous quantities. Two entrepreneurs named Jack Klein and Hy Dachevsky were producing the Pops in a small local plant. I commissioned the global marketing research firm ACNielsen to do a report, and the numbers were through the roof. My thought: *Let's buy this operation.*

When I pitched the idea in Minneapolis, the head of acquisitions said (with me in the room), "I don't know why Richard wants to wreck such a potentially great career on this acquisition." The Pillsbury CEO's response? "If Richard really believes in it, then we should let him."

I went back to Winnipeg and made a special trip out to the strip mall where the Pizza Pops were being made. I romanced the two co-owners of the enterprise and invited one of them to Toronto.

"We'd love to buy your company," I told him. We were in my Porsche, driving down the Don Valley Parkway in the pouring rain.

"No, it's not for sale," he replied. We were both bargaining now, and perhaps he said this to drive up the price. "We get along just fine the way we are."

"I'll launch my own," I said. That statement was meant to put some fear into him. I wanted him to ponder the possibility of a corporate giant effectively wiping out his company by creating its own version of his product. I was, in fact, bluffing. But the hardball play worked, and for some $5 million we bought the company. We changed the name to Pillsbury Pizza Pops and today it is a big seller right across Canada. Oddly, the American parent company never embraced the product, and the pizza pop is one of the few food products that are available only north of the forty-ninth parallel.

Finally, the reason for my success at Pillsbury had a lot to do with refusing to stand pat on the management cards I had been dealt—as I had done at Hostess. The first thing I did was to replace my CFO with the very solid Dick Pearson from Pillsbury US. Rob Hawthorne was a very good vice-president of marketing at General Mills, but he had been passed over for president. Despite being a peer, I talked him into becoming vice-president of marketing at Pillsbury, where he significantly upgraded the quality and sophistication of that department. I also told Rob that I would be president for four years only and he could replace me. That is exactly what happened. I also unleashed the vice-president of human resources, Jim Grossett, telling him that Henry Marchant's line, "Be daring, be different, be first," also applied to human resources. They say you can judge a university by the quality of its alumni; the same can be said about companies. At Pillsbury, we developed an outstanding management team. Seven managers went on to become presidents of their companies. (Just a note on managers: when I say "senior managers," I mean the directors plus vice-presidents; by "executive managers" I mean vice-presidents only.)

Across the company we upgraded the quality of evaluations, recognition programs and communications. Annual attitude surveys confirmed that morale and employee engagement were high. In my first year, I told my vice-president of operations, Paul Oliver, that I wanted to go into the plants and work on the lines. He didn't think it was a good idea and advised against it. Over the next year, however, I worked on many of the production lines. The employees loved that I was much slower and less skilled than them. The move was a hit—within a year almost all the vice-presidents were doing the same. We also introduced a practice called "corporate engineering" whereby every six months we reviewed all the managers and directors. We identified both the high promotables and the underperformers. We started doing cross-functional moves to grow the young leaders, and this worked well in many instances.

After four years, I was president and CEO of a company with 1,100 employees and some $210 million in sales. I was only forty-two and comfortable being in charge. The company was enjoying record sales and earnings, return on investment and market share. We had launched many new products, turned around employee attitudes and were named one of the *Financial Post*'s "100 Best Companies" in 1989. And I won a national award for marketing excellence from the American Marketing Association.

I was on a roll but getting bored. And, of course, I had not forgotten my basketball dream. One night in 1988, the senior team at Pillsbury gathered at a Toronto restaurant called Centro to celebrate our accomplishments that year. The Pillsbury senior management team was very good, and I knew we would not be able to keep all the team members together. I asked them what they wanted to do next in their careers. When it came my turn to speak, I told them I wanted to run an NBA team in Toronto.

# CHAPTER 5

# WILD DAYS, SKYDOME DAYS

On November 28, 1982, the idea was born of a closed stadium in the Ontario capital. The seventieth Grey Cup game, played on that Sunday afternoon between the hometown Toronto Argonauts and the visiting Edmonton Eskimos, unfolded under grey skies at the old open-air Exhibition Stadium. The day was so wet and miserable that this particular Grey Cup game would henceforth be known as "the Rain Bowl"—as in driving, freezing rain.

Throughout the game, thousands of numb fans retreated to the concession stands, making it look to the record-breaking Canadian TV audience of eight million that the game was spottily attended. Fans trying to make their way from the stands to the concessions or vice-versa clogged the narrow walkways and in some spots formed a near impenetrable gridlock. The washrooms overflowed, the fans froze, the Argonauts lost. At a rally next day outside city hall to honour the vanquished footballers, tens of thousands of people began to chant, "We want a dome! We want a dome!"

On June 3, 1989, they finally got their wish. A public and private consortium that included the Province of Ontario, the City of Toronto and thirty Canadian corporations had contributed to the costs of financing, designing and building the facility. Viewed on national television, the grand opening launched a multi-purpose sports and entertainment stadium with a truly retractable roof, the first of its kind in the world. SkyDome was state-of-the-art. And when it came time to decide who should be its new president and CEO, the last man standing was yours truly. I knew nothing about the sports and entertainment business. The new boss of this splendid facility was a complete and utter sports and entertainment rookie.

* * *

I had been toiling at Pillsbury while SkyDome was being conceived and built, and by 1989 I was bored with the consumer products industry. But, in a way, my hands were tied.

I couldn't go to another food company in Canada—not after pushing a "best food company" vision at Pillsbury. I didn't especially want to go to the United States with Pillsbury either, since my personal equity was in Toronto. My wife at the time, Trudy Eagan, had a senior position at the *Toronto Sun* and understandably did not want to move. I was quickly offered jobs as president at two Toronto advertising agencies, but I decided the ad industry wasn't for me. I did get on the short list for the CTV president's job and that truly did interest me. But the search was dragging on and I took my name off the candidate list. I then encouraged CTV to look at John Cassaday—he was then president and CEO of Campbell Soup UK. John was ultimately hired, and he has done a superb job in the broadcasting industry ever since.

SkyDome had just opened to wide acclaim in June 1989, but its president, Chuck Magwood, was a builder who had no interest in actually running the place. A high-profile search ensued. The headhunter who considered me was not enthralled with my resumé because I had no obvious connections to the sports and entertainment business. What I did have were powerful allies who pushed my name forward. Coca-Cola, Loblaw, Nestlé and Sun Media (owners of *Toronto Sun*) were all investors in the stadium and all pushed my candidacy. It's a small world: I knew the senior Coca-Cola people from my days at Hostess when Coke and Hostess were allies in the war against Frito-Lay and Pepsi. I knew the Loblaw executives from my time at Pillsbury. And Paul Godfrey, publisher and CEO at the *Sun* (and Trudy's boss), was especially helpful and instrumental in my eventual selection.

I understand that, in the end, it came down to three candidates—among them two Americans with facility experience (one was Michael Rowe, who ran the sports complex in New Jersey then called the Meadowlands and now, as MetLife Stadium, home to both the New York Giants and the New York Jets of the NFL). I couldn't match that, so I took a much different approach: I talked about branding, customer service, marketing and inspiring people. These were all skills that I had successfully demonstrated in consumer products. Was it my consumer products background, my contacts or the fact that I was a Canadian that got me the job? I will never know.

In any case, I got the job. From 1989 until 1994, I was president and CEO of SkyDome (now the Rogers Centre). My timing was perfect. The place was so hot then, so sexy. It seemed I was always leaving one job for another at just the right time.

Now I was in the baseball, football and music business. When I came in to the position, I wore my short hair slicked back. I looked like Michael Douglas in the movie *Wall Street*. But then I started to get the feel and fun of the place. Soon I was dressed all in black, I had an earring and—for one month anyway—a ponytail. My clothing changed according to who was playing that night: black for the rock and rollers, blue jeans for the country acts. I loved the energy of SkyDome in the early 1990s.

The Dome also churned with hormonal energy. Parents dropped off their teenaged daughters, who headed straight for the washroom to don revealing outfits or T-shirts with provocative messages across the chest that would have shocked Mom and Dad. The Backstreet Boys, New Kids on the Block and other groups were rolling through, and these girls were pleading with security to get back stage.

Rock groups would come to the Dome with riders—clauses in their performance contracts that stipulated special food and drink to be laid on, maybe fresh flowers in the dressing rooms, nice furniture, a Coke machine. The range of requests was dizzying. When the Rolling Stones came to SkyDome, they wanted the green room converted into an English pub, and what the Rolling Stones wanted, the Rolling Stones got. I'm not sure the result was all that authentic, but the trappings were there—including beer on draft.

For all the time I was at SkyDome and all the time I was at Maple Leaf Sports and Entertainment, riders made life interesting for those who had to deal with them, such as Patti-Anne Tarlton, then vice-president of live entertainment at MLSE (and now the new COO of Ticketmaster Canada). She has many, many stories to tell. She told me that Foo Fighters, Guns N' Roses, Madonna and André Rieu have all put Air Canada Centre to the test. The Red Hot Chili Peppers insisted on precise temperature and air flow and threatened to walk off stage halfway through their show if these conditions were not perfectly met.

The website thesmokinggun.com lists riders for a few hundred performers in its backstage section. It's irresistible reading. You might wonder, as I did, why Shania Twain needs ten pounds of carrots before every show. Or why the Red Hot Chili Peppers need not just four packs of Marlboros and twenty-four Heineken ("fully iced") but also four pairs of black cotton boxer shorts ("w/Button fly"). Guns N' Roses apparently required, among other things, Wonder Bread, a large pepperoni pizza, Pringles, store-bought cookies, two cases of Budweiser, a fifth each of bourbon and vodka and "assorted adult magazines (i.e., *Penthouse* and *Playboy*)."

Patti-Anne is very familiar with the stresses of staging Guns N' Roses. She was working the show at Olympic Stadium in Montreal the year lead vocalist Axl Rose walked off stage after telling fans he was "fucking out of here." The crowd rioted inside and outside the stadium and throughout the city. Vancouver suffered damages the year Axl cancelled the first date on the tour well into the night— he never even flew into the city. Patti-Anne staged Guns N' Roses three times at the Air Canada Centre and each was a nail-biter. On the last occasion, it was 12:30 a.m. when Axl's personal assistant advised that he would not leave the hotel for the venue unless we could confirm we had a massage therapist available for him when he arrived at the ACC, twenty minutes from then. Magically, we found an usherette who was considering going to school for massage therapy, and we had her in waiting, uniform and all. For the record, Axl Rose arrived and walked straight on stage, and our employee never did have to pretend to be something she was not.

André Rieu, the celebrated Dutch violinist, conductor and composer, presented what Patti-Anne calls "another event experience sure to have shortened our lives." As chance would have it, Rieu's annual tour stop coincided with the G20 summit in Toronto in 2010. Although the show slated for June 26 had been booked well in advance of confirmation of the G20, Patti-Anne tried to talk him into rescheduling his show date as she learned of the magnitude of the security measures to be implemented in the city. He insisted that he would continue with the event because our government had not declared the city unfit for business. Even at midday the day of the show, as public transit was being shut down and reports of violence spread across news outlets locally and internationally, Rieu insisted on following through with the performance for his fans. We continued to load in the production, and he completed a sound check, business as usual. It was not until he left the stage for his final preparations in his dressing room that he took in the live media coverage of burning police vehicles and vandalism only blocks from the venue. It was then that he hailed the venue manager and we decided to postpone the show, less than two hours before showtime.

Barbra Streisand, Crosby, Stills, Nash and Young, Cirque du Soleil and Super Snowcross have all stretched the limits of the Air Canada Centre. As Patti-Anne once told me, "Whether it is the weight of the production that is installed in our ceiling or the ever-growing dressing room requirements for executive chefs, workout facilities, medical facilities, hospitality, VIP parties, meet and greets, meditation, vocal rehearsal, wardrobe, makeup, animal grooming, babysitting, video edit or office requirements and more, the shows and their requirements continue to grow to meet the expectations of their fans, and our footprint seems increasingly smaller in comparison. But bring it on, we'll make it happen."

\* \* \*

Sometimes we let rock groups use the SkyDome boardroom as their green room, taking a chance that the place would be trashed. It wasn't the group itself I worried about; it was the entourage. When the Russian circus came through town, its reputation for stealing stuff preceded it. But the circus surprised us, not by lifting things but by leaving things behind—including fridges, all manner of clothes and clutter from a long tour. We were the last stop and so became the dumping ground.

There were challenges to running SkyDome, and I'll come to them. But especially in the beginning what I felt most was exhilaration. I had that rare combination of vocation and avocation: I was in my early forties, I loved sports and concerts, and I felt like I was very much at the centre of things—especially in 1992 and 1993, when the Blue Jays won two World Series pennants in a row. The atmosphere then was surreal.

As president of SkyDome, I believed I had to be there for almost every event. Originally, the experts said we could not manage even 200 events a year, but by 1993 we were hosting more than 250 a year. I was a hands-on president who made his presence very obvious. To every stranger I met at the Dome, my first utterance was always the same: "Welcome to SkyDome!"

Before many events I often got my exercise (this was the tail end of my marathon days) by running the concourses, ramps and even the exterior of the building—about eight kilometres all told. That way I knew what kind of shape we were in before the doors opened. I also became known as the boss who was always picking up garbage—a habit soon emulated by staff. (I continued that tradition at the Air Canada Centre—though I drew the line at Kleenex.)

During the 1993 World Series, we opened up SkyDome so fans could watch the away games in Philadelphia on the Jumbotron. We worried that fans might run on the field, become a distraction or damage the turf. Most of the full-time staff volunteered to work the event. I stationed myself as a security guard on the field and, sure enough, one intoxicated fan ran onto the field near me. I tackled him and turned him over to police. The next week, my staff gave me a small trophy with "world's greatest tackle" printed on the base.

We were a non-union shop at SkyDome, so everyone pitched in during events—from putting up chairs to sweeping up after a show. More than 40,000 fans came to see Simon and Garfunkel.

Before the show, in my walk around the building, I realized that we were heavily backed up at one door, so I simply opened another turnstile and started taking tickets. On many of these occasions, some fans recognized me and expressed surprise that the president would be doing such tasks. One thing is certain: facility management is not a spectator sport. To do it right, you have to get involved—especially for live concerts.

A thirty-one-storey roof did not make for good concert sound, but the cachet of the building helped draw large crowds. One of the first things I did at SkyDome was sign a lucrative and exclusive concert agreement with the legendary Michael Cohl and Bill Ballard, two veteran promoters with Concert Productions International. I had also hired Paul Clark, one of the marketing directors from Pillsbury.

Sometimes things can go very wrong during a concert. Michael and Bill were unflappable on these occasions, Paul and I less so. Take, for example, the concert that took place on October 2, 1989, when everything that could go wrong did go wrong. One of the first concerts with me at the helm was to feature Frank Sinatra, Sammy Davis Jr. and Liza Minnelli. SkyDome's roof was then not yet finished, as one small roof panel was not yet in place. In our wisdom we decided to tarp it. The wind came up that night, and the tarp flapped loudly and annoyingly all evening. Sammy Davis Jr. bowed out at the eleventh hour after being taken to the hospital. I suspected that Frank Sinatra was drunk (he blew some lyrics near the end of the evening, and I worried about him falling off the stage).

Then there were the bugs. SkyDome's seating area was always spray-washed after events, with some of the sections movable on rails, much like train tracks. This allows the stadium to reconfigure for baseball games, football games and concerts. But there is no drainage at SkyDome and water collected in the tracks, where bugs then hatched in enormous numbers. They plagued the fans sitting in the floor seats all night. They swirled around Frank Sinatra's head. And when Liza Minnelli came out for a medley, she came armed with a can of bug spray.

At one point, Minnelli removed her eyelashes. "I always knew they were good for something," she told her audience. "They're for catching bugs."

In his review in the *Globe and Mail* (under the headline "Dome Can't Daunt Electric Pair"), music critic Robert Cushman said that Sinatra and Minnelli were magnificent. But he ended his piece with this: "Ground level at the Dome was an insect's paradise; this, plus the acoustics and the distance and the fact that the orchestra sounded like it was playing on an adjacent planet, drove some people to ask for refunds. This, to understate matters, was a shame."

Truth is, we were still figuring out the building's acoustics. (We never did resolve that issue.) We kept claiming that the sound in the building was great, but it was actually quite poor, and even worse that night because the microphone the artists were using was picking up signals from the CN Tower. The fans had paid a hefty price for their tickets, and some were close to rioting—especially those way up in the 500 level. So up I went with Ballard and Cohl to talk to the disgruntled fans.

"What should we do?" I asked Ballard and Cohl as we climbed the stairs.

They came back with a question of their own. "What would you do?"

"Well," I said, "in the consumer products industry, we would give them their money back."

"You sure are new to this business," they said. We dealt with the fallout as best we could. One thing that was obvious to me back in the early 1990s was that the industry and the artists often didn't care about the fans. They would hold back fans from coming into the building in cold, wet weather so a roadie could take his time adjusting a stage light. Guns N' Roses would have a show start time of 9 p.m. printed on their tickets, and then not go on until midnight. (They quickly earned the nickname "Guns N' Refunds.") This aspect of the business really bothered me—though I have to say that country artists were better at appreciating their fans than were the rockers.

Lots of acts complained about wonky acoustics at SkyDome. Elton John once paused during a concert to register his complaint about sound quality. "This is awful, isn't it?" he asked fans. "You should ask for your money back!" Elton John was getting 80 per cent of the take. Was he willing to take less money if fans followed his advice? I doubt it.

When Madonna arrived on her Blond Ambition Tour, the sparks flew. *Rolling Stone* magazine called her show "an elaborately choreographed, sexually provocative extravaganza," and not only the best tour of 1990 but the greatest concert of the 1990s. A blend of music, cabaret and performance art, the show in support of her *Like a Prayer* album was clearly meant to offend—and it did. "The tour's goal," Madonna said at the time, "is to break useless taboos." A crucifix figured in the choreography, and a dominatrix outfit was one of Madonna's costumes, with backup singers dressed as priests and nuns. There was also simulated masturbation and, of course, the now famous bullet bra. The Pope called for a ban of the show when it arrived in Rome, and one of three scheduled shows in Italy was cancelled. He also called on the worldwide Christian community not to attend the show.

During a sound check on the morning of her first show at Sky-Dome, Madonna insisted that no one be in the bowl. And no one was. The show played to a packed house three nights in a row (May 27, 28 and 29). During the last show, I got a call. Better go backstage, the caller said, because the vice squad is here. What I witnessed was a confrontation between the police and the promoter, with the former insisting that changes be made to the program or obscenity charges would be laid. The tour manager, John Draper, famously told police, "Cancel the show and you'll have to explain to 30,000 people why." The show went on, unaltered.

I loved SkyDome concerts—sometimes even more than the Blue Jay games, and definitely more than Argo games. Apparently, I was not alone in my fervour: recent research by Live Nation, the California-based events promoter, suggests that 24 per cent of concert fans would rather go to a concert than have sex. I don't know about that, but this I can say with certainty: running SkyDome was a lot of fun, and my four years there connected me with important people in the live entertainment industry, such as Riley O'Connor and Arthur Fogel at Live Nation. Those connections would pay off mightily twenty years later when I was with Maple Leaf Sports and Entertainment.

I cherished being at those concerts in the Dome, but I feared I would be put on the spot. What if the guy beside me lights up a joint? I'm the CEO—do I ignore him? Do I call him out? What if I don't call him out and security is watching me? My solution: watch the concert not among the fans but from a suite or standing behind the barricades near the stage.

The hotel also sometimes presented a problem during concerts. During one concert, I was in the pit below the stage with Bill Ballard when we both noticed a red light from a hand-held camera shining at one of the hotel windows looking down on the stage. Somebody was filming the concert, and that's not allowed. I called security and told them to go up to the hotel and confiscate the camera. Minutes and minutes went by and the guy kept filming. Ballard and I were getting angry. Before we went up to the room, I had the good sense to count the windows so I would know which room it was when I got to the hotel. Sure enough, Ballard and I went up to the floor and security told us they couldn't find the room—but I knew which one it was. Confidently (with six burly security guys behind me), I knocked loudly on the door. A man answered. I accused him of shooting bootleg footage and grabbed his camera. We closed the room window and locked it. Out we went; problem solved. Bill was now my best buddy. The next day, the man returned to get back his camera (minus the film) and told me that what I did—confiscating the camera and destroying the film—was illegal. He was probably right. On the other hand, we always made it clear to fans that only the performers had the right to film their concerts—so the fan was in the wrong too.

* * *

After a few years at SkyDome, I was feeling more confident about my concert knowledge, and was one of the keynote speakers at a four-day conference in California put on by *Performance Magazine.* I was to speak during the afternoon of the second day, so I sat through all the meetings leading up to my spot on the agenda. It took to noon the second day before any speaker even mentioned the importance of the fans. The agent for Barbra Streisand in his remarks actually asked participants, "Who is the most important person in the industry?"

"The artist," everyone responded. In my talk later that afternoon, I challenged that belief and the lack of focus on the fan. The next week, *Performance Magazine* accused me of calling out one of the most important agents in the business. Oops. Things, thankfully, have changed a great deal since then.

* * *

With its magnificent clamshell top and glamorous looks, Sky-Dome was four times (consecutively) named Stadium of the Year in North America in the time I was there. In that period, the Dome hosted more than 1,000 events and attracted some twenty-nine million patrons. I was named North American Facility Manager of the Year in 1992. But when I arrived at the newly minted facility in the fall of 1989, the place had no history, no established operating procedures and a very young workforce that was almost as green as me. And, to top things off, the stadium was way over budget and still not finished. The new dome was an operational mess, and its new president was a complete sports and entertainment rookie who was clearly flying by the seat of his pants.

By the time of my introductory press conference, I knew I was in a completely different world. Print reporters, radio reporters, TV cameras. Pillsbury and Hostess were never like this. And no one at SkyDome prepared me with Q & A rehearsals beforehand. To questions from the media I gave naive answers about filling the building every night of the year, and about how I was confident that the debt was manageable. Thankfully, I was still in Sky-Dome's honeymoon period. The questions were all lob balls and my answers were not challenged.

I soon learned that we had no clue how to run the building well. No one was quite sure what his or her role was, resulting in the building being double-booked a few times. Construction costs continued climbing as we finished the roof, the 348-room hotel and the health club. Construction claims were flooding in. We joked that our lawyer, Lisa Novak, should have a sign over her office door that read, "Over 1,000 liens served." The thirty companies that each invested $5 million to help finance the building were complaining about not getting a return on their investments, and fights were breaking out over who exactly had certain rights.

McDonald's, for instance, had the right to quick-service food. Restaurateur John Bitove Sr. controlled fine dining. So tell me—when is a chicken sandwich fast food and when is it not? That question was never resolved to anyone's satisfaction, nor was the hot dog conundrum. Both McDonald's and Bitove sold hot dogs, yet Loblaw was the official hot dog supplier of SkyDome and got to set the price—which Bitove and McDonald's argued was too high.

I called all this The Food Wars, as they were utterly unpleasant. I wanted vending machines to dispense at least some food—especially at night, when staff converted the facility from, say, a baseball stadium to a football stadium. But that too was a problem. Everything at SkyDome was a problem. The place seemed not meant to work.

When rockers came through town with their entourages, the promoter would want to lay on a spread using a caterer he knew or had been told about. But Bitove and McDonald's fought me on that too. They were wholly concerned with their rights as food providers, and they could not agree on what constituted a fair price. Things were a mess. We had a saying at SkyDome: "Thank God it's Friday—we only have two more days to work."

When I look back at my time at SkyDome, I can see that what marked my tenure was lack of control. I learned from that. If the Dome experience was about never really gaining control, I was determined at Maple Leaf Sports to get control—and keep it.

Despite all the challenges at SkyDome, we set about tackling them. We were guided by vision and values. We created a "world's greatest entertainment centre" vision, with three core values captured by the initialism QSP: *Quality. Service. People.* After about six months of using this vision and these values, I overheard one board member saying, "When is Peddie going to sell something and quit focusing on this vision and values thing?" Some people think vision and values are just warm and fuzzy statements. But if you religiously adhere to them, they are hard and demanding and cannot be ignored.

\* \* \*

At two points in my time at SkyDome I was offered the helm of the Toronto Argonauts. By this time, the Argos had left their old digs at Exhibition Stadium and were playing in the Dome, but the terms of their lease were unclear and had to be renegotiated. This brought me head to head with the tempestuous Harry Ornest, who owned the football team between 1988 and 1991. One time we were in his office at the Canadian National Exhibition, and the temperature was rising.

I got angry, Harry got angry. He stood up, I stood up. He swore, I swore. I was forty-three years old, fit and trim. Harry was sixty-seven, but he was not backing down one inch, and had he swung at me in anger, it would not have been the first time. That same year, he and actor John Forsythe got into a fistfight at Hollywood Park racetrack in California. And I was thinking, if we did come to blows and he felled me, I will have been beaten up by an elderly man. If I downed him, I would be accused of abusing a senior. I couldn't win this battle. Finally, Harry calmed down, and I soon did the same. We postponed our discussion, but we never did resolve the lease issue.

Ornest sold the Argos, and soon the celebrities were flying in from Los Angeles. The new owners of the club included Bruce McNall, a multi-millionaire who also owned the Los Angeles Kings of the NHL and who made his fortune collecting (smuggling, actually) rare coins. The others included Wayne Gretzky, who was then playing for the Kings; Janet Gretzky, his actress wife; and John Candy, the Canadian actor and comedian. There were end-zone parties after games, with lots of expensive Scotch. It was all heady stuff.

Months and years passed, and still no headway was being made on the Argo lease negotiations. McNall was a smooth operator, the ultimate salesman. His CFO was a tiny dynamo of a woman named Suzan Waks who, well along in her pregnancy, was willing to delay her scheduled Caesarean section to get a deal done. In the middle of negotiations, her side offered to hire me. Sign on, they said, and we'll bring an NBA team to town—and you can run that too.

In the end, I declined thanks to what I can only call my spidey sense. When Suzan forgot her shoes in Los Angeles, a plane was sent to fetch them. These LA folks thought we were all hicks in Toronto. Something was not right—and, indeed, my instincts were correct. Suzan Waks went to jail after pleading guilty to single counts of bank fraud, conspiracy and tax evasion. Bruce McNall spent almost five years in prison after pleading guilty in 1993 to five counts of conspiracy and fraud.

* * *

By 1994, the year that marked the end of my tenure at SkyDome, I had acquired a score of useful skills (I was getting, I would say later, my ticket punched). I was by then quite comfortable steering a big ship, and I could even right a leaky one. But SkyDome was taking on far too much water. On the one hand, the Dome was pulling in $15 to $20 million a year in operating profits, with 250 events annually and the Jays winning World Series before packed houses. On the other hand, the debt load was huge, and we could not make the interest payments on the loan, never mind tackle the principal, so the debt just kept on growing. The whole financial model was broken. That was true when I arrived and true when I left. So much thought had been given to building the Dome and so little to actually running the place in a way that made economic sense.

When it came time several years later to think about how best to operate the Air Canada Centre, I thought about all the mistakes made at SkyDome and how I might learn from them. What follows are lessons learned, ones that can generally be applied to many companies.

First, a facility of this magnitude has to be seamless. SkyDome had so many seams that got in the way of delivering quality service to fans and promoters. For example, a promoter seeking to book an event at SkyDome had to deal with the two food service firms, plus another company for chairs, and yet another company to arrange electrical hookups and show staging. Years down the line, when the Air Canada Centre was being built, the board at Maple Leaf Sports and Entertainment agreed with executive management's recommendation to go seamless and run everything (with the sole exception of suites) ourselves. So when we had a problem or an opportunity, it was ours to solve or realize. There was no third party stopping us.

Second, there was what to do about disgruntled fans. At Sky-Dome, there was no system in place. So I implemented one I called All Out Recovery. My thinking was that delivering great service is critical. The odd fan getting a cold hot dog, while not excusable, is inevitable. Try as you might, you will make mistakes. The normal fan reaction to more egregious mistakes was "I am never coming back to SkyDome again." We could not let this happen. We also knew (in those days prior to the Internet, blogs and Twitter) that every miffed fan told his or her story to about ten people. Today such fans can electronically tell thousands.

The good news for any company is that if you put in a solid recovery program, you can almost always change customers' minds and in many instances make them even more loyal. Accordingly, we put in a system whereby SkyDome service people would ideally contact unhappy fans the very next day. Apologize. Invite them to a future event of their choice for free. Give them free food coupons and apologize again. Initially, our service people were worried they were going to get ripped off by phony complainers. I pointed out that even if a small percentage were taking advantage, saving the other 90 per cent was worth it.

I invited Michael Bregman to speak to SkyDome staff on the subject of service. Michael had experience owning mmmuffins and Second Cup. He said something that resonated with everyone: "Do not judge your customers. You really don't know what they are thinking."

Third, I learned that the building is not the show—though for the longest time we thought it was. Today, SkyDome seems just a little tired and passé, and most of the concerts that used to go to the Dome now go to the Air Canada Centre. The Dome was the last of the multi-use facilities; stadiums built these days tend to be single-purpose. Fifteen years after SkyDome went up, the questions began: Is the Dome now obsolete? Is it time to replace it?

SkyDome was a very sexy building for a long time. A roof that opened. Largest indoor video board. The Hard Rock Café. SkyDome Hotel. It was a remarkable building, and people wanted to see it and even tour it. We soon believed that there was a SkyDome factor—that an event in the Dome would draw 40 per cent more fans than it would were that same event held in another building. And this seemed to be true, as that great Blue Jay team of 1991 drew four million fans in one season, the first Major League team ever to do so. Forty thousand came to see the last episode of *Cheers* on SkyDome's Jumbotron. We joked that we could throw a birthday party for one of our vice-presidents and draw 20,000 fans.

However, the Dome's technological and design breakthroughs quickly become dated. The act is the draw—not the venue. Later, when we opened the Air Canada Centre, we believed there would be a 20 per cent factor tied to the building. But by 1999, when that facility opened, suites, restaurants overlooking the playing field and high-tech video boards were all the norm. The ACC is a great facility, but the arena, I repeat, is not the show. Fans simply want to see great sports and entertainment.

Related to the point about staying current with design and technology is this critical point, the fourth on my list: you have to keep modernizing. (Ironically, I am something of a Luddite myself, but I fully understood the importance of technological change and surrounded myself with people in the vanguard.) I liken the modern arena to the Boeing B-52 bomber. The airframe of the Stratofortress has not materially changed since it was introduced in the 1950s, but the American military has constantly upgraded its electronics, its computers and its weapon systems. Built correctly and to the right basic design, arenas and stadiums can last for years and years. But to stay current and justify fan spending, owners have to constantly spend capital dollars on refreshing restaurants, installing new score boards, upgrading suites, building new operating systems and so on.

Back in the 1990s, SkyDome's capital budget was only about $2 million a year. That's far too little for a 54,000-seat stadium with its many amenities. At the Air Canada Centre, we spent in the $6 to $8 million range per year. Today, the ACC looks better and *is* better than when it opened in 1999. SkyDome had gone downhill because of lack of capital dollars until Rogers and the Blue Jays started spending in the past few years. Yet the media and the fans don't take into consideration capital spending when talking about profits. Media reports on profitability focus naively on operating profits rather than net income; there's a big difference between the two. The former measures how much an enterprise is taking in from normal day-to-day operations; the latter is calculated after subtracting interest, taxes, depreciation and amortization. Net income is the true measure of profitability (every company listed on the TSX, for example, reports on net income).

Fifth on my list of lessons learned is that not all events are created equal. On some large concerts, SkyDome could make as much as $200,000. On others, we might have made $25,000 or, in some cases, lost money. Family shows such as Disney on Ice can give a venue twenty or more events, but you might only make a total of $200,000 on all those shows combined. Developers still pushing for a new arena in Markham, north of Toronto, in 2013 were claiming the place could be profitable with 130 shows. Not a chance. The key to a facility's profitability is having one or two top-tier professional sports teams. You simply cannot make enough money on concerts and family shows to cover your expenses. Also you cannot sell suites or club seats without a major sports tenant. Finally, you need to sell building title sponsorship and significant sponsorships if you hope to be profitable—and without a major sports tenant, the price you get for them will be very low.

Even were Toronto to get another NHL team (which I rather doubt because the total franchise and new stadium investment could approach $800 million—but I suppose it's a possibility if such a new team became a third major tenant at the Air Canada Centre), simply having a professional sports team as an arena tenant is no guarantee of financial success. Fans and the media point to New York and Los Angeles/Anaheim as examples of cities that support more than one team; yet these cities' teams, with the exception of the New York Rangers, all lose money—the Los Angeles Kings, the Anaheim Ducks, the New Jersey Devils and the New York Islanders are not profitable. And remember, New York City and Los Angeles are significantly larger than Toronto.

Lesson six: Don't nickel and dime. When SkyDome opened, it charged extra for everything. It charged the promoters extra for chairs, phone lines and stages. It charged suite holders for extra events such as concerts, for the hostesses in their suites and even for the design and construction of their suites: some clients spent a million dollars on their suites, ordering expensive light fixtures from Italy—which meant importing bulbs when the old ones burnt out. It was insane, like custom building 201 houses. And SkyDome had to maintain those suites, a job that was both pricey and problematic, since each suite was different.

We learned from this mistake and built all those costs and amenities into our offerings at the Air Canada Centre. We also made every suite exactly the same.

Lesson seven applies to any construction project: architects need to put their pencils down before construction starts. Sky-Dome was a unique and complex project, with its moving roof and its many amenities, such as restaurants, hotel and fitness club. In the hotel, for example, as with the suites, no two rooms were alike—so that dramatically drove up construction costs. No one really knows how much it cost to build SkyDome, but my best guess is $570 million. The cost could have been trimmed considerably had constraints been put in place from the beginning. Despite all the fussing, the place has flaws: the elevators in the hotel are all at one end, so room-service food was cold by the time it reached the far end of the hall. Further, the whole project was being fast-tracked so the Blue Jays could get out of Exhibition Place and start the 1989 season in their new digs at the Dome.

Architects' drawings were being done and redone all the way through the project, and this too added to cost overruns. When Maple Leaf Sports and Entertainment built the ACC and BMO Field, we were on budget and on time. With Maple Leaf Square we weren't quite as good. That's because too many cooks were in the kitchen, with us and third parties arguing over things such as the cost of shower heads: would we install ones that cost $100 or $1,000?

Finally, what I learned at SkyDome was that vision and values really do work as guiding principles. One of the best at this approach is Disney. When I was at SkyDome, I joined several of our vice-presidents in taking the course at the Disney Institute in Orlando, Florida, where the professional development arm of that company is based. Many new owners and presidents of franchises and facilities naively claim they are going to operate like Disney; it's not that easy. For more than sixty years, vision and values have guided Disney. Consistent with its family values, Disney has strict rules on everything. For instance, the earring I was wearing didn't fit with how Disney wants staff ("cast members," as they are called) to appear to customers ("guests"). And when, as part of my education there, I worked in customer service, I was asked beforehand to remove the earring. Had I worn a beard, that too would have had to go: the rule then at Disney was no facial hair. Classes are offered on the Disney approach, and the course price is not cheap. But it's an excellent course that offers lessons on how to incorporate a creative and collaborative culture in the workplace. What struck me was the makeup of the attendees. As expected, there were lots of people from the hotel and entertainment industry, but there were also a great many individuals who worked in the health and medical fields in the United States.

In 2012, Frank Supovitz, the National Football League's senior vice-president for events, hired Disney to prevent a seating debacle that had marred the 2011 Super Bowl game from happening again. Hundreds of fans with tickets for that 2011 game were turned away from Cowboys Stadium in Arlington, Texas, when it was discovered that hundreds of temporary seats had not been properly installed in time, rendering them unusable—forcing triple-face-value refunds to 400 disgruntled fans and giving the stadium, the league and the Super Bowl a black eye. Disney came in and created a training program for the 20,000 staff members who would work at the 2012 game. The goal was to instill a sense of pride in those individuals, with the aim of every fan, in turn, being treated like a VIP. Supovitz also hired Disney for staff training leading up to the 2013 Super Bowl in New Orleans. I imagine those staff members were put to the test when the stadium lights went out in the second half of the game.

* * *

During my four years at SkyDome, I received an education in so many areas that would help me immeasurably at Maple Leaf Sports and Entertainment. Some were important best practices; others were worst practices that I had to make sure we avoided. Another key benefit for me was working with the Toronto Blue Jays. They were the lead tenants and without them, SkyDome would not have been profitable at the operating line. From Paul Beeston, then and once more the team president, I learned the following.

*Put all your games on TV.* The CFL, the Expos and, most recently, the Chicago Blackhawks did not do that, thinking that to do so would negatively affect the gate at home games. This dubious practice hurt those franchises immensely. I believe that one reason for the older demographics of the Argos is that they lost a generation of fans because of those blackout rules. Beeston believed that all games needed to be on television, to generate awareness and long-term interest for the team. I took that concept to MLSE and applied it to the Raptors right off the bat. To this day, MLSE even tries to get as many Marlie games on TV as it can.

*Don't get too close to your players.* They are younger than you and different. You can't hang out with them. They are also assets, and you need to be comfortable trading them or letting them go. That point was made clear to me whenever I walked into the Leaf or Raptor dressing room and had to say thanks and goodbye to players I had come to know.

*Live sports is leverage.* Many people who say they watch little TV are nevertheless drawn to live sports on television; this is the great appeal of sports. There is an inherent drama in a close game. A favoured team can be upset by one lower in the standings, and even a so-called meaningless game may contain moments of pure grace and surprise. This is what drives fans to pay subscription fees to sports specialty channels such as TSN and Sportsnet. These channels need you, and you can play hardball with them to get the deal you want for your broadcast rights.

I would learn that lesson at TSN. We took that even further at MLSE by launching our own specialty channels such as NBA TV and Leafs TV, and by buying Gol TV to show football (soccer, that is) games. In fact, merely preparing to launch a regional sports channel that featured the games of all four MLSE teams (Leafs, Raptors, TFC, Marlies) was one of the major drivers that helped the Ontario Teachers' Pension Plan command a high enterprise value price for the company when it sold its shares in August 2012 to Bell and Rogers Communications. The selling price for almost 80 per cent of MLSE stock was a handsome $1.32 billion.

*Spend money on your dressing room.* What may seem like a small thing is actually an important recruiting tool and an important place to address any small issues with your players. This was critical when we built the Air Canada Centre. Since then, just about every owner in every sport has spent millions on opulent dressing rooms, so it isn't a point of difference anymore—unless you do it cheaply.

During the lockout of 2012, the Leaf dressing room underwent a major makeover, with new skate-friendly flooring, maple seats and trim, whiteboard spaces near the ceiling, where coach Randy Carlyle can post inspirational messages, and a graphics board, where life-sized images of players can be posted as a way of recognizing and honouring them. When I went for a look-see in late

2012, there were photos of winger Joffrey Lupul and defenceman Dion Phaneuf. Carlyle plans to rotate player pictures throughout the season. Each player continues to be assigned his own locker, one made of fine, polished Canadian maple.

*Stagger your leases and your sponsorships.* In November 1998, SkyDome filed for bankruptcy protection. One factor (aside from the crushing debt load and the recession) was that most of the 201 SkyBox tenants had signed ten-year leases, and now they were all up for renewal at a time of recession and flagging fan interest in both the Blue Jays and the Argos. Lesson: as the owners of office buildings well know, never have all your tenants' leases expire in the same year. In the enthusiasm that marked the design and construction of SkyDome, no one foresaw the risks involved in having all the leases expire at the same time. At the Air Canada Centre, we launched with three-, five-, seven- and ten-year leases.

*Marketing matters.* I thought the Blue Jays needed better marketing, customer service and community outreach. "Where is your marketing?" I asked Paul Beeston. To which he replied, "Pat Gillick [the team's general manager] and a winning team." He was right to a point: the team is the engine, and all the marketing and customer service in the world cannot turn around the business fortunes of a bad team. But great marketing, solid customer service and aggressive community initiatives can mitigate a bad team's revenue downturns and put topspin on a great team's revenue momentum.

I'm not sure that all the SkyDome partners ever truly embraced the concept of customer service. Maybe that, in part, is why some called it The Mistake by the Lake. (Not an original moniker but arguably apt nonetheless.) The Dome had something called the Founders Club, created as a place where owners and major stakeholders could gather for food and drink. But it was stuck deep in the bowels of the building, so deep it earned the nickname "the Flounders Club." Similarly, we sold T-shirts and other gear, but that store too was unwisely situated. So lasers and smoke machines were tried to generate interest and foot traffic, but I questioned the expense of these gimmicks and I wondered why we were selling American college jerseys. The store was called Major Attraction, but it got dubbed Fatal Attraction. The space was eventually taken over by Ticketmaster. It's still there.

\* \* \*

From 1989 through 1993, the Stadium Corporation of Ontario—as SkyDome was legally named—did pretty well. People were travelling from far and wide to see one of the world's great entertainment venues. The Meadowlands in New Jersey had a lock on the North American Stadium of the Year award—until SkyDome came along.

Operating profits were solid, but, as I've said, net income is the line that matters most. The cost of building the Dome added up to around $570 million (again, my best guess), requiring the provincial government to finance the cost overrun with debt. SkyDome could not begin to cover the interest costs of the debt. The premier at the time, David Peterson, agreed that we needed to explore refinancing the building, but he first wanted to call a summer election. Voter polls indicated that he would win, but I wasn't so sure. Many believed that his support was a mile long and an inch deep. Sure enough, the New Democratic Party, led by Bob Rae, surprised everyone by winning the election.

Quickly the NDP realized that, despite the Dome's popularity, the facility was a drain on provincial finances. The new provincial government also believed that SkyDome management was too cozy with its many corporate investors. So it placed on the board two men more to its liking. One was socialist Bruce Kidd (he doesn't mind me calling him a socialist, but for the record he then taught—and still does teach—in the department of kinesiology and physical education at the University of Toronto). The other was Bob White, head of the Canadian Auto Workers union.

I loved seeing White in action. I learned he was a superb actor. One moment he was as professional and as well behaved as could be, and then to make a point he would throw a switch and swear like an army sergeant. Early on, both White and Kidd did not want to trust management, but they soon realized that we were pretty good at what we were doing and that we were actually fighting many of our corporate partners about their sponsorship rights. I developed a good relationship with both men.

When I retired from MLSE, Bruce Kidd wrote me a letter to say how much he enjoyed our time together on the SkyDome board. We had forged a relationship, one that has endured to this day. He remembered the very first meeting in Ontario treasurer Floyd Laughren's office in the fall of 1990, during the turbulent early days of the NDP government, when SkyDome was one of its major challenges. At that meeting someone—either White or Kidd—suggested that the government appoint a commission of inquiry to examine the huge construction overruns that burdened SkyDome with so much debt. Kidd recalls that I had more than a twinkle in my eye when I countered, "You mean like the Dubin Inquiry?"

I was referring to the exhaustive, lengthy and hugely expensive commission led by Chief Justice Charles Dubin in the wake of the 1988 Olympic Games scandal, when Canadian sprinter Ben Johnson was stripped of his gold medal after testing positive for steroids. I knew that Kidd, a former track star, would immediately get my point—and he did.

That comment, as Kidd described in his letter, had a domino effect. Laughren was persuaded not to go the inquiry route. The chairman of the board immediately submitted his resignation.

With White and Kidd now representing the new government, the next meeting of the SkyDome board went on for six hours, four hours longer than scheduled. There was some election-style grandstanding and speech making.

Here was another case of respect first, affection later. Years later I asked Bruce to head up the MLSE Team Up Foundation (a charity dedicated to improving the lives of youth by building facilities, giving to sustainable programs and empowering youth through sports and recreation) because he was a contrary thinker, and I knew he would champion the foundation's vision very aggressively.

* * *

The year 1994 was my last at SkyDome, and while I was still there, one final attempt was made to fix what was clearly a broken model.

The Dome was at that time owned in part by Labatt, which had a 41 per cent stake. The Canadian beer giant also owned 90 per cent of the Blue Jays and 100 per cent of the Argos. Labatt CEO George Taylor asked me to create a long-term strategic plan that projected the operating profits for all of those properties if they could be synergistically and efficiently managed together. Taylor would then use the plan to approach potential buyers about buying into the new larger entity, and Labatt could take its ownership position down to 41 per cent of the new company.

The SkyDome team prepared just such a plan and quantified a number of other ideas that we thought could drive the profitability of the new company. We quantified, for example, purchasing a Major League Soccer team, selling title sponsorship to the building and reopening the suite leases so they would not all expire in 1999. Finally, we quantified what owning an NFL team that played at SkyDome would look like. In 1993, I thought that one could buy an NFL team for around $200 million. (Today, the price tag exceeds $1 billion.) I went on Fan Radio in Toronto and bet broad-caster Bob McCown $100 that Toronto would have an NFL team by 1999. He has never asked to collect on that bet (though I suspect he will now).

In the plan, SkyDome prognosticators also identified the risk and impact of a new arena coming to Toronto. We knew that a new facility would take away all concerts from the Dome and compete in a major way for sponsors, suite holders, ticket sales and employ-ees. What I could not have imagined at the time was that I would be a part of the team that would build and lead that threat.

I made my presentation to George Taylor and others on a Mon-day. On the following Friday, the Ontario Teachers' Pension Plan and Onex Corporation announced a hostile takeover of Labatt that resulted in Labatt selling to Interbrew, the Belgian beer com-pany (which would later merge with a Brazilian beer company to become the largest brewer in the world). With that announcement, the strategic concept of merging SkyDome, the Blue Jays and the Argos died.

By this time, I was bored again. I was seeing seventy ball games a year and about twenty Disney on Ice shows and I had had enough. George Taylor knew I was getting anxious, and he talked to me about joining the Labatt family. So in 1994 I joined Labatt Communications, working for Gordon Craig, the chairman, CEO and founder of the hugely successful and groundbreaking TSN.

# CHAPTER 6

# INTO THE BROADCAST BIZ

Timing is everything. I left Hostess just before the American potato chip giant Frito-Lay woke up and decided finally to crush the Canadian upstart. I left Pillsbury just before its Canadian office became an American branch plant. I left SkyDome just after the Toronto Blue Jays had won those World Series pennants and just before the baseball strike in 1994 when the bloom came off the rose for both the team and the sport. And one month before I left Maple Leaf Sports and Entertainment, the company sold for a small fortune—with a nice payment coming my way because I had helped grow the company. (I would, in effect, be getting paid a bonus for all the work I had done to build MLSE. This is a standard clause in CEO contracts, with the bonus greater or lesser depending on how much time passes between the executive's departure and the closing of the sale.)

Likewise, I got a small taste of the sports broadcast business just when it was really coming into its own and just when CEO

Gordon Craig at TSN—then owned by Labatt Communications and a major player in that world—was looking for someone to ultimately replace him. This was in 1994.

The year before, I had taken a six-month leave of absence from SkyDome to be part of a consortium that had made a valiant but failed bid to bring an NBA franchise to Toronto. (Labatt had been part of that bid.) To have had my dream come so close and to miss out at the end was tough to swallow. The day after the NBA announcement, I read in the newspaper about a senior executive who had lost out on a bid for a certain company. He said something like, "They won . . . We lost . . . Next." So what was next for me?

As I've said, after four years of running SkyDome, I was bored. The facility was operating well, but I was losing interest. Thirty corporations had put up $5 million each to fund the design and construction of the Dome, and each player—none of whom believed they were getting anything like a proper return on their investment—had a seat on the SkyDome board, a kind of shadow board to the Dome's other board, that of the Stadium Corporation of Ontario. The latter was concerned about the Dome's debt; the former was concerned about profit, or rather, the lack of it. My job as CEO was to herd all these cats, but they were smart, aggressive cats and I was weary of tangling with them all.

I had even tangled with Labatt CEO George Taylor, though my fights with him were no more and no less fractious than they were with everyone else. The battles were inevitably about control and price. I had a good relationship with George. He was a solid businessman who always wore a suit and tie, he was smart and even-keeled and professional—but he could laugh too. And I was a buttoned-down business guy, his kind of guy. We got along fine. And my running of the Dome for four years had won me some credibility with him.

I told George I was looking around for some new challenge, and he suggested that I work for him at Labatt Communications Inc. (LCI), the owners of TSN, RDS (Réseau des sports, the French sports network) and Dome Productions. Labatt needed potential backups not only for the CEO and chairman of LCI (Gordon Craig) but also for Labatt Breweries and maybe even the Blue Jays someday.

I knew Gordon from his involvement in the Dome. He was a Canadian broadcasting icon who had created and successfully grown TSN when everyone wondered how the channel could possibly fill twenty-four hours of broadcasting daily with just curling, darts and tennis. Gordon and I had frequently crossed paths at SkyDome, since TSN had broadcast-production rights for the stadium. I had tangled with TSN too, but our relationship remained cordial. Gordon's retirement was on the horizon, and there was no clear backup for him.

Ultimately, I went to LCI as president of business development reporting to Gordon.

I have always liked and used the products I sold—from potato chips to soap to corn. I could never, for example, have worked for a cigarette company. I need to feel a personal connection, and I had that with TSN. My initial assignment was president of development. Really, the job was a president's role in name only, but I had already been a president for ten years at Hostess, Pillsbury and SkyDome and had no interest in giving the title up. (Besides, the optics of going from president to vice-president would look lousy on a resumé.)

Gordon Craig understood that here was a comfortable way for me to join a company full of experienced broadcast experts. However, after a few months I got tired of not being in a leading role. When George Taylor asked me one day how I was doing, I said, "Okay, but you know I am used to wearing the president's hat, and

I think I am going to move on." Actually, I was about to be offered the job as president of YTV, a Canadian specialty channel aimed at the nation's youth.

I had already tossed my hat in the ring over at YTV. If I couldn't steer a broadcaster aimed at sports fans, I would steer a broadcaster aimed at children. The hiring committee at YTV had comprised five people, and I was quizzed by all five at once. In preparation for the interview (and I am a bear for such preparation), I had watched YTV for a solid week and prepared a thick binder as a primer. I told the hiring committee that I had a lot of questions, but that I'd be saving one key question for the end. This was tactical, and it worked. They all wondered, what could that question be?

My last question was this: What would you have liked to have done as a broadcaster in the past five years but did not do? In the end, I was offered the job and I might have taken it had George Taylor and Gordon Craig not promoted me to president and COO of Labatt Communications.

I had the presidents of TSN, Discovery Channel, RDS, Dome Productions and LCI Sales all reporting to me. All of them knew a lot more about broadcasting then I ever would. They were pretty set in their ways and not too interested in a new reporting level between them and Gordon. I can't say that in my brief tenure at LCI/NetStar I did much leading, but I did learn a lot—about rights deals, about producing games and newscasts for television, about ad sales and the CRTC.

I watched, for example, how Trina McQueen successfully launched the Discovery Channel and how she was the first to start using the new emerging digital platforms to market and engage her audiences. By her example, I learned just how important a TV website was and is. This was early days in the whole digital revolution; I vividly remember putting my email address on my business card and thinking that this was a major step forward.

Trina was also an icon, a much admired broadcast executive who was seen as a powerful player and presence at the annual Banff film festival. When she spoke, everyone listened. Technically, she was working for me, but I was the rookie. I learned from her.

I participated in LCI's pitch to the CRTC to introduce a specialty history channel. We lost, but I got a close-up look at both the CRTC and all the work that had to go into the launching of a specialty channel. I found the whole application and review process bizarre. You pitched your idea, and all your competitors got a chance to tell the CRTC why it should not be allowed. I liked the less-regulated US model a lot better (in the United States, Fox Sports and ESPN, for example, compete head to head). In Canada, we have the Friends of Canadian Broadcasting and all other vested interests weighing in.

TSN was a groundbreaker in the 1980s, but no one gave it much chance of succeeding. A channel devoted exclusively to sports twenty-four hours a day, seven days a week? In the early days, the channel really was filled with minor sports. Baseball was seen exclusively on CTV and Global. In those days, cable had far fewer subscribers than the over-the-air broadcasters and it was largely off the radar of Major League sports. All that changed. Today, most sports are on cable.

About a year after launching TSN, Gordon Craig was called to the Labatt headquarters in London, Ontario. He went, convinced HQ was going to put a bullet in TSN. It didn't, and by 1994 TSN was a huge success, with a roster of major sports, especially the Blue Jays, making TSN easily the most profitable specialty channel in Canada.

While at LCI, I talked Gordon Craig and senior management into doing a relaunch of TSN. I had come from the world of consumer products, where you regularly revitalized products with a new package design, some new special ingredient that made the product better, new shapes and sizes, and new advertising. With difficulty, I talked them into relaunching TSN. Sportsnet was about to be launched and would be competing with us, I said. We need to freshen the product.

"Let's at least change the graphics," I said. The late Jim Thompson was then president of TSN. Jim was pretty set in his ways, and he fought me the whole way on the relaunch. He just could not grasp the concept of revitalization. Jim liked the status quo.

"This is sports, Richard," he said. "Not Jell-O." If memory serves, this line was delivered with eyes rolled.

Here was the kind of touching up I sought. Today, the little sports bug graphic indicating scores and time remaining in Major League hockey, baseball and football games is in the corners of every sports broadcast. ESPN had just begun the practice, and early audience research was favourable. Jim didn't like the bug and asked why I wanted to do it. Because audiences want it, I replied. To my way of thinking, you give the consumer what the consumer wants. ESPN in those days was doing a lot of cool new stuff, such as launching a website, a radio station, the X Games (coverage of extreme sports) and a magazine. These were all best practices out there for the copying.

The bug was incorporated, marking this as one of the few battles I won with Thompson. As a president, I had a certain way of approaching new ideas. When I ran an idea past colleagues it struck me that there were three possible responses:

1. I love it, let's do it.
2. It's okay, but this is how we can make it better.
3. No thanks, your idea stinks.

If responses from an individual were balanced among those three options when I ran ideas past him or her, I was generally pretty happy. When, down the line, we merged the Leafs and Raptors, the Leafs had a food and beverage director who was neither confident nor very good. He liked *all* my ideas despite my definitely not being a food and beverage expert, so I knew he had to go. Thompson was pretty much a "No thanks, your idea stinks" kind of guy, and accordingly the TSN relaunch was a shadow of what it could have been. We had slightly revised graphics and a new sell tag, but it could have been so much better.

One thing we did do as part of the relaunch was introduce Canada's first sports website—tsn.ca. Initially, it was the digital equivalent of a brochure, totally one-dimensional and lacking anything interactive, such as fan polls and videos. But it was a start, and the night we launched it the traffic (though extremely low by today's standards) caused the site to crash. I was learning about something new called the Internet, and I started reading *Wired* magazine. That website experience was something I took with me several years later to Maple Leaf Sports and Entertainment.

Later in my career, when the Air Canada Centre was up and running and MLSE was making decent money, the MLSE board essentially came to me and said, "Richard, whaddya got?" What I had was a vision for the future of the enterprise—a future with broadcasting as the centrepiece.

The Ontario Teachers' Pension Plan, TD Bank, Larry Tanenbaum and Steve Stavro had by this point bought the Toronto Raptors of the NBA and merged it with the Toronto Maple Leafs of the NHL. I started thinking about how we could grow the enterprise. It was time to branch out with new ideas.

I gathered the senior management team at the Harbour Castle Hotel to brainstorm ideas. I had laid on nothing more fancy than Danish pastries and orange juice, and had set up a flip chart at one end of the meeting room. Using an approach from the consumer products industry, I wrote "Leaf brand" in the middle of the chart.

Out from it I drew lines like the spokes of a wheel. Collectively we wrote down concepts such as leafs.ca website, Leaf radio, Leaf merchandise, Leaf magazine and, most importantly, Leaf television. Years later we came up with the idea of extending the Leaf brand into Maple Leaf Square, condominiums and a hotel. We then did the same thing with the Raptor brand. We also agreed that we wanted to launch websites and a specialty TV network. But all of that started with a crude drawing of spokes of a wheel.

We debated whether there should be one channel for each sports team and kept brand-focused, or whether we should combine the Leafs and Raptors in one channel. But we didn't like the brand implications of that combination, and we also worried that the CRTC would not allow the channel, since it would start to compete against TSN and Sportsnet. We thought we had a big and unique idea. Other than Manchester United, no other professional team in sports had a channel devoted exclusively to it. And Manchester United's channel largely comprised reruns and team promos. Our channels would feature live games.

There was only one problem: none of us had broadcast experience save me. And I knew what to do, but not how. Worse, a broadcast facility to produce and transmit our channels was going to cost more than $7 million. So we reached out to third parties to see if they might be interested in teaming up with us. Both The Score and Corus Entertainment (with John Cassaday at the helm and my brother, Tom, as CFO) made us offers. We chose Corus contingent on board approval.

Steve Stavro was then the majority shareholder of Maple Leaf Sports and Entertainment, and he loomed as a potential major wrench in the works. Steve had come to Canada from Macedonia as a young boy and started as an entrepreneur running a Greek restaurant on Danforth Avenue—a major thoroughfare in Toronto's east end and home to many Greek restaurants. The restaurant was at one point poised to go under but he somehow kept it afloat and he went on to launch Knob Hill Farms—the first big box store devoted to groceries. But for all his success as a builder and entrepreneur, he was not a sophisticated man. He ran Knob Hill Farms as a one-man show, and he was famous for checking up on his stores at six o'clock in the morning.

He was not keen on big presentations or strategic plans; in fact, he was not keen on even meeting with me to discuss the proposed new channels. If I insisted, he said, make it a Saturday morning. I always wondered about that. Did he think we would not want to work on a Saturday and therefore forget the idea completely? We met on a Saturday at the old boardroom at the Air Canada Centre. (I say "old" because the board stopped using that space, in part because it was too dark and in part because its close proximity to the ACC bowl meant for a noisy room when rock groups were doing sound checks. Another boardroom was created elsewhere in the building, but the board eventually outgrew that space; these days, the board typically meets in an expansive room on the sixth floor, where there are lots of Smart Boards on the wall.)

Imagine the scene that Saturday morning. Rare wood panelling, a photograph of Conn Smythe at one end of the room, the blinds drawn. The windows looked out onto the ACC bowl, where the Leafs were doing their morning pre-game skate, but the players were invisible to us. I was not looking forward to the meeting. Steve could be difficult, and he was notoriously unable to grasp complex financial scenarios and befuddled by technology. With him was his lawyer and confidante, Brian Bellmore. I called him (not to his face) Steve's *consigliore*.

My senior management and I pitched them on our idea for both Leaf and Raptor television channels. Steve was not big on the Raptors, so we mostly focused on the Leaf channel. We showed them two scenarios. One had us doing it ourselves. It would cost us

$7 million to lease and build a broadcast studio, and we would lose money on the venture for several years. The other scenario had us doing a joint venture with Corus, using its broadcast studios and saving us the $7 million capital investment but still giving us a majority position in the new company.

Now, Steve never truly understood what we created with those two channels. For the longest time, he thought they existed only on a computer. We even sent staff to his house to set up the channels on his cable box, and he still didn't get it. But on that Saturday morning, he made two big decisions that would dramatically affect the future of the company. He said, "Why do we want partners? We can afford to do it ourselves." And second, he said, "Let's launch both Leafs and Raptors TV."

The rest of the board—with the exception of Brian Bellmore—got the concept immediately and were an easy sell, but as majority owner we needed Steve's approval. On that day, Steve was a very pleasant surprise. Bellmore thought more short term that day; he wanted to spend any available money on acquiring a defenceman (such money was always available to Pat Quinn and Ken Dryden. Steve never turned down Pat Quinn).

When we made the pitch to the board that day, our broadcast strategy had three clear objectives:

1. Make money and grow enterprise value.
2. Promote our brands, tickets and merchandise.
3. Grow the value of our broadcast rights by keeping the other networks honest in their negotiations.

Leafs TV and Raptors TV (later renamed NBA TV to give the channel a broader national image) were a small investment for MLSE but, as it turned out, probably the most important one we made in the fourteen years I ran the company. We used our two channels as stalking horses to make sure there was competition for the rights to broadcast our games. We kept the bidding networks honest.

If they would not pay what we thought the games were worth, we would put the games on our own channels. This dramatically drove up our broadcast rights revenue. It also forced us to build up an experienced broadcast team of sixty-plus people who learned how to shoot, produce, transmit and sell live games and non-game programming. To our portfolio consisting of Leafs TV and NBA TV we added Gol TV, purchased so we would have the same leverage with our TFC games. We now had core broadcast competency. We could compete with anyone.

So when the CRTC changed the rules to allow us to compete with TSN and Sportsnet, we applied for a fourth channel that could broadcast all the Leaf, Raptor, TFC and Marlie games not broadcast by their respective leagues. We were going to call it Real Sports TV and synergistically market it with our Real Sports Bar & Grill and our Real Sports stores—with the first ones in Toronto and others to follow across Ontario. To get ready for the launch of that channel, we made sure all our rights deals terminated in 2015. Launching a channel such as Real Sports TV is definitely not for the faint-hearted. Such a venture has major distributor and audience—therefore fan—issues. We knew what ugly public battles we would likely go through with distributors and fans by witnessing what the NFL channel and the New York–centric YES Network went through in the United States. In the case of the 2002 launch of YES, which televises Yankee and Brooklyn Net games, fans were enraged when premium prices were charged. You couldn't watch unless you subscribed to a package, and soon fans were angry with the Yankees, the cable companies and the YES Network.

On the other hand, the money involved in cable television and sports is staggering. A 49 per cent minority share in the YES Network sold late in 2012 for $3 billion, so its enterprise value is worth more than twice that. In California, Time Warner paid $3.7 billion in 2012 to gain the rights to broadcast LA Laker games for the next twenty years. Then, in January 2013, it turned around and signed a lucrative television deal with the Los Angeles Dodgers to start its own regional sports network, with a commitment to pay the Dodgers between $7 and $8 billion over the next twenty-five years.

The decision on Real Sports TV was still two years away. We imagined two scenarios. One had us actually launching it. This would have meant living through a public relations disaster for months until the distributors gave in, but ultimately creating a channel that could be worth $1 billion all by itself. The other scenario was that the threat of what I called a "category-killer, big sports box" network would cause Bell or Rogers to pony up for a huge jump in rights fees. The existing Leaf rights deal with Rogers was very good—equal to what the Los Angeles Lakers were getting for their games in those days. But when the Lakers threatened to launch their own channel and Time Warner stepped up and bought the broadcast rights, that blew the existing Leaf deal out of the water. Significant competition and growth continue in the United States, with Fox announcing the launch of a national Fox Sports network to go head to head with ESPN.

\* \* \*

In 2001, when Steve Stavro made those two important decisions, we never knew that our broadcast strategy would realize an even larger fourth objective. Instead of fighting with us, instead of paying a huge price for games, Bell and Rogers bought a majority share of the company in 2012. I don't know if MLSE would have ever launched Real Sports TV. MLSE was certainly capable of it. But a lot of things can change in two years. I believe that Bell and Rogers, two tough competitors, would never have teamed up in this unlikely partnership and paid so much for MLSE without the very real threat of Real Sports TV. That said, I believe that Bell and Rogers got a superb deal when they bought Maple Leaf Sports and Entertainment, and I might even argue that they underpaid—by about $1 billion.

With the decision back in 2001 to get into broadcasting, MLSE also got heavily into other digital platforms. The Leafs had a history of being first in airing their games. First it was radio in 1931 with Foster Hewitt. Then it was TV in 1952, again with Foster Hewitt. The NHL worked with the CBC to broadcast *Hockey Night in Canada* on Saturday nights, and almost all those games featured the Leafs. Today, the Leafs consistently draw the biggest hockey audience in the world at two million viewers a game. But the competition for viewers today is bigger than it has ever been.

Children and young adults especially want to consume their sports and talk about sports in the way they want and when they want. Teams such as the Leafs cannot take future Leaf fans for granted. Having a broadcast division allowed us to synergistically create a number of new platforms that would keep fans engaged in our teams and make us a little money. Today the Leafs, Raptors, TFC and Marlies are among the digital leaders in their respective leagues. MLSE has invested heavily in digital media (including Facebook, Twitter and YouTube ) to ensure that their teams are talking to and with their fans, however and whenever those fans wish. While all the company's teams are registering healthy traffic on their individual digital platforms, the Leafs in particular have an incredible digital following. For instance, mapleleafs.com has almost two million visitors per month. And every month, the team's mobile app draws approximately 160,000 unique users, with 350,000 followers on Twitter and about 1,800,000 interactions on Facebook. Clearly, the Leafs and the rest of the MLSE teams have come a long way since the early days of Foster Hewitt.

And as MLSE invested in and launched Real Sports Bar & Grill, the e11even restaurant and the Team Up Foundation, among other undertakings, all were being marketed through their own websites and social media platforms. With three TV networks, with video boards and websites, we had all these tools to market our teams and our ventures, and to appeal to fans today and into tomorrow. And the more we invested in these digital platforms, the more we increased the value of the company.

Broadcasting, then, is critical to the financial success of sports teams in the twenty-first century and still represents the largest revenue opportunity in the near future.

* * *

One point I find myself stressing repeatedly in this book is the importance of emulating best practices, and sometimes many years transpire before you get a chance to act on an idea long admired. And if broadcasting and sports made for a good pairing, so did food and sports.

When I was at NetStar and working on TSN, I wanted to have a close relationship with ESPN. It was the clear leader in sports and had a number of things going for it. It was, for example, line extending into restaurants, with websites, with ESPN2 and with a great many other ideas. In the consumer products industry, I had quickly learned that US head offices were not interested in Canadian ideas (remember Pizza Pops?). But I proved to myself that if I took the ideas I developed in Canada and the best ones from the United States, my business results were better than those of my US counterparts.

Inspired by the ESPN example, I wanted to launch a TSN-themed restaurant. Since TSN had no food and beverage expertise, management had to search out a third party to do it for us. I thought we had a deal, but the company went back on its word and bailed on us. When I left LCI (by now it was called NetStar) for the Raptors in 1996, the project quickly died.

At NetStar, I had watched Rick Brace—then a vice-president of programming at TSN and now head of specialty television at CTV—hammer out a broadcast deal with Ed Desser of the NBA. I had often spoken with Rick about my plans for a sports bar and restaurant.

Fast-forward fourteen years. On the night in June 2010 that MLSE launched its brand-new Real Sports Bar & Grill in Toronto, I greeted each of our guests on the red carpet at the restaurant's entrance. Rick Brace was one, and as I shook his hand, I said, "I told you I would launch a sports bar." I just hadn't said when.

In the meantime, a second Real Sports Bar & Grill opened successfully in the ByWard Market in Ottawa in November 2012. Good ideas do find homes.

* * *

While I was working for TSN in 1996, my basketball dream was still very much alive. I had methodically been going about the business of educating myself in all the areas necessary to run a sports franchise. The dream was like a candle burning—a small point of light that was simply there, refusing to be snuffed. Consumer products had taught me about marketing, branding, finance, sales and general management. SkyDome had taught me all about running sports facilities. My work with Larry Tanenbaum on applying for an NBA franchise for Toronto taught me a lot about the NBA. And LCI/NetStar had taught me a bit about broadcasting.

So when Allan Slaight asked me to have lunch with him to talk about the possibility of me becoming the president of the Raptors, I knew exactly what to do.

# CHAPTER 7

# THE RAPTORS ARE COMING!
# THE RAPTORS ARE COMING!

When I was a boy growing up in Windsor, I loved basketball. I was a big fan of the Michigan Wolverines (the University of Michigan's NCAA basketball team) and the Windsor Lancers. I was clearly not good enough to play on my high school basketball team, but I nonetheless practised my game all the time. I shot hoops in the driveway of the Johnsons, who lived across the street and two doors down. They had a cement drive, with a hoop over the garage door. When I missed the hoop (often the case), the ball banged the garage door. The Johnsons seemed not to mind.

Sometimes we'd play two on two with my brother and a few neighbourhood kids, but most of the time it was just me and my fantasies. "With two seconds remaining, the ball is in Richard Peddie's hands, he shoots . . ." We'd go to Detroit Piston games (the team was awful in those days) and we'd buy the cheap seats, then slide down to the better seats later during the game. One of my favourite players was Dave Bing, now the mayor of Detroit.

As poor as I was at basketball, I was worse at hockey. We did play a lot of street hockey (I remember picking cinders out of my shins), and we skated on the backyard rink my father built (there was little organized hockey then in Windsor), and we followed the Detroit Red Wings and the Toronto Maple Leafs and got their sweaters as Christmas gifts, but there was something about basketball. In hockey, you might score three or four goals once in a blue moon; in basketball, a gifted player might score thirty or more points (Kobe Bryant of the Los Angeles Lakers once scored 81 points—against the Raptors—and Wilt Chamberlain once scored 100 points in a game). There were so many measurements to basketball: points, assists, blocks, rebounds. My affinity for the sport started in my childhood and I never lost it. At Colgate, we had a basketball team and we'd play against Procter & Gamble. In those games, I played to win. I was feisty and aggressive.

Watching the Windsor Lancer basketball team win three national championships when I was a student at the University of Windsor in the late 1960s stirred a dream: What would it be like to run a basketball team—an NBA basketball team? I articulated that dream in a private journal—the one my girlfriend had given me—and the dream stayed with me as I headed off to the world of consumer products, and where I stayed for almost twenty years. My aspiration neither faded nor surged; it was simply there.

The flame flared a little when I took the job at SkyDome: the facility played host to numerous NBA exhibition games, and I talked to parties interested in bringing an NBA team to play in the stadium. Then, in 1993, I took a six-month leave of absence from my duties at the Dome to join a consortium led by Palestra (Larry Tanenbaum's group) that made a vigorous attempt to bring an NBA franchise to Toronto. When the league rebuffed that proposal, it looked for all the world like my dream was finally done.

Why did that attempt in 1993 go wrong—despite all our hard work and despite the expenditure of some $2 million?

Larry Tanenbaum, who made his fortune in the construction industry, has had more influence on me and my career than any other single person. I never worked as long or as closely with anyone else. For most of my fourteen years with Maple Leaf Sports and Entertainment, I reported to the board and not to Larry, but he was my de facto boss. We have had our battles in the past two decades, but no one has been more supportive or more generous. He was the one leading the charge in 1992 when the Denver Nuggets were up for sale. And when Larry decided to go for them, I was thrilled that he asked me to join his band.

Our first mistake was trying to dictate the timing. All commissioners in professional sports want to control league expansion and especially possible franchise transfers from one city to another. When the league pushed back on the Denver sale, Larry wisely listened and he passed. We then decided to submit an unsolicited bid for a *new* franchise.

We thus came face to face with the formidable David Stern, commissioner of the NBA. (He announced in October 2012 that he would be stepping down on February 1, 2014—precisely thirty years after commencing his tenure as commissioner.) If you ever watch the NBA draft, you will see Stern, all five feet, eight inches of him, happily shaking hands with a player who may be six feet, ten inches tall. But there is nothing small about David Stern. He's smart, he's aggressive and he uses fear to his advantage. When he took over the league, the NBA had little TV exposure, drug use among players was rampant and its reputation was in tatters. Stern made it all right.

He would often come last into the room, preceded by his entourage. The entrance was meant to be grand, and the tone in the room changed on his arrival. He always came in swinging; in later years, often at me. When we finally did get an NBA franchise, Stern would enter a meeting, eye me and say, "Richard Peddie? You still here? What are you trying to sell today?" At governors and owners meetings, the hired team managers seldom asked questions. For a while, I was the exception. "Oh," he would say, "Richard, you have a question. You always have a question, don't you?" At one negotiating meeting, Stern said, "I know what's going to happen today. I'm going to get angry, Peddie is going to get angry and nothing will get accomplished."

Stern's lieutenants, Adam Silver (who will succeed him as commissioner) and Joel Litvin, worked exceptionally hard for Stern, and they were exceptionally loyal to him. I didn't so much like Stern as admire him.

In 1993, we forced Stern's hand. He did not want to consider our entry into the league but he could not ignore a thoroughly prepared application and a significant dollar deposit. He had to take it to the twenty-eight NBA governors. The last two expansion franchises, in Charlotte and Miami, had each paid $33 million for their teams. Existing teams could not ignore a new franchise fee of around $100 million—especially since all would get a share of that fee.

We started romancing and lobbying the other twenty-eight teams in the belief (mistaken, it turned out) that the NBA worked as a democracy. I visited twenty franchises, introducing myself and learning about best team and arena practices. I was clearly looking for their votes. Larry Tanenbaum and his partner Joel Rose did the same thing with many of the owners. By the end, we thought we had about twenty or more owners on our side. As it turned out, we were probably too visible, too enthusiastic. And the NBA, we would discover, does not function as a democracy.

There was a vote all right, but the way it goes is this: An expansion committee is formed with a few owners who work closely with Stern and his staff. The committee makes a decision and takes it to the full board, and the board always agrees with the committee's recommendation.

Our mistake was in not really listening. Sure we asked the league if it was okay that we visited teams while we worked on developing a team name and logo and created potential corporate promotions. What we should have done is ask them: Is this what you want us to do? Instead we said: This is what we are doing—Is that okay? Big difference.

We made no end of tactical errors. Our presentation materials were too finished, too slick, too commercial. We showed the NBA an impactful TV ad that introduced our name for the team—the Toronto Thunder. During the screening, Stern turned to one of his lieutenants and said, "Where the hell did that name come from?" It came from thousands of dollars of fan research and design work, but we missed the key point: *the league* picks franchise names and designs team logos. We also had mock-ups of national fan promotions that were, we later learned, not entirely within league rules. Palestra had submitted a comprehensive application for a franchise, making a compelling case for Toronto (demographics, economics, head offices, corporate sponsors, transit, broadcast, even how the exhibition games drew at Maple Leaf Gardens and SkyDome).

The main competition for the Toronto franchise was coming from another consortium comprising three parties: restaurateur John Bitove Jr., broadcast executive Allan Slaight and Scotiabank. As I understand it, the consortium's bid was more low-key and personal. John Bitove had done a smart thing by agreeing to host the world championships of basketball in Toronto at SkyDome in 1994. He took the financial risk and did most of the grunt work to put it on. Because there was a US team of NBA players in the championship, the league wanted the competition to go well. The NBA owed Bitove for all his efforts, and we initially underestimated the importance of this IOU.

At the end of our presentation, Stern asked us what we would pay for a franchise. George Taylor of Labatt, part of the proposed ownership group, gave a rational answer: "We will pay a fair price that will give us a return on our investment."

When the same question was put to it, Bitove's group said, "Whatever you think is a fair price." In the end, Bitove et al. got the franchise for US$125 million—overpriced by our calculations by about US$40 million—but they got it fair and square.

A look at more recent events in professional sports suggests that some have learned from our mistakes and some continue to make them. The Winnipeg Jets owners worked perfectly with Gary Bettman and the NHL while transferring the Atlanta Thrashers to Winnipeg. On the flip side of the coin was the clumsy, arrogant and failed attempt by Jim Balsillie to move an NHL franchise (first the Pittsburgh Penguins and then the Phoenix Coyotes) to Hamilton. He went down there as if he were the cat's meow. He knew the rules but started selling tickets using the Pens' logo before anything had been signed or settled.

On September 30, 1993, the NBA was set to announce its decision on who would have the Toronto franchise. The Palestra team was meeting at Larry's house to hear what we were certain would be the good news. I had stopped at a liquor store in midtown Toronto to buy champagne to celebrate. As I was getting out of the car, The Fan radio station broke the story that the Bitove-Slaight group got the franchise. I was numb. I felt ill. I was angry and depressed. I got back in the car, slammed the door and drove to Larry's house, where the mood was funereal. We were all in a state of shock. I woke up the next day so sad.

The basketball dream that I had nursed for years was dead and buried. Coincidentally, the person who had headed the NBA expansion committee was Jerry Colangelo, father of former Raptor president and general manager Bryan Colangelo. Larry

Tanenbaum also took the loss hard, and he too was extremely angry and disappointed. His relationship with Jerry Colangelo was frosty for years afterward, although today they are close friends again.

Although our bid failed, we did succeed in hammering home to the NBA that it made perfect sense to bring pro basketball to the city of Toronto—and to Canada. Ultimately, Vancouver rode our coattails when the NBA needed a balanced thirty-team league.

\* \* \*

Bitove and Slaight were now the owners of the newest NBA franchise, the Toronto Raptors. Isiah Thomas, the legendary former point guard with the Detroit Pistons, was brought in as a minority shareholder and as general manager. Bitove and Slaight at first set their sights on Dundas Square as the location of their arena but wisely changed their minds and purchased the old post office building at Bay and Front Streets. This prime location was near the Toronto subway line, the main train station and the GO Transit station (the regional public transportation system); right beside the Gardiner Expressway; and within walking distance of the Bay Street towers and sponsor head offices. Setting the arena here was a brilliant decision.

On the other hand, storm clouds were forming. Bitove and Slaight were having trouble getting the finances to work: the financial projections for a stadium that was going to cost the owners around $214 million of their own money was not very attractive to lenders. On top of that, the US$125 million they paid for the franchise needed to be financed, and, as mentioned, it was too high by about US$40 million. They were starting to fall behind their promised arena construction start date. And their title sponsor, Air Canada, was worried that it was not going to be built at all. While construction was under way, the team played at SkyDome, but early ticket, sponsor and broadcast revenues were soft. And finally, Slaight and Bitove were not getting along.

In their shareholders' agreement they had what's called a shotgun clause. Either party could take the other out by offering a higher price than the other. When the partnership did break down, this clause was triggered. Bitove scrambled to find investment partners, but the arena and franchise costs did not make for an appealing financial proposition. Slaight, on the other hand, was a billionaire thanks to his very profitable Standard Broadcasting. He would have preferred that Bitove come up with financing—offer a fair price for Slaight's shares and take him out. But it was clear that Bitove was having trouble coming up with the money. Complicating things was the fact that Bitove was the president of the team. If Slaight took him out, he needed a president.

And that's when my basketball dream resurrected itself.

I had met Slaight only very informally once before, but as he started asking around, my name kept coming up. Other than Paul Beeston, there probably was no one more qualified for the job in Canada than me. Slaight invited me to lunch at a restaurant at St. Clair and Yonge, near his office. I brought one piece of paper. Not a resumé but more of a checklist of all the skills and disciplines that a successful Raptor president should have. I put the paper on the table and showed it to him.

- Marketing/sales skills. Knows potential sponsors. Nineteen years in consumer products.
- Financial skills and general management skills. President of four companies.
- Facility management (music, suites, food and beverage). SkyDome.
- Facility construction. Some at SkyDome.

- Broadcast skills. NetStar.
- Sports knowledge. Learning from Blue Jays, Argos, TSN and NBA bid.
- Public Relations. SkyDome and NetStar.

Allan Slaight and I had a great discussion over that lunch. He didn't offer me the job on the spot, but I think I got it then. The official news came at precisely 11:30 p.m. on November 26, 1996, when I got a call from Allan. "You're the new president and CEO of the Toronto Raptors basketball club," he said. I went back to bed, turned off the lights and smiled in the darkness for the longest time.

There were times early on when I knew I was in over my head as president of the Raptors. A week into the job, I realized that the man brought in to be executive vice-president (Isiah Thomas) was both the real deal (he had been named among the top fifty best NBA players of all time) and a powerful adversary. Here I was, a guy who had sold soap and crescent rolls, crossing swords with the man nicknamed the Smiling Assassin. He was charismatic, he had a flashing smile and the media loved him. The flower shops all saw a drop in business when he left town. Someone very senior in the Piston organization had called to warn me about this man, that I was not to trust him. I wish now I had listened more carefully.

Thomas thought he could assemble a team of reputed "bad guys" and reform them. It did not work out. Thomas did design the Raptor dressing room at the Air Canada Centre, and he did draft two superb players in Damon Stoudamire and Tracy McGrady, but those are about the only things he did right.

Allan Slaight never included Thomas—a minority shareholder, after all—in the search for president. That was a mistake. A typical arrangement in the NBA is to have a basketball guy named president of team operations and someone such as me named president on the business side. I had been given both positions, and when I suggested to Slaight that the team president position be offered to Thomas, he agreed. Thomas, a keen player of Machiavellian gamesmanship, turned him down. This allowed Thomas to play the role of wounded party.

Initially, Thomas had media support in Toronto. By the end, and especially owing to the team's poor record, most wanted him out of town.

Isiah Thomas never did fully gain my trust. He would do things such as this: the two of us were chatting at an All-Star game one time, and people were passing by and saying hello to him. Making conversation, I just said, "Everybody knows you, Isiah." Now Isiah had the ear of a certain Toronto reporter, and next day a story ran that suggested I was flabbergasted that everyone knew Isiah. The story made me look naïve. Who was the source of that quote? Unless a reporter was within earshot (unlikely), the source was Isiah Thomas.

He had the media and fans believing he was a good businessman. I saw no evidence of that in the one and a half years we worked together. I think he went to only one ACC construction meeting. The input he gave was on the dressing room—he had a good idea to make it round so that all the players could look in to the coach and to one another.

The dressing room was one tiny component of a much larger task—getting the Air Canada Centre built. That was my first job with the Raptors. I looked at the architects' drawings and made a couple of important changes. Bitove was a Big Ten Indiana University grad. He went to school loving the big university field houses and planned for around 23,000 seats—way too many for basketball in any market, let alone Toronto. I scaled them back as much as I could, to about 21,000. Scarcity is a great sales tool.

Unbelievably, the capital budget did not include an ice plant, nor ice surface and boards. I said, "You can't build an arena in Canada without ice." I was already thinking that we had to get the Leafs in the building if the Raptors and ACC were going to be financially viable. We put ice in the budget. The Bitove plans included a large cigar area bar; I changed it to a microbrewery and pub. SkyDome had an undeserved reputation for watery beer. I figured that having a brewpub would speak to freshness and quality and would be more successful in the long term, especially since the city was in the process of banning smoking in all public places.

We did not have a budget for a Raptor practice court, but I was optimistic. I had work crews put in a strengthened floor so it could accommodate one at a later date. When the Leafs bought the ACC and increased the capital budget to $265 million, we added the court.

I reflected on many of the best practices I had gathered on my tours of twenty NBA arenas while working on the failed Palestra bid. For instance, when I went to a game at the Palace of Auburn Hills outside Detroit, I noticed the powerful lamps on the roof beaming columns of light into the night sky. We added those to tell Toronto when there was an event at the arena. We also incorporated floodlights into the building's logo design. The budget was now $214 million. I reworked the financials (optimistically) and with a lot of help from Scotiabank and Slaight's Standard Broadcasting CFO, David Coriat, we got financing.

Air Canada, meanwhile, had committed to an important upfront payment that we needed for cash flow, but they were very hesitant about giving us the money because they worried the building would never be built. Slaight and I had dinner with Lamar Durrett, Air Canada's CEO. The two of us hit it off, in part because I had put myself through school working for Air Canada and spent the summer of 1969 working at its head office in Montreal. Durrett looked me in the eye and asked in his deep Southern accent if we were definitely going to build ACC because he himself had his doubts. "That dog won't hunt" is how he put it. I said, "We are going to build the Air Canada Centre. Absolutely. You can count on it." He gave us the money.

The Toronto Maple Leafs, in the meantime, were now owned by the Ontario Teachers' Pension Plan, Larry Tanenbaum and the TD Bank—with Steve Stavro as the majority shareholder. They were looking to build an arena of their own. We couldn't have that. With two arenas in town, the Leafs and Raptors would have to share suite holders, sponsors, season seat holders and other events, such as concerts. And ACC would definitely get the smaller share. The Vancouver Grizzlies of the NBA were soon to fail in Vancouver. I strongly believe that if two arenas had been built in Toronto, the Raptors would have failed too.

We had a saying—a strategy, more like it—that spurred us on: "The first one with a shovel in the ground wins." We started construction on February 4, 1997.

Our strategy paid off. Slaight was able to sell the Raptors and get out from owning a franchise he never truly wanted. The city got a much better arena that would be one of the world's best concert venues and attract hundreds of events, including the NHL All-Star game and the World Cup of Hockey. Maple Leaf Sports and Entertainment got a building with two major tenants and no serious competitor. My aggressive building strategy and speaking out about the Leafs possibly getting government funding did not put me in a very good position with the new owners. I had been in the enemy camp, and now suddenly I was in the enemy's employ—or maybe not. About two weeks after the sale, Larry Tanenbaum and Ontario Teachers' Pension Plan director Dean Metcalf asked to come see me. I thought I was toast. So much so I began cleaning out my office.

To my surprise, they offered me the job as interim president and CEO of Maple Leaf Sports and Entertainment. The plan was to give me six months to prove myself. There were two conditions—lose the earring I had acquired at SkyDome and get a haircut (I had long hair and sometimes wore a ponytail. Both the long hair and earring were about me fitting in and liking the music business). I agreed immediately. Did I sell out? Hardly. Who wouldn't give up those things, given what was on the table? I was getting a chance to run both the Leafs and Raptors—making true Gordon Craig's prediction during his announcement to the NetStar senior management team that I was taking on the president's job with the Raptors.

"One day," he told the NetStar team (with me present), "Richard Peddie will end up running the Leafs too."

* * *

My first year as president of the Raptors was a difficult one. At thirty wins versus fifty-two losses, the team's record was okay for a new entry to the league. However, Isiah Thomas was keeping Slaight and me away from the players by not inviting us into the dressing room or encouraging us to have any interaction with the players. I understood why Thomas was doing this to me (he and I were like oil and water), but I could not understand why he seemed to want Slaight to look uninterested and uninformed.

What is often misunderstood by fans is that NBA basketball players and NHL hockey players do have an interest in getting to know the owners of the team, so Thomas putting a wedge between owners and players was more than just a slight. When Larry Tanenbaum arrived on the scene, he started the tradition of an annual dinner at his (rather magnificent) house. At first, only Raptor players were invited, but later the invitation was extended to Leaf players as well. It's a pretty cool evening. I remember Colleen and I sitting beside a hockey player originally from Saskatchewan and a basketball player from the American South. These two athletes seemed worlds apart, but I was amused to discover that one thing they shared was a passion for the video game Call of Duty.

In year one with the Raptors, the big surprise for me was learning that Slaight did not really want to own the team and was looking to sell it, as I mentioned.

I had left NetStar to follow a dream. I also was leaving a guaranteed multi-million-dollar payout when NetStar was sold or did an IPO—an initial public offering, when shares in a company are sold to the general public. I would not have left if I thought I was to be only a basketball president for twelve months. Slaight first of all lined up a potential owner from Chicago. I might have had a chance holding on to my job if that had transpired, but that plan failed. Slaight then worked out a deal with Isiah Thomas to sell him the team contingent on Thomas getting financing.

If that succeeded, I was gone. Thomas and I simply did not get along, and there was no chance he was going to keep me on. All spring and early summer of 1997, Thomas worked hard to find financing. He was having trouble because he had few dollars to contribute himself, yet he wanted to be in control. The Raptors had a large employee meeting scheduled for a couple of weeks before the projected closing date. I figured if Thomas was to own the team, he should address the employees on his vision for the team, the arena, who his financial partners were going to be and how he intended to run the business. He wanted to cancel the meeting. It's scheduled, I told him.

Thomas did speak that day, but there was nothing in the speech about his vision for the business or about his partners. He just talked in generalities about the team, proving to me once again that he had no vision for the business and no business expertise. Hell of an All-Star point guard and a winning, alluring smile, but when it came to business, he was the hollow man. Thomas never closed the deal. Slaight stayed on as owner.

Thomas resigned as team president and sold his shares in the company in the fall of 1998. The 1997–1998 Raptors team, with Thomas calling the shots, won sixteen and lost sixty-six, with an ugly seventeen-game losing streak.

Thomas left the Raptors to run the Continental Basketball Association; it went bankrupt. He then became an on-air NBA commentator, but that only lasted two years (though he did return in December 2012 as a part-time studio analyst, appearing twice a month). He coached the Indiana Pacers from 2000 to 2003 before being fired. He went to the New York Knicks, made terrible trades and was named in a sexual harassment suit that cost Madison Square Garden dearly.

That case was finally settled in December 2007. The terms meant that Anucha Browne Sanders—the former Knicks' senior marketing executive who had accused Thomas of verbally abusing her and making unwanted advances—was paid $11.5 million in damages, plus $4 million in legal fees. The Garden paid the entire amount, and in a statement called the result "a travesty of justice." For his part, Thomas maintained that he did nothing wrong.

Finally, Isiah Thomas was fired in 2012 from his head coaching job at Division II Florida International University after a losing three-year record of 26–65.

More recently, Isiah Thomas has been involved in a basketball-related campaign to stem gang violence in his hometown of Chicago. And I give him credit for this. Thomas helped raise $500,000 to fund "Peace Game" basketball tournaments in which gang members competed on the court.

During the months that Thomas was chasing the ownership of the Raptors, the media were depicting me as the lame-duck Raptors president. My long-time assistant, Alda Byers, had a wicked sense of humour. She gave me a toy duck with its leg bandaged. Slaight, who loved a good joke, saw it and had a laugh—though

I didn't think that the chance of losing my dream after only a few months was so funny. That night when I got home, there was a bottle of Baby Duck on my porch with a note from Slaight.

Isiah Thomas was gone, but Allan Slaight still wanted to sell the Raptors, and the natural buyers were the Leafs. In the spring of 2008, Steve Stavro, Larry Tanenbaum, the Ontario Teachers' Pension Plan and TD Bank purchased the Raptors and created Maple Leaf Sports and Entertainment (MLSE). The Air Canada Centre, which was just over 40 per cent complete, was given a new expanded construction budget of $265 million, with the additional monies allowing us to put in a better video board, expand the number of suites to 150, put in additional amenities such as an escalator and significantly upgrade the stadium finishes.

This new infusion of capital also allowed us to operate our own food and beverages, which turned out to be a huge strategic move. The seat colours were adapted from the Maple Leaf Gardens (gold, red, blue, green), with the upper greys (what used to be the cheap seats at the Gardens) turned into platinum seats that were the closest to the court/ice and the most expensive. In the United States, most arenas and stadiums are largely built with government money. The teams get the keys, pay a nominal rent and then take all the revenues. I was always proud that MLSE paid its own way. (Frankly, I don't understand why Daryl Katz in Edmonton or Pierre Péladeau in Quebec City—both very rich men—are seeking major funding from government for new arenas in their cities. Katz owns the Oilers and Péladeau wants an NHL franchise back in Quebec. Both men can afford to finance their buildings themselves.)

The next few months in 2008 were incredibly busy—merging two organizations, building ACC, selling suites and sponsors. The management team was largely Raptor people. Plus Leaf personnel such as Tom Anselmi, Ken Dryden and, as it turned out, the best CFO I would have in my twenty-nine years as a president, Ian Clarke.

I was feeling pretty good about my chances of becoming the permanent president and CEO of MLSE, but I had heard that Stavro was talking to a number of other people about the job. So I invited Larry Tanenbaum to lunch. We met at Il Posto, an upscale place in the posh Yorkville district. He reviewed my progress in the job, which was excellent, he said. But I told him what I had heard about Stavro looking to replace me, and I handed Larry an envelope with my resignation inside. I had had it with Stavro. I was working very hard, and the newly merged company was making good progress, but he was still looking to replace me. My move was a bluff: I thought I had leverage, and I was emboldened by a contract I had with MLSE that would have paid me a handsome severance even should I resign. (Though I tried, I never managed to negotiate such a clause again.) Still, I was hoping that Larry would not accept my resignation. And he didn't.

Within a week I had the permanent job. Years later, MLSE directors Dean Metcalf at the Ontario Teachers' Pension Plan and John MacIntyre at TD Bank told me that I had the job right from the start. It would have been nice had you told me that from the start, I kidded them.

In the 2001–2002 season, at the height of Vinsanity (the buzz created by Vince Carter), the Raptors would sell out all forty-one home games and win forty-two games. However, their record under my watch was only 493 wins against 685 loses (and I watched almost every one of those games in their entirety). And only three playoff appearances after 172 players, six coaches and four general managers. The record is disappointing, it's unacceptable and it wore me down. Losing was the toughest part of my job.

\* \* \*

I tried to follow Paul Beeston's advice about not getting too close to the players, but most Raptors stood out as "good guys."

There was Alvin Williams, who gave his all every game but had to retire far too early because of his knees. I was delighted that he was the first alumnus to work for the team and very sad to see him let go in the summer of 2013. Alvin was a great player. Talented and hard working, personable and accommodating, he played through pain; I admired him as a person and I admired his values. I understand that a new manager wants to make a stamp on a team when he first arrives, but letting Alvin go might have been a mistake. He was and is a quality guy, and I think MLSE is going to miss him.

There was Jerome "Junk Yard Dog" Williams, who displayed non-stop enthusiasm. Fans loved him barking like a dog, his fellow players not so much. He was great in the community. I think he should have kept playing after the New York Knicks bought him out.

Antonio Davis was actually a power forward playing out of position at centre. Still, he carried the 2000–2001 team on his back into the playoffs.

Doug Christie was a heck of a defender. He scored the highest on the fitness beep test, which measures cardiac fitness: a player is given so many seconds to run from one foul line to the other, and as the test unfolds the beeps keep coming faster and faster. Christie went farther and longer than anyone in team history. A few players could manage three minutes of this; Doug was still going strong after thirteen.

Charles Oakley was a rugged and durable power forward who played for the Raptors between 1998 and 2001. We picked him up in a trade to add toughness to a young, soft team. He was a tough guy with an even tougher reputation. Charles was famous for not taking any guff and for having a teammate's back. The team had never had anyone like him and has had no one like him since.

He was, hands down, my favourite Raptor. Quirky, smart, street smart. I would still have Charles as the second colour guy on the Raptor TV broadcasts. He was our version of Charles Barkley except you would need closed-captioning to translate the Oakisms, such as: "We needed that win like a hog needs slop." Or this one, when he was offering his take on Isiah Thomas: "It's like he's got a puzzle and he dumped pieces in the trash in ten different places." Or his opinion of young players coming into the league these days: "They've just given them more avenues, they've given them everything, and they don't have anything to look forward to, so when you want them to do something that's tough, they can't do it. The league is just like daycare."

Charles would say outrageous things. Once he told the media that 50 per cent of NBA players smoke marijuana. The next day, NBA deputy commissioner Russ Granik phoned me. "What the hell is Oakley doing?" he asked. "Where does he get off saying that?"

Coincidentally, I was having lunch with Charles that day. "Charles," I said, "where did you get the information that 50 per cent of NBA players smoke dope?"

"Oh, I don't have research—I just know."

"Does that mean 50 per cent of the Raptors smoke?"

"Oh no—none of the Raptors smoke up," he told me. I just laughed.

Charles was also a clotheshorse who wore stylish, made-to-measure suits and often a huge fedora. It was a pretty impressive look on a muscular six-foot, nine-inch man. Charles noticed what I wore—he'd even open up my jacket to check the label. One early spring day, it was unseasonably hot. I did ponder as I dressed for the Sunday game whether it was too early for a light-coloured spring sports jacket. I actually worried that Charles would say something. After the game I went into the locker room. Charles saw me and simply said, "Too early."

Tracy McGrady was a wonderful talent, and I wonder how good the Raptors could have been had he stayed. But he was set on leaving the team as soon as he could. At the NBA governors meeting the day we voted to end the 1998–1999 lockout, David Stern and the NBA Players Association head, Billy Hunter, were sitting at the head table facing all the governors. They said, "We will get what we expect from the players. If we set the bar low, we will get low behaviour on and off the court. If we set it high, we will get the best behaviour." I decided right then to create a "business of basketball" presentation for the players. I clearly remember presenting it to the team and watching as McGrady slouched and fell asleep in the back row.

And then there was Vince Carter. He had amazing athletic talents but he did not work hard—at all. Bill Simmons wrote about Vince Carter in *The Book of Basketball*: "I've never been a fan of gifted offensive stars who thrived in dunk contests vs. playoff games." Vince had little heart, and no ability to rise to the occasion in the way that Michael Jordan of the Chicago Bulls did and Kobe Bryant of the Los Angeles Lakers still does.

Vince had no desire to spend the extra time in the gym or the weight room to get better. On the other hand, Vince put us on the map. His electrifying dunks and his All-Star credentials made our team a must-see in Toronto and across the NBA. One season, the ACC sold out forty-one consecutive times. He was instrumental in creating what we called irrational exuberance. People who were not even fans wanted to come to the games.

When I was house hunting in Caledon, north of Toronto, my real estate agent told me he was getting season tickets to the Raptors. "Great," I said, "are you a big fan?" No, he had never been to a game, but he said everyone was excited about them, so he wanted to be there. Few players can sell tickets, but during his short career with the Raptors, Vince sure could—at least at the start of his career. When he started getting injured and taking his time going back on the court, when he started laughing and goofing around on the bench, when he started frequently saying "I don't care" when asked about his behaviour or giving less than his all, the fans and media began to turn on him.

In the beginning, we tiptoed around Vince and gave him whatever he wanted. He laughed and joked around a lot. We'd get blown out, and he'd be sitting on the bench with a towel over his head tickling the guy next to him.

His agent at International Management Group was Mark Steinberg, also Tiger Woods's agent. This was long before Tiger's very public meltdown, when he was still a PR dream—always saying the right things about the sport, his game and the fans. One time the fans were booing Carter, and when the press later asked him about it, his response was "I don't care." I once sent to his agent a clipping with every one of Carter's "I don't care" comments highlighted in yellow. I also offered to give him tapes of interviews Carter did. My efforts went for naught. Carter's behaviour did not change.

As for the parking space given Vince Carter's mother at the ACC Centre and all the jealousies and negative press it inspired, file it under pilot error. In the CBC-TV comedy series *The Newsroom* (which ran intermittently between 1996 and 2005), Ken Finkleman played the role of a self-obsessed executive producer at the CBC whose primary concern was his choice parking spot in the underground lot. Parking was and remains a huge issue at the Air Canada Centre. There are only 214 spaces available—to be divvied up among owners, players, coaches, managers, board members and suite holders. These spaces are valued because they offer security, shelter in inclement weather, and the guarantee—if you're a player on game day—of a quiet and safe walk to the dressing room without being besieged by fans or media. The NBA, in fact, mandates secure parking for athletes.

And when there were arguments at the ACC about parking, those issues landed on my desk. I sometimes had to say no to some very important people—owners sometimes sought parking for their children. For better or for worse (in this case, for worse), Glen Grunwald gave Carter's mother a parking spot. This came back to haunt me because media in Toronto were trying to make the case that Peddie cared more about the Raptors than he did the Leafs, and here was "the evidence."

Vince was a Mama's boy, and his mother was a force. The Directors' Lounge at the ACC, for example, is meant—as the name suggests—for directors, as well as owners and invited sponsors. Larry Tanenbaum told Carter's mother to come in "any time you want." And she did. Mrs. Carter got used to going there, and even after Vince was traded in 2004, she attempted to go into the lounge. It was suggested to her that this was now inappropriate.

In the early days of his career, they would say of Vince that he was half man and half amazing. One year he won the NBA dunk contest with three dunks that will never be replicated; I swear he went ten feet in the air.

In those days, whatever Vince wanted, Vince got. Today, every team in the NBA has security to protect players from being blackmailed, from death threats, from organized crime—and from themselves. Today, the Raptors' security person is a former member of the Toronto police force, and he's a pro.

In the days of Vince Carter, we didn't have such security. Vince had his own: a lumpy guy called Peanut, whom I nicknamed "the fan prevention department" because he was so rude to fans and so adept at keeping them at bay and away from Vince—who was also often rude and arrogant to fans. Case in point: our last game against the Grizzlies (March 11, 2001) before they left Vancouver in 2001 and moved to Memphis. When we won the game 101–84, many fans wanted to embrace the Raptors as Canada's team. After the game, the team bus was surrounded by fans chanting Vince's name, for he had been dazzling that afternoon, scoring twenty-five points. They wanted him to come out and sign autographs. He would not do it. I was on the bus, and I have always regretted not forcing him to go out and sign programs. Bad judgment on my part.

Vince Carter had not graduated from the University of North Carolina but had gone back to school in the summer and finished his degree. I remember someone coming up to me in the dressing room, also in 2001, saying that Vince wanted to go to his graduation ceremony.

"When is it?" I asked.

Turned out the ceremony would fall in the middle of the second round of the playoffs. I said no way. But I later learned that Larry Tanenbaum and Glen Grunwald said okay. As it happened, Vince's graduation ceremony was on the same day as the seventh game of the second-round playoffs with the Philadelphia 76ers in May 2001.

Vince, who had flown to North Carolina on Larry's plane for his graduation the night before, only spent a brief time at the ceremony itself. After posing for photographs with his classmates beforehand, he proceeded with them into the stadium and left shortly after to fly back to Philadelphia in time for the pre-game team meeting. His coach, Lenny Wilkens, had warned Vince he would come under intense criticism if he played poorly after deciding to attend his graduation, and Lenny was certainly right about that. Most of his fellow players refused to metaphorically toss Vince under the bus, but two of the team's fiercest competitors—Antonio Davis and Chris Childs—had terse "no comments" when asked by the CBC about Vince's decision.

The new Raptors GM, Rob Babcock (among the worst hires in my entire career), finally traded Vince Carter to the New Jersey Nets for Eric Williams, Aaron Williams, two late first-round draft picks from the Nets and the injured Alonzo Mourning (whom we bought out before he ever played a game for the Raptors). The board at MLSE did not like the trade. I did not like the trade. But to veto it meant we were meddling. Whenever the media accused me of meddling, I'd point to the Carter trade as proof that I didn't. The two Williams never contributed much to the team. The draft choices never turned into key players, and Mourning went on to win an NBA championship with the Miami Heat. This was a horrible trade, one of the worst in the history of the NBA and one that set the Raptors team back years.

Rob Babcock as GM of the Raptors was in over his head. He did not have what it took, at least not then, and the press could see right through his inexperience, his naivete. This is Toronto: you have to have confidence and a body of work. I hired him in June 2004; fifteen months later, he was gone. Since 2006, Rob Babcock has been an assistant general manager with the Minnesota Timberwolves.

Hiring Rob Babcock really strained the relationship I had with Larry Tanenbaum. He was livid that I hired Babcock and livid with Babcock's performance. And he had a right to be; I should have listened to him. Larry would have fired me right then and there if he could have, but the shareholders' agreement dictated that replacing the CEO required unanimous agreement among all owners. That clause probably helped me last fourteen years because over that period there were a few times that one shareholder or another was unhappy with my performance.

Larry and I were estranged for about a year, and the media picked up on it. But eventually we sat down and had a professional and candid conversation. I apologized. Larry had challenged me to be a much better CEO. He really threw down the gauntlet, accusing me of being a chief operating officer and not a chief executive officer.

"Where's the creativity?" he asked. "Where are the new ideas for growth?" We agreed to always be honest and candid with each other. After that, our relationship got much stronger. The media continued to say our relationship was in trouble, but actually it was better than ever. I liked working for Larry. He listened to my ideas and almost always supported me. I listened to his ideas, and I helped him in any way I could. And his challenge to be a better CEO caused me to dial up my efforts to grow the company.

The Vince Carter trade also reinforced in my mind that I had made a big mistake in hiring Babcock. Rob was a good guy with just okay credentials. Jack McCloskey, who was acting as the Raptor interim GM after we let Glen Grunwald go, was a huge fan of Babcock. McCloskey had solid credentials: two NBA championships as GM of the Detroit Pistons, and his point of view influenced me strongly. But Rob had no clue about how to be a general manager in the NBA.

Rob did do two things right. He signed point guard Jose Calderon and he hired Wayne Embry. Wayne was a five-time NBA All-Star with the Celtics and the Bucks, so he had earned his spot in basketball's Hall of Fame. He was also the NBA's first African-American GM, a successful GM of both the Cleveland Cavaliers and the Milwaukee Bucks. Wayne was a big help to me as I dealt with the general Babcock issue and the horrible relationship between coach Sam Mitchell and Babcock. When I fired Babcock, I made Wayne the interim GM, and he was able to quickly trade Jalen Rose and his big long-term contract to the Knicks. This freed up significant cap room for Bryan Colangelo to make the important moves he did in dramatically improving the team in 2007.

Chris Bosh was a good kid, a player we nurtured and an All-Star player who generally gave his best. He was never an issue until the spring of 2010, in his final season with the Raptors. After

Christmas, he changed. Chris was an unrestricted free agent, and Colangelo would have loved to re-sign him. But it seemed that someone had whispered in his ear about the bright lights in other markets. He was legitimately injured (broken nose) at the end of the season, and it's not for me to judge whether he might have been able to play. All I know is this: some athletes play through injury, some don't. All we had to do was win one more game that season to make the playoffs.

As an unrestricted free agent, Chris had every right to leave for the team of his choice. And his choice, the Miami Heat, made him a two-time NBA champion fair and square. But his exit bothered me for three reasons. One: he would not sit down and listen to our presentation to re-sign him. All we were able to do on the first day of free agency was to send to his house a recorded pitch on a customized iPad. Two: Bryan Colangelo and especially Larry Tanenbaum were really good to him. Yet he never had the class to talk to either man as he was leaving. Three: when Bosh signed his second contract with the Raptors in 2006, he pledged a $1 million charitable commitment to the Boys and Girls Clubs: $500,000 to Toronto and $500,000 to his hometown, Dallas (the total pledge was later reduced by $250,000 when Bosh left Toronto before his contract had expired). Bosh's agent, Henry Thomas, assured Bryan Colangelo in an e-mail in February 2011 that "Chris has always had every intention to honour his commitment and he will do just that." But as I write this in the summer of 2013, there is still more than $150,000 owing on that pledge in Toronto. I have confidence in Chris Bosh. I trust he will pay it, and soon.

* * *

The list of Raptors' coaches is an interesting one.

The second coach in Raptors' history, Darrell Walker, was

hired to replace Brendan Malone. Walker had no coaching experience when Isiah Thomas chose him for the job. The suspicion was that Thomas could control him more easily than he could Malone. After going 41–90, Grunwald fired him.

Butch Carter replaced Walker, and his 73–92 record demonstrated genuine potential to be a good NBA head coach. He got the Raptors into their first playoffs and helped develop Vince Carter and Tracy McGrady. However, constant controversy and off-court distractions finally did him in. Just prior to the playoffs in 2000, he filed a $5 million defamation of character suit against ex-Raptor Marcus Camby (who was playing for the New York Knicks, the Raptors' opponent in the playoffs). The NBA informed Butch that his action was "unprecedented and inappropriate." After lots of media, fan, MLSE management and NBA criticism, he dropped the suit five days after filing it.

At the end of the 2000 season, Butch Carter tried to talk me into making him the GM and Glen the team president—if he could get McGrady to re-sign with the club. This struck both Grunwald and me as an end-around, one that would seriously undermine Glen's effectiveness. Glen and I called him in and told him we were letting him go. He seemed relieved and said, "What took you so long?"

I could not understand why he seemed to have a coach's death wish. "Butch," I told him, "do you know what you are doing? You are an NBA coach. There are only thirty of them in the world. It's pretty special." He said he did not want to coach anymore—and was true to his word for many years.

After three rookie coaches, Grunwald wanted to go with a proven, big-name coach. He hired Lenny Wilkens. Lenny was at the time the NBA's most winning coach—he had 1,332 wins by the time the New York Knicks let him go. He coached for thirty-two seasons, made the playoffs in twenty of them and won an NBA championship with Seattle. Lenny started out very well, as the Raptors made the playoffs in his first season, and he took the team to the division semifinals before losing to the 76ers (when Carter missed his shot from the corner on his graduation day). The Raptors made the playoffs again the next year, but Lenny seemed to be losing his desire to work hard and develop the younger players after the grind of so many years as a coach. In the 2002–2003 season, the team only went 24–58 and Grunwald let him go.

Now Lenny still had a couple of years to go in a contract that paid him a few million dollars a year. The Raptors had him under contract and, as accounting rules dictate, we had to write off the millions owing in the fiscal year 2003. Given the length of Lenny's career and his age (he was sixty-six), I figured he would never get a coaching job again and we would be paying out the cash owing to Lenny for the next few years. Much to my surprise, one evening in the winter of 2004, as I sat in my office, I got a call saying that the Knicks had signed Lenny.

NBA (and NHL) coaching contracts usually have mitigation clauses that allow the teams that fired the individual to get off the hook for paying some or even all of the contract once the individual signs with a new team. So this was great news to me. It meant that we would have a significant positive financial variance in the 2004 fiscal year.

Interesting how the New York Knicks GM, one Isiah Thomas, handled this. First of all, if we wanted to file a tampering complaint with the league, we could have. Even though Lenny was not coaching for us, he was still under contract, and NBA tampering rules prevent any discussions unless there is written approval from the team in question. Thomas had never asked our permission to contact Lenny, but there was no way I was going to bring that up. Second, Thomas should have played a little poker with me. He should have called me or Grunwald and said that he was considering hiring Lenny but that he also had another quality candidate, and unless we agreed to pay some of Lenny's contract he would go with the other person. Glen and I would have bought that story in a second and been very happy to save 50 cents on the dollar. But Isiah Thomas never asked. So we saved 100 cents on the dollar. Thomas could have saved the Knicks a million dollars easily.

After Lenny Wilkens, Grunwald went back to a rookie. Following a thorough consideration of numerous young coaches, Glen hired Kevin O'Neill. As mentioned, O'Neill really prepared for the interviews. He had a large binder detailing the things he would do on and off the court to make the Raptors successful. I remember the session we had to discuss whether we should hire O'Neill. Glen wanted O'Neill, and I supported him. Only long-time scout Jim Kelly voiced his concern. Jim wasn't specific, but he made it clear that in his opinion this hire was a mistake. We didn't ask him why; in hindsight, we should have.

As it turned out, we should have done a lot more due diligence. O'Neill was a complete disaster. His team played boring basketball and finished 33–49 after winning only eight of their last thirty-two games. He was hot-tempered (he once destroyed a hotel lamp after learning that a key player was injured and unable to play), and he rode his players mercilessly. Unfortunately, the hiring of O'Neill contributed to the end of Grunwald's career with the organization. (O'Neill, by the way, would go on to coach several American college teams, most recently the University of Southern California Trojans—who fired him in January of 2013. ESPN on that occasion called him "one of the top defensive minds in the country." But his temper still dogged him. In 2011, he got into a shouting match with an Arizona fan in a Los Angeles hotel, and security guards were called in to escort him off the premises. O'Neill later apologized.)

The new GM, Rob Babcock, then hired Sam Mitchell. Mitchell

had a great reputation as the type of a player who could be a very good coach someday. Even though Babcock and Mitchell had a good history together in Minneapolis, their relationship was soon dysfunctional. By November, Babcock told me he was going to fire Mitchell. I said no to that.

"Sam was your hire five months ago," I told him, "and you have to work with him to be an effective coach." But the relationship between the two men was awful. Wayne Embry and I started having regular sessions with the two men together to try to get them on the same page. It didn't help.

"Rob can't teach me a thing," Sam told us. Wayne and I clearly told them that if they didn't work it out, we would have to fire one or both of them. As it turned out, Babcock got fired first. When Bryan Colangelo came in, he kept Sam on, and in the 2006–2007 season, Sam won the NBA Coach of the Year award. I still don't understand the practice, but seldom in professional sports does a new GM keep an incumbent coach on, and after only a couple of years together, Colangelo replaced Sam with Jay Triano.

Jay had survived the craziness of being an assistant coach with Lenny Wilkens, with Kevin O'Neill and with Sam Mitchell. Jay was a proven Canadian Olympic basketball player, national team coach and so well regarded in the NBA that he had been an assistant coach with USA Basketball. With his hiring, he became the first Canadian head coach in the NBA. Jay's teams, though, never had the success that he or anyone else hoped for. Still, he was always a quality guy within the team and the community. I was delighted that Bryan kept him on with the team after removing him as coach in June 2011.

Jay stayed on as vice-president of pro scouting until August 2012, when he moved on to become an assistant coach with the Portland Trail Blazers.

Dwane Casey was the final Raptor coach I got to know—for a

short while, anyway. He was hired in the summer of 2011 just after he helped the Dallas Mavericks win an NBA championship as an assistant coach. Because of the lockout, Dwane started coaching Raptor games only in the last week of my tenure with MLSE. I have been optimistic about all our coaches at the start of their careers with the Raptors but, dare I say, I am actually the most optimistic about Dwane.

He has done his time developing his coaching skills with Kentucky, Seattle, Minnesota, Dallas and even the Japanese national basketball team. He is excellent on the defensive side of the game, which he proved in helping the Mavericks win a championship. He also is a proven winner with his Dallas championship ring. There is a league-wide belief that Dwane is the right guy to develop the Raptors into a contending team. I too have very high hopes for him, but time will tell.

* * *

The NBA is a tremendously well-run operation. League staff are hard working and very sharp. They watch everything you do and have rules on everything from the uniforms to game operations, from broadcast to sponsorships. The NBA is the David Stern show, for sure. Stern is one of the toughest, brightest and most demanding people one will ever meet. He deserves a lot of credit for the very successful international giant that the NBA is today, and for making basketball arguably the world's second most important sport after football (soccer).

As the Palestra team learned, you don't want to cross him. For most of my fifteen years working with the NBA, there was not much transparency in the league. It was difficult to understand how the Women's National Basketball Association (WNBA), the NBA store or even the NBA development league were doing financially—never mind the NBA itself. The huge annual NBA operating budget was approved without much dialogue.

But a few years ago, certain owners—Mark Cuban in Dallas, Michael Heisley in Memphis and James Dolan with the Knicks in New York—championed more disclosure, and now a team owner or governor gets to see all that information. During the last collective bargaining negotiations that I was part of, in 2011, there was terrific transparency. Everyone knew what every team was making, right down to the net income line. And a lot of owners, even new owners, got a chance to weigh in on the terms of the new collective bargaining agreement.

I disliked Mark Cuban when he first joined the league as the owner of the Dallas Mavericks. At one early Raptor game against the Mavericks, the Dallas players were gathered in a huddle during a time out, and there in the huddle, on the court, was Mark Cuban. I immediately emailed a message from my seat to Joel Litvin at the NBA: "What's Cuban doing? He's on the court, he's talking to the refs!" At an NBA board meeting, the late Bill Davidson, long-time owner of the Detroit Pistons, called him a "snot-nosed rich kid."

Mark came into the NBA after buying the Mavericks in 2000, and I did not like the very vocal and visible approach he took. He was always critical at league board meetings, and I was told that he phoned the NBA almost every day to complain about things. Cuban was criticizing the referees, and he was getting heavily fined by the league for ignoring clauses in the collective bargaining agreement (by sending limos to chauffeur players around and by sending chefs to cook for them in their homes). Cuban once famously criticized the manager of the league's referees, suggesting that he was incapable of managing a Dairy Queen. The latter took offence and invited Mark to manage a Dairy Queen outlet in Coppell, Texas, for a day—which he did, drawing huge lineups of fans in the process. Owners in the NBA are (mostly) rich men. They're all A-types, but they do observe a certain decorum and civility, and Mark Cuban was not playing by anyone's rules. But over time I changed my mind about him.

Mark passionately championed better refereeing. He pushed for more training and accountability. He was one of the first to push for video reviews of shots at the end of the game, and that has been a very good move. Along with some other owners, he pushed for more league financial transparency. He kept the league people and David Stern on their toes. He also did everything he could to help his team win, sometimes breaking the rules. But in the end, I appreciated and applauded his passion. If other owners had been the first to come off the team plane in their own city carrying the NBA trophy, they would have been criticized for upstaging the team. In 2011, Mark came off the team plane beaming and holding the trophy high. He deserved it.

The NBA is in great shape today, and the new collective bargaining agreement will level the playing field somewhat. But I do believe it will be much tougher for the Raptors to win their first championship than it will be for the Leafs to win their next championship. In the NHL, there already is incredible parity—with seven different Stanley Cup winners in the past seven years. In the NBA, I don't believe that the same parity will ever exist. With a soft cap (meaning that teams have several ways to exceed the current spending limit of $58 million), the big teams will always spend more money. In the NHL, there really isn't a market everyone wants to play in. In the NBA, on the other hand, New York, Miami, Los Angeles and a few others will always be preferred over Minneapolis, Detroit, Portland, Cleveland and Toronto.

The NBA comprises largely American players, who generally would rather play in the United States. In the NHL, American players make up approximately 20 per cent of the NHL, as compared with Canadian players, who make up 50 per cent of the players. One could thus argue that Canadian cities, with their strong hockey following, are actually a slightly preferred place to play. On the other hand, some players don't want to be constantly recognized on the street, nor do they want the constant pressure to win.

And finally, the NBA is a star league where two to four players will plot to play on a team in the brightest cities in the league. Bryan Colangelo is very good and I had thought he might pull off a winner, but that was not to be. In May of 2013, Maple Leaf Sports and Entertainment announced that while Bryan was staying on as president (though I had to ask—responsible for what?), the hunt was on for a new general manager. On May 30, the team announced that Masai Ujiri was the new GM. (And just over a month later, Bryan stepped down—though he would remain a "consultant" to the team.)

This marked a kind of homecoming for Masai. He had been the Raptors' director of global scouting and was an assistant general manager from 2008 to 2010. But now he was coming from the Denver Nuggets, where Ujiri—the first African-born GM in the history of North America's four major sports (basketball, baseball, football and soccer)—had been for three years the general manager and won an NBA executive of the year award.

I remember him as a soft-spoken man, with excellent character and values. Masai was personable and well liked; he's patient and listens to the advice of others. He'll fit in well in Toronto and with MLSE. And, given his success in Denver, he can clearly develop a broad strategy to win. He did an amazing job turning around a team of bad-apple stars into a younger team with fewer stars but a lot more success on the court. I will say this, though: given the high altitude, Denver is a tough place to play, and the home team—accustomed to playing a mile high—has the advantage. Masai Ujiri won't have that benefit in Toronto.

That said, I do know that winning teams drive larger TV audiences, so both Bell and Rogers will be supportive of giving the new GM the resources he needs.

* * *

Two final thoughts, one on women's basketball and one on refereeing in the NBA.

MLSE once applied for a WNBA team but was turned down. This was early in the history of MLSE, and the league didn't think that we were ready for one yet. Most of the time since, I have been glad we were turned down because we would have lost a lot of money, as most teams have done. I remember asking Tom Wilson of the Detroit Pistons and the Detroit Shock (a WNBA team) how his team was doing. He said, "Our tickets are so cheap, fans can afford not to show up."

As much as I was happy that we didn't have a women's basketball team, the 2012 Olympics have me reassessing our decision. The Canadian women's team qualified for the Olympics after an absence of twelve years and for the first time qualified for the quarter-final round. This type of performance helps the future of women's basketball in Canada and also helps create future Raptor fans. But why has it taken Canada so long?

In most countries, young women can move from their club teams or universities and play in professional leagues. But Canada is one of the few countries without a pro league where our young women can stay in the game and earn a living while still developing player skills. Just as the new TFC Academy in Toronto will help Canada be more successful in world football, I think a Toronto-based WNBA team would help Canada be more successful in world basketball. And what helps create players and future fans helps the Raptors. I would suggest to MLSE that it think of owning a WNBA team as an investment in marketing to present and future fans—as well as helping Canada win more Olympic medals.

As for refereeing in the NBA, my question is this one: Why is it so variable?

In the NBA, the stars get the calls. I hear on-air announcers talking about this or that player "not having earned the calls yet." That drives me crazy. Fouls are fouls—whether the player is DeMar DeRozan or Kobe Bryant, the calls should be the same. And since the Raptors don't have any All-Stars (other than Rudy Gay) at the present time, the team also doesn't get the calls. In the spring of 2013, I was watching a lot of Raptor games, and while I am still definitely a big fan, I believe I can watch and judge things a little more objectively. During the season, I saw a number of missed calls at the end of games that cost the Raptors the win. In fact, the league has already apologized twice for game-changing calls that went against the Raptors—and the season was only half over.

A lot of fans and league people likewise believe that the stars get the calls. A few years ago, Houston Rockets GM Daryl Morey brought up that question at a league GMs' meeting. David Stern tore a strip off him up one side and down the other.

\* \* \*

Running an NBA basketball team was a lifelong dream of mine and I got my chance. Initially, my focus was all basketball, but with the growth of MLSE and the hiring of Bryan Colangelo, I got further and further away from it. I remember talking to Stan Kasten, who is now the president of the Los Angeles Dodgers. Stan had responsibility for baseball's Atlanta Braves and the NBA's Atlanta Hawks. I was running the Raptors, and I said to him, "I wish I had two teams instead of one." Then I got responsibility for the Leafs to equal Stan's, and he promptly got responsibility for the Atlanta

Thrashers, in the NHL. I joked with him that I had caught him only to have him pass me again. To which he said, "Actually, I wish I was still running only one team—it's more fun."

I now understand what he meant.

CHAPTER 8

# THE FOOTBALL PITCH

On May 12, 2007, there was a home game against the Chicago Fire at the brand-new BMO Field for the hot new team in town—TFC. Toronto Football Club. This was only the second home game in the fledgling club's history, and there was a buzz in the air.

I was then living in a condominium in the old Tip Top Tailors building near the foot of Bathurst Street, about a kilometre from the new soccer (i.e., football) stadium at Exhibition Place. My wife, Colleen, and I decided to walk to the game, joining throngs of other fans who were all decked out in red and white (TFC colours) and marching loudly and gleefully to the stadium. Many were wearing the scarves they had received in the mail as season seat holders. But it was also clear from the sea of red and white that many TFC jerseys had been sold. The bars near the stadium were packed, the mood was ebullient. Just as in the heady days of the Vince Carter Raptors, "irrational exuberance" was the phrase we used at MLSE to describe the over-the-top fan avidity.

At the twenty-fourth minute of the game, played before a full house of 21,859 fans, TFC's Danny Dichio scored the club's very first goal. He also got an assist that game—which Toronto won 3–1—and was red-carded (ejected from the game) after getting into a fight with a Chicago player. Were this hockey, he would have been credited with a Gordie Howe hat trick (a goal, an assist and a fight). And with that goal, a tradition was established. At the twenty-fourth minute of every home game, TFC fans break out into a song—one created to honour Dichio and that moment in history for the club. Dichio retired in the fall of 2009 and is now head coach of the U19 TFC Academy team. He remains the most popular player in team history.

That game was marked by something else too. As I walked into the stadium, I was handed—as all fans were—a white seat cushion meant to be kept as a souvenir. Uh-oh. We had tried handouts at Raptor and Leaf games (mini-basketballs, noisemakers), and many of them had ended up on the ice or the basketball court, so we had stopped the practice. If a giveaway could be converted into a projectile, we'd hand it out at the end of the game.

None of this (the scarf to season seat holders, the seat cushions at the gate) was my doing. I had handed off the TFC file to my then COO, Tom Anselmi. My thinking was that one day he would succeed me and that running this little football operation would be an easy entry into the big job. I was wrong on both counts. Tom and his team had come up with the idea of the scarves and the cushions, and now we would see what would become of them.

The scarves stayed on necks; the cushions did not stay on seats. When Dichio scored the goal, hundreds and hundreds of white seat cushions flew into the air—and then rained down on the field. The game was halted for ten minutes while the field was cleared. My first thought: *Let's gather them all up so we can resell them.* My second thought: *The commissioner of Major League Soccer is not going to like this and may fine us heavily.* Were this a basketball game, David Stern of the NBA would have hit us hard—with maybe a $100,000 fine.

Over the phone the next day, Don Garber, commissioner of Major League Soccer (MLS), did give me grief, but I thought I could detect a smile behind his tough approach. Video of the seat cushions flying through the air had made sports broadcasts all over North America, so MLS had to be happy about that. How do you explain the avidity of Toronto football fans? BMO Field is intimate, it's football-specific, it's the game itself and it's the Red Patch Boys—the diehard, slightly crazed fans who occupy one end of the stadium and who keep things from ever getting dull. Our own research suggests that 77 per cent of fans attending the game believe that supporter groups such as the Red Patch Boys significantly enhance the game experience.

Even though the product on the pitch has not been good, fan support and the number of season seat holders have been exceptional. Paid attendance has always exceeded 19,000 per game, with 2011 surpassing 20,000. TFC has the highest revenue per game in MLS, so much so that in several MLSE strategic plans, management has studied the capital expense of expanding the stadium to around 30,000 seats. With the interest in football in Toronto and now the rivalries with Vancouver and Montreal, once TFC starts winning, don't be surprised if BMO Field dramatically expands in the next few years.

I had played soccer in grade eight, but without really understanding the game's grace or structure. When I was working with TSN, I was in Giants Stadium in East Rutherford, New Jersey, to watch Ireland beat Italy in World Cup play. The game mattered a great deal in the Irish and Italian communities of New York, but frankly I found the match boring. The day was stifling hot, and the stadium ran out of bottled water before the game even started.

I had also seen an MLS All-Star game in 2006, and I couldn't get excited about that game either. So I had by this point watched a grand total of two football games.

On the other hand, I had seen Toronto bars fill as Greece met Portugal in the 2004 Euro Cup, and I had felt the frenzy. I knew that bringing football to Toronto could work. But May 12, 2007, was something else: 20,000 Toronto fans marching and singing their way to a game. I had never seen anything like it.

* * *

On a Saturday morning in the spring of 2005, I was sitting in the lobby of an airport hotel. The word "ratty" seemed to apply: worn carpets, no-frills furniture, reproduction art on the walls. This was a hotel that had clearly changed hands often. I had time to survey my surroundings because it was now 10:30 a.m. and my meeting was to have started at 10 a.m.

I was there to make a pitch to the Canadian Soccer Association (CSA), the national governing body for football in Canada, then with second-tier teams in Vancouver and Montreal. As per FIFA (Fédération Internationale de Football Association) rules, we had to secure approval from the CSA board before we could field a team in Canada. I knew that the board members were not thrilled that Maple Leaf Sports and Entertainment wanted to bring a football team to Toronto. They wanted us to hold off so that all three Canadian teams could enter MLS at the same time.

Now, after the short delay, I was in with them, in a long salon, the tables covered with white tablecloths that had seen better days, juice boxes, bran muffins and candies scattered over top. The men looking up at me were all volunteers, and they had reason to be skeptical about football in Toronto. The Toronto Lynx had failed to draw much more than 2,000 people since starting in 1997 and then dropping into a fourth-division league. The Toronto Blizzard had failed twice—in the 1970s and the 1980s—and had likewise struggled at the gate. The Toronto Falcons, the Toronto Metros, Toronto Metros-Croatia: the list of failed football enterprises in the city was long.

The first words out of my mouth were "I know nothing about football." I paused to let that truth sink in before adding, "But I do know a lot about how to run a successful sports and entertainment business, and I am confident we will be successful with our team." The CSA approved the application with only a little discussion. No surprise, really. I wasn't there to negotiate; we were going ahead—with or without its approval.

For Maple Leaf Sports and Entertainment, why football? Why not?

By 2005, MLSE was operating very successfully. The Leafs were playing well, and we were averaging more than five very profitable home playoff games per year. The Raptors were enjoying mixed success on the court, but our ticket, suite and sponsorship revenues were very solid and we were consistently registering some of the highest revenue numbers in both leagues. However, we were running out of revenue runway. Our suites were sold-out. Our Leaf games were sold-out. We still had Raptor inventory (gaps to fill in sponsorship and advertising) but not much. We needed all our teams to start moving toward winning championships, and we needed to come up with new business ideas.

In the meantime, the board at MLSE looked to management to grow enterprise value. And Larry Tanenbaum, remember, had challenged me to be a much better CEO, so I was very motivated to come up with new growth ideas. In the consumer products industry and in many other industries, management has to create a long-range strategic plan in addition to an annual financial plan. Long-range plans, though, are rare in sports. Gary Bettman told me once, during a Leaf game, that more than half of NHL teams do not create an annual plan, let alone a long-range strategic plan.

MLSE had started doing five-year strategic plans in 2003. I remember the first one we did with Steve Stavro, and as one does in strategic plans, we talked about the strengths and weaknesses of our competitors—the Blue Jays, the Argos and SkyDome. Steve was aghast, as if we had committed a faux pas. "You don't talk about your competitors in a strategic plan," he said.

As previously mentioned, Steve had created Knob Hill Farms, which initially was an incredibly big idea—well before its time. He had started in 1954 with a fruit stand on Danforth Avenue in Toronto, but then he sold that and, in 1963, launched a series of ten "food terminals" with 800 employees and a valuation of $100 million. Long before it became fashionable, Steve was buying local produce, catering to Toronto's ethnic populations with non-traditional foods in a no-frills atmosphere and keeping stores open until midnight. His were among the first of the so-called big box stores.

On the other hand, Steve was decidedly old school. Long after the competition had gone electronic, Knob Hill Farms was still relying on handwritten orders. "That computer stuff," he once declared, "is not for us." The strategic plan we showed him was probably the first one he had ever seen. If Steve had had a sophisticated management team that mapped out an aggressive, long-range strategic plan for Knob Hill, he could have created a grocery retail giant. He had had a good idea but had not followed it up very well, and soon all his competitors were executing the large discount store format better than he was. Knob Hill Farms ceased to exist in 2001.

I had been aware of Major League Soccer since writing the major SkyDome strategic plan in 1993. We had created a weekend football championship that involved the Canadian national team and three lesser international teams. It did okay, with crowds in the 20,000 range. Football is the number one sport in the world and growing quickly. In Canada, more kids were now playing football than hockey. A study of the heritage of Torontonians showed that more than 60 per cent of the city's population were from football-playing countries. So SkyDome had some interest in professional football.

However, as we soon discovered, Major League Soccer was in legal battles over its unique single-entity ownership (the case was eventually settled, in the league's favour). This arrangement means that although owners own a team in MLS, *the league* dictates salary totals, or the salary cap, as it is known. Each team is also allowed to designate three players who don't count against the cap and who command the highest salaries. Essentially, there are no restrictions on what an owner can pay those three players; on the other hand, the league will turn down overly lucrative contracts for the rest of the players. The legal battle was actually being funded by the National Football (North American football, that is) League Players Association, since they realized that a league controlling all player salaries posed a real danger to the growth of NFL player salaries. Consider these numbers: in the NBA, Major League Baseball and the NHL (under the new collective bargaining agreement signed in January 2013), revenues are shared fifty-fifty between owners and players. In Major League Soccer, by sharp contrast, well less than 40 per cent of revenue goes to players. You can see the appeal for owners.

In the end, the Labatt takeover in 1995 killed the MLS concept for SkyDome. Nevertheless, I parked the idea of football somewhere in my brain.

In 2005, as now, emerging demographics in the Greater Toronto Area were disposed to football. So much so that in future strategic plans at MLSE we identified a risk to the Leaf fan base because most immigrants to Toronto had little or no experience with ice hockey. Also, the very affordable and controllable salary structure of MLS strongly appealed to us. The NHL was in a lock-out that year, and the inflationary trend in NHL salaries was a critical issue for us.

So in the lead-up to the strategic plan, I went to New York and introduced myself to MLS commissioner Don Garber and his deputy commissioner Mark Abbott. Of course, they knew about MLSE and, of course, expansion into Canada via Toronto interested them. The franchise fee at the time was a very affordable US$10 million. Before meeting Garber and his team I had a morning meeting with Gary Bettman. Gary had invited me to lunch, but I told him I would have to pass because I was meeting with MLS to buy a franchise. Gary told me that I should not spend money on the franchise and instead the league should give it to us for free. Interestingly, TFC would go on to make more annual operating profits than most NHL teams.

Seven years later, Don Garber sat on a panel at the Bloomberg Sports Business Summit in New York City, where he had this to say: "Richard Peddie is in the audience today. I sold him a franchise for $10 million; it's now worth $100 million. That's the worst deal I ever made, and the best deal he ever made."

Not having national rights for the Leafs or Raptors severely limited our ability to sell national advertisers, so it was imperative that our MLS football team—should it come to pass—be granted national rights for television and consumer promotions. The league understood that failure to acquire such rights was a deal-breaker for us and it eventually agreed.

The next issue was a place to play. MLS was pushing for football-specific stadiums, and we agreed that such a stadium was key to long-term success. There was some push for us to consider Sky-Dome, but that facility was completely unacceptable. Not only was that stadium not intimate, our team would be the third tenant for dates and, worst of all, it sat 54,000 for football. Once again, we believed that scarcity would be a good sales tool.

Initially, we partnered with the Argos and focused on building a stadium to replace the old Varsity Stadium at the University of Toronto. Getting the right location for our stadium was now the potential deal-breaker. If we could get the right stadium design in the right location, an MLS franchise was a go. If not, we would have to pass on the opportunity. We liked the Varsity site for all its positives: proximity to the subway, right on Bloor Street. But there were issues, including having to deal with the university and its student body. That meant potential restrictions on who could advertise, the sale of alcohol, the tricky notion of the university teaming up with corporations. The site was also land-locked and small. We were extremely worried that local ratepayers would be up in arms over such things as noise, bright lights and traffic and would prevent construction.

The university, meanwhile, wanted the stadium to contain a 400-metre track; that would have increased costs and reduced intimacy for football fans. Finally, brokering a deal with the university administration proved elusive. We thought we had a deal, until the new president changed the financials and the terms were simply not acceptable to us. (The university went on to rebuild Varsity Stadium, and today it is a wonderful facility for its students and athletic programs.)

We then commissioned fan research that measured interest in three sites: York University, Downsview Park (both in the northwest quadrant of the city) and Exhibition Place, down by Lake Ontario. The latter was easily the fan favourite. York University scored the poorest in our research, so when the Argos announced a deal to build a stadium there, we were not interested at all. That initiative later died without our involvement. We did have negotiations with Downsview Park, land that was in federal hands, but its management team of bureaucrats was incapable of making a decision.

Exhibition Place, site of the historic Canadian National Exhibition, was our overwhelming choice. The city had been awarded the 2007 World Under-20 Men's Football Championship, but it was going to lose the event unless a stadium was built—and quickly. The federal and provincial governments had already committed to $35 million in funding ($27 million and $8 million respectively). I met with then Toronto mayor David Miller several times to get the city involved. Miller was a huge football fan and eventually one of our loyal season seat holders, but there was friction among the three levels of government. I had a few meetings with the mayor using a "city builder" theme that was consistent with our "bring pride to the community" corporate value. The aim of the meetings was to persuade the mayor to team up with the provincial and federal governments to get the stadium built. Ultimately, he agreed with a number of reasonable conditions that continue to this day to work out very well financially for the city.

This was the arrangement we reached: the city would provide $10 million and the land, and would retain ownership of both the building and the land. MLSE would contribute $19 million and get to sell the title sponsorship of the stadium, which we did in August 2006 to BMO Financial Group. We named the stadium BMO Field. The city would receive 50 per cent of the annual operating profits from the stadium. As of January 1, 2013, the city's return on the stadium investment is already over $2 million.

MLSE would be responsible for building the stadium on budget and on time. Bob Hunter, executive vice-president at MLSE, working with PCL Construction, did a great job building a no-frills football pitch on the approved $65 million budget and on time for the Under-20 games and the 2007 TFC inaugural season. MLSE being responsible for construction overruns was a major commitment. Stadiums coming in on budget are not the norm across the world.

BMO Field is the only case in the history of Maple Leaf Sports and Entertainment where it received government funding, and even in that case MLSE contributed 29 per cent of construction costs and the city already has had 20 per cent of its $10 million paid back. *Toronto Star* columnist Dave Perkins continues to write about all the financial breaks MLSE has received from the government. That's simply not true. MLSE paid for 100 per cent of the Air Canada Centre and its surrounding infrastructure. I could go on, and I will: MLSE became the lead tenant at the MasterCard Centre and attracted the Hockey Hall of Fame as tenant (it has offices and stores some of its archives there) and Hockey Canada so that the city could build its first new ice pads in years. We also agreed to take on a dramatically above-market-value lease of more than $4 million a year to run the Ricoh Coliseum. In the past I have said publicly that if anyone wants to take on the Ricoh lease, they are welcome to it. While running MLSE, I made many good deals; the Ricoh lease was easily the worst. But it bailed out the city. If not for MLSE, the arena would be largely dark and costing the city millions to operate and maintain.

The BMO Field deal was negotiated just in time. Any later and there was no chance it could be built in time for the World Under-20 Men's Football Championships, and the city would have lost out on a major international event. When the Argos heard that we had done a deal with the city, one of their owners, Howard Sokolowski, phoned me to ask to be included in the deal. I had to say no for two reasons. One, bringing in another partner would have necessitated more negotiations, which would have delayed construction. And two, the $65 million budget could not accommodate the larger 110-yard CFL field and the required changes to the end zones. There simply was no budget and no time to redesign the stadium. Howard and I would end up having numerous arguments over BMO Field while he owned the Argos. And although I irked him many times with my lack of support for the Argos, we somehow remained friends.

So the franchise price and territory were agreed upon, the Canadian Soccer Association had approved us, and stadium construction got under way. But now the naysayers came out. The owner of the last Toronto team to fail, the Lynx, went on Fan Radio in Toronto to criticize us and to predict that we too would fail.

But I was confident for many reasons. The MLS league was far stronger than the National Premier Soccer League, the Premier League, the North American Soccer League, the Canadian Soccer League and the United Soccer Leagues—all the ones that had come before it. MLS had an excellent collective bargaining agreement, and the single-entity structure helped prevent out-of-control salaries. MLS had very strong and passionate owners with strong professional sports expertise: Robert Kraft, who owned the New England Patriots of the NFL; Lamar and Clark Hunt, who then owned the Kansas City Chiefs of the NFL; Phil Anschutz, who owned numerous sports teams and facilities, including the NHL's Los Angeles Kings; and Stan Kroenke, who owned pro teams in the NHL, the NBA and the NFL (in November 2012, *Sports Illustrated* ran a piece on him entitled "The Most Powerful Man in Sports"). MLS had a sharp young commissioner in Don Garber, who learned his sports and entertainment expertise at the NFL. We in Toronto were building the stadium in the right place. BMO Field would become a best practice emulated elsewhere as new MLS teams went on to build or renovate stadiums in downtown urban markets such as Vancouver, Philadelphia, Portland and Montreal. Another reason we knew we'd succeed was our expertise at MLSE: we knew the business of sports, and not everyone had our resources.

BMO Field was intimate, with great sightlines. When MLSE invested $5 million of its own money to convert to state-of-the-art natural grass, the stadium became football-authentic and a real plus to attract free agents. Heated grass involves an underground system of pipes that can bring water and nutrients to the grass as early as March. Artificial turf, on the other hand, is hard on players' bodies and extremely hot in summer. Players don't like it; they believe it causes injuries. Real grass, on the other hand, boosts team morale.

To get out of the multi-use obligation, we had to win the approval of three levels of government—the City of Toronto, the Province of Ontario and the federal government—and we got all three. We built a new artificial pitch in Etobicoke for $1 million, and we installed a bubble at Lamport Stadium so that city soccer players were not out of places to play in winter or summer.

Finally, the time was right for Division One football in Toronto. The World Cup was a huge event in Toronto. Canadian television showed hours of football all year. New Torontonians love football so much that it's easy to imagine the day when TFC and MLS will be bigger in Toronto than the Argos and the Blue Jays.

From the start we wanted to create an authentic club that would resonate with the millions of "footie" fans in Canada. In doing our best practices research on football team names and logos in Europe, we quickly realized that we wanted to use the word "football" in the team name. We decided on Toronto Football Club—TFC. When it was announced, we actually received a call from the president of the Argos complaining about the name. There's only one *football* club in this city, he as much as said, and that's the Argonauts of the Canadian Football League. He worried that CFL fans might be confused.

We told him his franchise was almost 100 years old, with equity—he shouldn't be worried about a small competitor coming into its market. We developed a logo after studying logos in the English, German and Spanish leagues. Our name and logo were football-authentic. Not for us North American sports names such as Heat, Raptors, Grizzlies or Magic.

As I said earlier, TFC games were famous for the antics of the Red Patch Boys—a TFC support group that primarily occupies sections 111 and 112 of BMO Field, an area nicknamed The Bunker. With the Red Patch Boys leading the way, fans would toss streamers at visiting team players when they tried a corner kick in the south end of the stadium. The streamers were often so thick around the feet of the player that it was tough for him to actually get the kick away. No doubt the league objected in some fashion, at least for the record, and the announcer at BMO Field would dutifully ask fans not to toss streamers. In fact, MLS essentially looked the other way, happy to see such enthusiasm for football.

None of this—the Dichio song and the singing and chanting, the streamers, the Red Patch Boys—was planned by Paul Beirne and his marketing people. They just happened, and became part of the team's personality and equity. TFC games at BMO Field were soon the place to be in Toronto.

TFC fans know their football, and while they are loyal they are not shy about giving advice. Neither Raptor fans nor Leaf fans are as organized as TFC supporter groups, which view their supporter-group membership to mean ownership and responsibility to the city and club. They even feel partially responsible for the team's win or loss as part of their "job." You want to listen to them and you want to take action on some of the things they suggest, but you can't just give in to their every whim and desire. They see themselves as ambassadors for their club but not always for the league itself.

This forces an interesting and sensitive balance for management. The fans' bias is definitely toward MLS league games.

Although they like following the big international clubs, they are not that interested in meaningless friendlies (exhibition matches between teams from different leagues with no bearing on standings), with their higher prices and only part of the visiting team's real roster on display. Fans have also not quite embraced the Confederation of North, Central American and Caribbean Association Football (CONCACAF) matches.

When it comes to hardware up for grabs, football is a lot better than the NBA and NHL. In those leagues, a team has only one cup for a club to win. In the case of an English Premier League team, it can win the Premier League title, the FA Cup (Football Association Challenge Cup) and the UEFA (Union of European Football Associations) Champions League. There is more than one parade in football. TFC has already won four Nutrilite Canadian Championships (the only team hardware won while I was CEO) and went deep into the CONCACAF playoffs in 2012 (46,000 saw a match in March 2012 against David Beckham and the Los Angeles Galaxy at the Rogers Centre), but the fans are lukewarm on this series. I think and hope that, with more time, this series can rival European championships for fan interest.

When we got the MLS franchise, I decided to give the responsibility for overseeing the on and off pitch business to my executive vice-president and COO, Tom Anselmi. I knew I was retiring soon and was interested in creating a possible successor. I thought that Tom having responsibility would give him experience dealing with teams—hiring a general manager, helping the GM navigate through budgets and board presentations. Not making the coaching or player choices but making sure the individual did his due diligence and created a solid plan to win us an MLS championship. I thought it would be a nice, simple, easy task for Tom. I was so wrong.

Although TFC is a much smaller franchise in financial terms than the Leafs or Raptors and in a much smaller league than the

NHL or NBA, the issues of player performance, coaches and GMs, media and fan reaction are all very much the same. Tom's first hire was former Glasgow Rangers and Celtic FC star Maurice (Mo) Johnston. Mo was a good guy who was having some early success despite three coaching changes. In 2009, we came very close to getting into the playoffs and only missed out by losing badly (5–0) on the last day of the season to a very inferior team. Mo decided that he needed a much tougher coach and hired Preki (yes, it's just "Preki").

The team Preki inherited was pretty good. Some modest changes and superb coaching would have got us over the hump and into the playoffs. The GM is supposed to make player moves in a patient and strategic fashion. He should listen to the coach but not necessarily heed his advice because some coaches are too reactive and want to make roster changes after every game. That was Preki. Mo was too weak, and he let Preki blow up a good team. Preki was fired, Mo was fired and the fans went crazy— especially after ticket prices were hiked in the summer of 2010. It was an ugly time for the team, for MLSE and for Tom Anselmi. The months-long uproar was bad and it culminated in what we called the October Revolution.

Adding to the mix was that the team's star player, a Toronto-born mid-fielder named Dwayne De Rosario, had gone public with his desire for a raise. He was, no doubt about it, an extremely talented player who would eventually leave the team and earn an MLS Most Valuable Player award in 2011 with DC United, in Washington. But during the October Revolution, he scored a goal against the San Jose Earthquakes at BMO Field and then made a cheque-signing gesture to drive home his wage demands. Fans were divided, with some arguing that we should sign De Rosario at all costs and others believing that his best days were behind him (De Rosario turned thirty-five in 2013).

Tom Anselmi remembers this all too well, especially the part where MLSE kept tearing up old contracts with this player who originally wanted $1 million a year. Tom told me that De Rosario had a long wish list of impossible demands, including a guaranteed four-year extension, a condo at Maple Leaf Square and tickets to all MLSE events.

Credit Tom. He met with numerous groups of fans over many nights and professionally took their criticism and anger. Most pro teams avoid such town halls because they tend to be a bloodletting. Tom then hired Jürgen Klinsmann, a former player and current manager of the American national football team, to advise him on what to do next. After a full assessment, they picked Aron Winter, who added Paul Mariner to help him run the club.

By now, TFC had an academy but one without a real home. Winter brought world-class football credentials with him; he was chosen in part for his experience leading the famous Ajax Academy in the Netherlands. For all of 2011 and part of 2012, Winter tried to get TFC to play his style of play, but it wasn't working. In June of that year, Tom replaced Winter with Mariner, who fared no better. TFC ended the 2012 season with a 5–21 record—worst in the league.

So Tom Anselmi truly did get more team experience than I imagined he would. He made the wrong hire with Mo Johnston and, as I did with John Ferguson, he kept him on one more year than he should have. He hired Aron Winter, who had football credibility, but his leadership skills as a coach or GM were significantly undeveloped.

* * *

Football academies are the norm all over the world. In the fall of 2008, TFC announced the formation of its own academy and

Brampton, Ontario, native Doneil Henry became the first graduate of the TFC Academy to sign a contract with TFC. In 2011, Toronto-born Ashtone Morgan became the first graduate of the academy to earn a spot with the Canadian men's national team. Originally, the Toronto academy players were nomads moving from one facility to another to practise and play; they had no home. But in preparation for a strategic plan presentation, TFC and MLSE management toured the better academies in Mexico, England and Europe—with special attention paid to the Ajax Academy in the Netherlands. Armed with some international academy best practices and an understanding that the way to develop a winner and manage your player costs was to develop a bricks-and-mortar academy, management presented to the MLSE board a recommendation to invest $22 million in an academy at Toronto's Downsview Park.

Today, the academy has three natural-turf fields, one synthetic-turf field that has a bubble over it in winter, and a 40,000-square-foot academy building that holds dressing rooms, a large strength-and-conditioning centre, offices and food and beverage amenities. It is arguably the best academy facility in North America and, with time, I believe it will help TFC annually compete for an MLS cup.

* * *

Six years and no playoffs gave truth to my comment to the Canadian Soccer Association back in 2005 that "I know nothing about football." The people we hired to navigate us through the formation and development of the team into a winner did not work out. At the same time, we proved that we did indeed know how to launch and run the business side of a football team. We took a franchise and stadium investment of $24 million and created a franchise that is worth close to $100 million today.

In a 2010 email Don Garber wrote to me, he said, "I mentioned to Mark [Abbott] several times during that day how fortunate we are to have you and your company involved in Major League Soccer. It's not just what you do, it's how you do it. TFC set the stage for our success in Seattle and will help create a business for us in Canada we never contemplated." Garber would later observe that the launch of TFC was a turning point for the league and, further, that the launch is widely viewed as a business school model for other professional sports teams to emulate.

That said, TFC's struggle on the pitch just added to the weight of losing that I was experiencing with the Leafs and Raptors. By the end of November 2011, I had had enough.

# CHAPTER 9

# LEAFS NATION

When it came time to move season seat holders from their cherished old spots at Maple Leaf Gardens to their brand-new seats at the Air Canada Centre, we did so very, very carefully. We consulted old ledgers (wrested, no doubt, from some dusty vault in the bowels of the old rink) in which the earliest entries— dating back to 1931 when the Gardens opened—had been written by hand with a pen that had clearly been dipped in an inkwell. The alphabetical lists of names were gathered in yellowing, brittle binders, their edges curled. For each subscriber there was a name, a seat number, an address and a phone number. In the 1931–1932 ledger, I noted two telephone numbers: GL 3726 and WA 3344. The thing looked like something that Charles Dickens or one of his characters might have penned. What was remarkable about the book was the neatness of the script, how the names were so famil-iar (iconic Toronto names such as Ryerson, Simpson, Eaton that also became the familiar names of schools and stores, streets and parks) and the list of complimentary tickets that went to former Leaf players, including King Clancy, Red Horner, Syl Apps—and the chief of police. The Thomson family held fifteen pairs of tickets in the 1931–1932 season, when subscribers paid between $0.50 and $2 per game. Individual seats that season sold for between $0.95 and $2.95, and programs went for $0.15.

Some of the men and women listed in the ledgers had held these seats for many decades: they had come to befriend their neighbours in the stands, and they knew the names of the blue-uniformed ushers and usherettes in white gloves who worked their areas. Some 40 per cent of these fans had held the seats at least since 1970, and some 20 per cent had held the same seats since 1950 or earlier. The seats had been passed on from generation to generation, much like an heirloom set of dishes or a dining room set. They were precious.

When it came time to move the patrons, we had to explain to them the new seating arrangements—how, for example, grey (platinum, actually) was the new gold. Portables were set up outside the Air Canada Centre, then under construction, where we displayed drawings illustrating where their new seats would be, with that process starting in August 1998. Later, when the bowl was being formed and the seats had been installed, we took them into the building and had them sit in their new seats. It was like a form of feng shui. Did the vibes feel good in that seat? Would somewhere else be preferable? People who had held their tickets the longest got priority, and sometimes they swapped an old seat location for a different one.

The late Ken Thomson—a media magnate and art collector, and said to be the richest man in Canada at the time of his death in 2006—was one such patron. I knew him a little, and I knew from Steve Stavro that Ken had been very kind to Steve, who wanted to repay the favour.

"Help Ken Thomson pick out his seats," Steve said to me. "Centre ice. On the aisle."

So I helped Ken pick out two seats. But forty-eight hours later he came back, for he had decided to go up from platinum seats to gold. I found that interesting: he could certainly afford to sit anywhere, but by moving up one row he spared himself a club fee and a seat licence—while losing almost nothing in terms of vantage. Ken lived in Rosedale, about five kilometres from the Air Canada Centre. In my running days, I sometimes saw him walking his daughter's dog. He was a nice man and very sophisticated, as sophisticated a man as Steve Stavro was an Everyman. Yet they were friends. What brought them together, in part, was the Leafs. They were both members of Leaf Nation.

* * *

The rake (the angle from the bottom row of seats to the top row) is the same at the Air Canada Centre as it was at Maple Leaf Gardens, as is the set-up of the escalators. Even the Hot Stove Club, which dates from 1963, was re-established at the ACC.

I'm proud of the Air Canada Centre—proud that my name is on the cornerstone, proud of its design and location. I once timed it: you can get from the subway platform at Union Station and into a seat at the ACC in as little as ninety seconds. I'm proud that we took a dated, single-sport enterprise (the Leafs), an organization that was seriously outdated, and built a sports franchise empire that is recognized as one of the best run in the world. (Our record on the ice and court is admittedly less successful, and I'll come to that.)

Claude Lamoureux, formerly president and CEO of the Ontario Teachers' Pension Plan (once a major shareholder in Maple Leaf Sports and Entertainment), is a highly respected and admired businessman, and he often told me that our business plans were as good as any he had ever seen. Some 50 per cent of NHL hockey teams do not create formal, annual business plans, and none do strategic plans. That baffles me. At MLSE, we created annual business plans as well as strategic plans, and the latter changed every few years as something new and bold was introduced. When Maple Leaf Square was unveiled, reps from every Canadian NHL hockey team, as well as from sports teams from New York, Boston, Chicago and Phoenix, came to see what we were doing.

All that planning made a difference, one you could literally taste. At Maple Leaf Gardens, fans were served stale popcorn; at the Air Canada Centre, they can buy sushi and wraps and beer brewed in small batches right on the premises. There are 180 master sommeliers in the world and only three in Canada, including Jennifer Huether, who worked for the Air Canada Centre before leaving in 2012 for Cliff Lede Vineyards in California's Napa Valley.

* * *

The building of the Air Canada Centre meant 3,000 new seats for Leaf games. We had no trouble filling them. During my entire time with the Leafs, I had hundreds and hundreds of fans tell me that they were lifelong fans or that they were the "Leafs' biggest fan." Leaf fans are loyal, diehard, true blue. Season seat holders consistently renew every year—at a rate of 99 per cent. Divorces mean good business for lawyers because who gets the Leaf tickets is very much a bone of contention.

The Leafs' television audiences drive the CBC, with audiences surpassing two million viewers. Even the diminutive Leafs TV, which is restricted to most of Ontario, often draws audiences of more than 500,000—more viewers than many nationally televised NHL games in the United States attract. But what really staggered me, sitting in the stands at Leaf away games, and especially in Canadian cities, was the many jerseys worn on game night, the faces painted under blue wigs and the car horn honking after big wins. In my other life in consumer products, I had great iconic brands, but no one ever dressed up as the Jolly Green Giant or the Pillsbury Doughboy.

For years I didn't completely understand why Leaf fans were so loyal and so avid. It wasn't until I read Kelly McParland's *The Lives of Conn Smythe: From the Battlefield to Maple Leaf Gardens* that it all came together for me. The fan loyalty I inherited was a combination of things. It was Conn Smythe raising the money and working so hard to keep the team afloat despite serving in two world wars. It was the building of the iconic Maple Leaf Gardens in 1931. (Smythe's philosophy of "If you can't beat them in the alley, you can't beat them on the ice" applied to building the Leaf franchise as well.) It was Foster Hewitt, first on radio and then on TV introducing Leaf games with "Hello Canada and hockey fans in the United States and Newfoundland and to Canadian servicemen overseas." It was the 48th Highlanders marching out onto the ice to introduce every season—a Leaf custom still followed to this day. It was eighteen Leaf captains, such as Dave Keon, George Armstrong, Wendel Clark and Darryl Sittler. And, of course, it was thirteen Stanley Cups.

Recently, there has been a movement to rename some of the NHL awards because American fans and young Canadian fans can't relate to awards such as the Conn Smythe trophy, which honours the most valuable player in the Stanley Cup playoffs. This would be a mistake. Conn Smythe being successful with the Leafs helped the NHL be successful. Professional sports needs to recognize and go on recognizing the builders who got the league to where it is: individuals such as Conn Smythe, Georges Vezina, Jack Norris and Bill Masterton.

* * *

As the CEO ultimately responsible for the performance of the Leafs between 1996 and 2011, I can assure you that losing caused me the most pain. But what drove me the craziest were the fans and the media saying that the owners and the front office didn't care if the team won or not. After a while I would answer the question about our will to win with my own question: "Why *wouldn't* we want to win?"

Winning is definitely good business, since revenues are always better with winning teams. Winning championships is infinitely better because it sets up dramatic revenue increases for years to come. The Ontario Teachers' Pension Plan sold its 80 per cent share of MLSE in 2012 for an amount that translated into an enterprise value of almost $2 billion. If, at the time of the sale, MLSE teams had been consistently going into the second round of the playoffs, those additional playoff profits could have justified a sales price that would have been at least $200 million more.

Also, most of those who work for MLSE are big fans of our teams (though not overly so: the last people we wanted to hire were autograph-seekers and stalkers), so we really hate losing. I always said that employees had it doubly bad when we lost. Just like fans, we suffered emotionally. And as business people, we suffered from the negative fan and media reaction, and the way losses hurt our business results. Some journalists have argued that MLSE teams lose because they don't have to win. The thinking goes like this: Leafs have so many people on the waiting list for season tickets that they don't take new names anymore (absolutely not true), and that no matter what happens, we have a 99 per cent renewal rate. *That* is true, but players, coaches and general managers don't even think about renewal rates. So the argument holds no water.

After working in consumer products for nineteen years and in sports for twenty-two years, I am convinced that running a business is a lot easier than running a sports team. Business is not easy by any means, but you can control things a lot better. At Pillsbury, for instance, we created a crescent roll that tasted the same every time. With sports teams, the product on the playing field changes game to game and even period to period.

Unlike Kraft jam off the assembly line, the product's quality cannot be guaranteed. You also can't control your employees as easily. Admittedly, businesses have union and employee issues, but if you lead well, they are quite rationally dealt with. Not so professional athletes. These men have been told they are the best probably since they were nine years old or even earlier. Their average salary is usually the highest in the company. To the delight of the media, they speak their minds a lot more often and a lot more publicly than any employee.

When I was enduring the high-profile hiring, firing and trading of players, coaches and GMs, I recalled my time in consumer products and my letting go of or bringing in new vice-presidents, and remember thinking, *No one cared*. Also, in business there can be multiple winners in any one year. When I was running Pillsbury and having a good year, for example, the teams over at Campbell Soup and Nestlé were likewise enjoying success. Not in sports. In sports, to quote Brian Burke, "There is only one parade."

It's tough to win a championship. In sports, winning it all is definitely not the norm. The Detroit Red Wings have been a dominant team, with twelve straight seasons of 100-plus points and twenty-one straight seasons in the playoffs. But in the past fourteen years, all those incredible teams have won only two Stanley Cups, and I say "only" enviously.

* * *

My early Leaf years were easy. I was busy working on dragging the organization that time forgot into the twenty-first century. The Air Canada Centre was built, all the suites were sold and season seat holders had been with professionalism and courtesy moved down from Maple Leaf Gardens into their new seats. The Vancouver Canucks had difficulties when they moved their fans into the new GM Place (now called Rogers Arena), but we managed to avoid riling ours.

In those days, I was focusing a lot on the Raptors. As for the Leafs, Ken Dryden and Pat Quinn were having real success on the ice. I've heard some fans say that the Leafs haven't played well since 1967. But from 1999 to 2004, they played as well as or better than almost all NHL teams. From 1999 to 2004, they made the playoffs for six straight years, with two Eastern Conference appearances. In the 1999–2000 and 2001–2002 seasons, the Leafs recorded 100 points, and in 2003–2004, the Leafs set a team record with 103 points.

In four of those playoffs, we matched up against Ottawa. They usually dominated us in the regular season, but we owned them in the playoffs. One year after the Senators lost another series, Senators owner Eugene Melnyk was so angry that he punched a hole in the wall of the visitors' dressing room. When his then president Roy Mlakar phoned me to apologize, I said not to worry.

"We'll fix it," I told him, "and not bill Ottawa. We'll also keep it quiet." And I have kept it quiet—until now.

Over the ten years up to 2004, the Leafs averaged 5.5 home playoff games a season, so we regularly budgeted five playoff games in our annual fiscal plan. In fact, in the early days of MLSE, our financial plan counted a lot on playoff games to achieve our operating profits target. This was a very risky practice. Over time and as Maple Leaf Sports and Entertainment grew exponentially, we became much more conservative in our forecasts of playoff games.

In my last ten years at MLSE, we hit our earnings targets five times and missed them five times. I like those numbers; they suggest we were in the right spot. If you consistently hit or miss sales targets, something is off.

In one board meeting, a director, Dale Lastman, asked if being conservative with our playoff projections was sending the wrong message to the coaches and players. It was explained that our financial assumptions were confidential and that even if the team did learn about them, financial assumptions were definitely not what motivated them to succeed. I remember one NHL Board of Governors meeting where Gary Bettman showed us the budgets of all thirty teams. Almost all the teams assumed that they would be in the playoffs and indicated as much in their annual financial plans. Many teams assumed going two rounds. One even budgeted being in the Stanley Cup finals. Hope springs eternal. In reality, most teams needed playoff appearances to break even, and they needed profitable financial plans to show their banks.

In 2012, AEG (Anschutz Entertainment Group), which owns the Staples Center in Los Angeles, the Kings of the NHL and a 27 per cent share of the Lakers in the NBA (who share the arena with the Los Angeles Clippers), hit playoff pay dirt. All three teams were in the playoffs, with home games played at the Staples Center. For Phil Anschutz, the owner of two of those teams and the arena, this is heaven. This is what I dreamed of: the Leafs, the Raptors and the TFC team all in the playoffs.

During most of that successful period for the Leafs, Steve Stavro was the majority shareholder and chairman. He was a huge fan. Steve could often be seen standing up in the stands, cheering his "boys" or yelling at the refs. Face red, neck veins bulging, he definitely showed his passion. I did not want to sit beside him during a playoff game because he would often punch me in the arm to show his enthusiasm for a goal or a great play. I remember making it a point of *not* sitting beside him because my arm was getting too sore. After every playoff loss, no one was more disappointed in the company than Steve Stavro.

Steve had the corner office next to mine. He was the majority shareholder all right, but as CEO I reported to the board of Maple Leaf Sports and Entertainment, not to Steve. He never understood that. He was an uncomplicated man, with a grade nine education. He had a hardscrabble upbringing, yet he had come to own racehorses and a mansion in Teddington Park, a tony part of north Toronto near the Rosedale Golf Club. At first, he wanted me to phone him at 11 a.m. each and every day, and at first I did make the calls. Then I purposely missed one or two calls and eventually weaned Steve off that habit. It wasn't my job, nor was it productive, to talk to him every day. Then he started showing up at the office each day around 2 p.m. "Bring the boys in," he would say, meaning the senior management team of Tom Anselmi, Bob Hunter and Ian Clarke. This often meant hauling these guys out of meetings and disrupting their days. After a while, we got him off that habit as well. In the end, he came in only on Wednesday afternoons, and Bob, Ian, Tom, Steve and I would have a great hour-long chat about how things were going.

As I said in Chapter 1, during his tenure we had many fights. On the day of one of our biggest blow-ups, he walked into my office, the anger written on his face. He was beet red, leaning over me at my desk, and the veins on his neck were popping. But I had no fear. I was thinking: *I have no debt, I can always get another job, and I have no reason to muster anger to match his.* I remained very calm.

"Sit down," I told Steve. "Sit down or you're going to have a heart attack." He did—sit down, that is.

Managing Steve was definitely not easy. As I mentioned earlier, one time he kicked me out of a board meeting because he was angry about something I had done. I had come out the big oak doors, which someone had closed behind me. This time I was the one who was angry, and I threw the three-ring binder I had in my hands. The thing blew apart with the force of my toss and all the pages started drifting down, like leaves in autumn.

I survived that fracas and many others. Steve loved the players and was forever asking that they join him for roast beef and beers. The last thing they wanted was to rub elbows with the suits. Steve also loved Pat Quinn, the rough Irishman. I respected Pat's knowledge of the game as a player and as a coach—especially of the Olympic team. He had a wonderful career. But I never got close to him. I was the business guy and he was the hockey guy. I got to know Paul Maurice and Ron Wilson, both of whom came after him, a little better.

Steve Stavro was slow to warm to me. I remember one NBA All-Star break in February when the top four executives at MLSE (Ian Clarke, Tom Anselmi, Bob Hunter and I) went to Pebble Beach in California to play golf. Clauses in all our contracts gave us the right to attend the All-Star game of our choice, and we had decided as a group that after the game we would fly down to Pebble Beach and hit the links. I knew Steve would not like us all being away at once for four or five days, even though there were very capable people back at the office. He phoned me in San Francisco and really let me know his displeasure. When we got back, we all had our expense accounts audited. Everything was fine, for we had all paid our own way, but these were the kinds of battles that ensued in my early days with Steve Stavro.

By the end, we all had his loyalty—which was over-the-top. I was recommending salary increases for these three guys of 3 to 5 per cent. "I like him," Steve would say. "Give him five."

By the end of his tenure in 2003 (he would die, sadly, three years later), Steve and I had developed a good relationship. He trusted me and liked what the management team was doing.

"You look after the Raptors," he would say, "and I'll look after the Leafs."

When he was bought out of MLSE, he sat me down and said, "Richard, I am now counting on you to look after the Leafs too."

* * *

Although Ken Dryden and Pat Quinn were having success with the Leafs, cracks were starting to surface. And they would come back to haunt the team. For one thing, we had fewer scouts than the average NHL team. We did not have a goalie coach; 70 per cent of teams did. We would often trade first-round draft choices in the spring to pick up older players who might get us over the playoff hump.

Here's an example from 2003. At the trading deadline that spring, we gave up two good players (Alyn McCauley and Brad Boyes) and a first-round draft choice for Owen Nolan—a player who never found with us the form he had enjoyed in San Jose. It so happened that the 2003 entry draft offered a particularly rich crop of players, some of whom would become foundation players and/or leading scorers for their teams. Eric Staal, Ryan Getzlaf, Mike Richards, Jeff Carter, Thomas Vanek, Brent Seabrook, Zach Parise, Patrice Bergeron, Marc-Andre Fleury and Dion Phaneuf were all available in that first round.

Short-term gain meant long-term pain. Accordingly, our AHL (American Hockey League) team was mostly devoid of talent. Our annual plan for the Leafs was basically to list all the NHL free agents and go for them.

The MLSE board inevitably gave Dryden and Quinn all the money they needed. My joke was that the Leafs always took an unlimited budget—and then exceeded it. Ken was passionate about restoring the glory of the Leafs, on and off the ice. Regarding on the ice, he said he wanted to "remove every crutch that might prevent them from winning." As for off the ice, he very sensitively addressed the sex abuse scandal that had been hanging over Maple Leaf Gardens for years.

At one press conference, Ken essentially said, "We screwed up." He took the time to understand the abuse and how it was hidden, how unconscious memories can take years to appear. He was sincere and understanding. This was one of Ken Dryden's finest moments at Maple Leaf Sports and Entertainment.

And, with the help of Tom Anselmi, Ken brought the important Leaf alumni back into the fold after Harold Ballard had completely ostracized them from the team. Ken's mistake was to make Pat Quinn the GM as well as the coach. Pairing those positions was common in simpler, past times in professional sports, but it was no longer a formula for success. Coaching is a twenty-four-hour-a-day job. To have to worry as well about drafting players, developing future players, negotiating contracts, attending NHL meetings and so on is far too much for any one person to handle. After a few years of seeing that arrangement not work, we decided to split the job into two again.

In 2003, I quarterbacked a search with Ken to find a new general manager. We quickly boiled it down to a solid short list. Bob Nicholson: to this day, he does a great job running Hockey Canada. I sometimes wonder if he would have been a good choice. Neil Smith: he had won a Stanley Cup in New York as a general manager. Steve Tambellini: he was GM of the Edmonton Oilers for five years. Another person I wanted to talk to was Dave Nonis, then working for Brian Burke—then president in Vancouver. Burke was okay with it, but ownership turned me down.

In the end, we decided on John Ferguson Jr. As mentioned, I thought he had the right stuff to be GM of the Leafs, but I was wrong about that. In the back of my mind, I was worried about the dollars, worried about overpaying a new general manager. In hindsight, it was false economy.

When I hired Ferguson, he was, at thirty-six, the youngest GM in the NHL, and he had no experience as a general manager. Still, I thought he was the prototypical new manager, young and fresh. His DNA was excellent. John Ferguson Sr. had a solid NHL career with the Canadiens and had coached the New York Rangers and Winnipeg Jets. John Ferguson Jr. was drafted and played in the AHL for four years, so he knew what it took to succeed in the NHL. He had then decided to go back and get a law degree, which many GMs in sports today now possess. John had worked in the NHL's game operations and legal department over the course of two summers—including one when negotiations over collective bargaining agreements were under way. He had been a scout and an agent, and when we considered his candidacy as general manager of the Leafs, he was working as a vice-president with the St. Louis Blues.

John Ferguson was smart, and he had all the right credentials. Ken Dryden, the owners, me: we all thought he could succeed. Our big mistake? You don't put a rookie GM in charge of the Maple Leafs. John would have been much better starting his career with a team such as Columbus or Tampa, where the media coverage is far less and the fans are much less demanding.

John did double the number of scouts, and he did add a part-time goalie coach. He also brought in Paul Maurice, a very experienced NHL coach, to take over the Marlies. I tried to help John grow as a GM. Some would say I meddled. I did, I admit, help him write the plans he took to the board, but the content was his. My mistake was to often sit with him in the gondola looking down on the ice during games (which TV cameras duly recorded) and which may have given some the idea that I was meddling. In fact, I only wanted to hear what John and his management team were thinking. I never influenced him concerning a trade, a draft choice or a free agent.

Board expectations were high following the excellent run between 1999 and 2004. The team that John inherited, though, was not as good as the board believed it was. In business when a new president or CEO takes over, that individual has a chance to candidly reveal to the board what state the business is in. The new leader usually has a chance to clean house, close plants, write off bad debts, and so on. But John was too inexperienced to do the hockey equivalent, and even had he been bold enough, the board—blinded by high expectations—would not have accepted such moves. I strongly encouraged John to surround himself with an experienced management team, but his only step was to hire an ex-Leaf-turned-lawyer, Jeff Jackson. To top it all off, John was clinical and guarded with the media and therefore the fans.

We had hoped that a partnership of Pat Quinn and John Ferguson would click, but it never did. John should have been a great hire. He was prepared to be a GM—but not in Toronto. He also did not grow into the job enough during his five years on the job. Our conclusion after the 2005–2006 season was that the team was not prepared to be competitive under the terms of the new collective bargaining agreement. Suddenly we went from a team relying on a $70 million budget to buy free agents every spring to enable a playoff run to one with a $50 million budget. We were an older, slower team just when the crackdown on obstruction and interference was putting a new emphasis on team speed. Finally, we had no good prospects coming up from the Marlies.

Clearly, John Ferguson wasn't the man to lead the Leafs to success.

On January 22, 2008, we replaced him on an interim basis with Cliff Fletcher. As I had done with the Raptors, I brought in an experienced hand. Cliff had been the team's GM for six years back in the 1990s.

I remember the press conference where I introduced Cliff.

Somehow, I later became a target because of what happened that day. Before the Q & A with the press, I warned Cliff that a media mob would be waiting for him.

"Don't worry," Cliff said. "I've worked in this market."

"Cliff," I said, "it's changed."

He came out and gave a short speech—all off the cuff. Cliff barely looked at a few notes he had scribbled on a small piece of paper. But I have this habit apparently—one I was unaware of until this bizarre episode—of moving my lips when someone else speaks. The accusation in the press two days later was that I had written Cliff's speech and was just following along. "Richard Peddie, the Ventriloquist," was the headline.

Our plan was to put the word out that we were looking for a new GM so that any candidates whose contracts were coming up might consider the Leaf job before making any moves. I originally hired a search firm to help me. All businesses use search firms to help hire senior management roles, so why not professional sports?

Unfortunately, that is not the norm in sports, and there are no experienced search firms with a proven track record of success. The first search advisor I used did not work out. I then hired a PhD consultant who tried to rank all current and recent GMs using a statistical model, but his findings were directional at best. I then decided to hire sports lawyer Gord Kirke to do due diligence on a long list of candidates. Gord knew hockey and had great credibility in the NHL and in Toronto. My thinking was that third parties might be more candid with Gord than with me. In the end, both the statistical study and the Kirke analysis pointed to two men—one of them Brian Burke. He was our first choice: a former NHL executive with great connections to, and credibility with, Gary Bettman and the NHL office, a proven NHL GM in Vancouver and a Stanley Cup winner in Anaheim.

And he was definitely the type of individual who could handle the MLSE board and the Toronto media. Brian had been a friend of mine for years, and I was convinced he was the right man for the very difficult job of running the Leafs and the person to bring the Leafs their fourteenth Stanley Cup. Unfortunately, he was under contract with Anaheim. As per NHL rules on tampering, I asked Anaheim permission to talk to him. Understandably, my request was declined. But the board believed and I believed that Burke was the right guy, and we were all willing to be patient. Burke's contract would be up in a year. We had a proven interim GM in Fletcher and we would wait. Burke had family in the East, and Anaheim's West Coast location and the extensive travel that West Coast teams had to endure was not to his liking. He let Anaheim know that he would not be renewing his contract in the spring of 2009.

In early November, I was travelling with the Leafs on their annual West Coast swing through Calgary, Edmonton and Vancouver. One morning upon arriving at the Edmonton arena I was swarmed by the media and learned that Burke had resigned from Anaheim. It was a complete surprise to me. I immediately asked Anaheim for permission to talk to Burke and so informed the league, to make sure that the Leafs could not be accused of tampering.

Burke and I used to sit across from each other at NHL meetings and we hit it off right from the start. At one such meeting, the owners of the Anaheim franchise were sitting at a front table, with Burke behind them. I emailed him: "You know, Brian, if you were working for the Leafs, you'd be sitting in the front row, not back there." Was this tampering? I guess in a small way it was. But it was also indicative of the strong friendship we had.

When I started at MLSE and was going to NHL meetings, Brian was someone I could talk to. I was the new kid, and he was a guy who had made Vancouver into a 100-plus-points team. Then he moved to Anaheim, where his team won the Stanley Cup. Owners would change, general managers would change, and I would just get to know them and then they'd be gone. Brian, though, was a constant at those meetings. He and I would sometimes talk late into the night about hockey and the state of the NHL. He was so unlike John Ferguson Jr., who could not smile, who was so guarded and civil. In hindsight, what was I thinking hiring a reserved, taciturn coach for the Toronto market?

At an NHL meeting, when Brian Burke talks, people listen. He'll take on owners, anyone. There is no ounce of shyness in him. On the edge scale, he's 100 out of 100. I'm an 85 or lower.

We announced Brian's appointment on Saturday, November 29, 2008. I don't ever remember there being more cameras at a press conference in my time at MLSE. Brian had a clear vision on how to develop a Stanley Cup winning team in Toronto. If he had stayed, I am absolutely convinced that Brian would have rewarded MLSE owners with a team that competed every year for a championship and won more than its share.

After Brian was with MLSE for a few months, I asked him why our teams were not winning. He could talk only about the Leafs, but he said to me, "You give me all the financial support I need. You also give me all the moral support I need. If the Leafs don't win, it's my fault."

I really like Brian. He is incredibly generous with his time and his money. He's constantly giving speeches and then giving his speaker's fee to charity. I wish he would say "no" more. He is a very dear friend, an authentic, stand-up guy who always has your back. And he's a team player, whether by helping the entire organization do its business or by helping Gary Bettman and the NHL office. He's passionate and outspoken—sometimes to his detriment. There's a soft side to him, but he can also be bombastic and profane, and he can tell a story. I have in my possession three paintings by an artist named Brian Burke in Prince Edward Island; I tell Burke the Leafs' GM that I'm going to dash his macho image by revealing that he paints on the side. Brian is a hunter and a big supporter of Ducks Unlimited; I tell him he's building habitat to help ducklings grow up to be ducks he can blast away. He and I laugh a lot. Brian Burke should write a book; I'd buy it.

Late in August 2012, I dropped into his office at MLSE to say hello. The collective bargaining agreement talks were under way, and Gary Bettman was in town, so there were time pressures on him. But we spent about forty minutes chatting. He was wearing tan slacks and his trademark white shirt, which looked ironed. I had seen him earlier that spring—and the white shirt had looked slept in and it seemed that he wore on his face the pressures of the job. But this day he looked refreshed and relaxed.

I watched him dip into the mini-fridge in his office and pull out a can of Diet Coke from the great rows of the stuff stacked there. Right off the bat he pretended to be miffed because that morning Sportsnet had ranked the most prickly people in sports and New York Ranger coach John Tortorella had edged out Burkie for top spot. On the other hand, he laughed, "I beat Bobby Knight!"

We talked that day about the Leafs, about how they were not big enough or truculent enough, but that drafting was going to add both. "The cavalry are on the way," he told me, "you can hear the hoofbeats." He talked about the three pillars that are part of every team he has ever managed. "One, You run the team like a business. People will invest only if the money is wisely spent. Two, we play to entertain. We attack, we hit in all three zones, we fight, we score. We're a fun team to watch and we're a good draw. And finally, community service. The Leafs do twice what other teams are asking. We will give back. It's a demand. You don't do it, you don't get to play here."

Players on all four teams—the Leafs, Raptors, Marlies and Toronto Football Club—make visits to the Hospital for Sick Children. And that can be tough, sitting on a bed beside a child with no hair. Burke made the point that, in terms of community service, the hockey player is a breed apart.

"An NHL player," Brian reminded me, "is a special kid. They do this community work gracefully. Other athletes in other sports are not like that. The difference is night and day. I listen to other GMs in other sports. They tell me how hard it is to get their players into the community. It's unbelievable to watch here. It's cultural. The game of hockey has always given back. It's a wonderful side of our game. There is not one player on the Leaf team I would not send to a family's house."

We also talked that day about the GM's life, and the challenges he faces. "It's hard," he said, "to turn a team around, to change the culture. What's acceptable and what's not? Too many players here accepted losing. Even in beer leagues, losing is not acceptable. Coming here as GM, I was not prepared for the lack of privacy, how I can't walk the street or have dinner in a restaurant. And the fans here are frighteningly knowledgeable, so sophisticated. The bigger mistake would be to try to bullshit these people."

He also reflected on his skirmishes with the media. People think that talking to the media is sexy. "It's not," says Brian. "It's a pain in the ass. Reporters in this city have a tremendous fear of being last to report something. Not being right is one thing; worst is being last. So there are tremendous time constraints, the quality of journalism is lost and people with average skills come to be viewed as authorities. Some young guy starts by covering high school football, then he's a stringer for a big Toronto newspaper. Then he's the number two guy reporting on the Leafs. He has acquired a veil of authority. I have cut way back on interviews."

* * *

Burkie and I also talked that day about Gary Bettman. Brian called him "the most misunderstood person in North America. He's seen in Canada as an American basketball guy. He's a wonderful human being. If he asked me to drive him to New York, I would do it. If he needed $10,000, I'd give it to him. He's brilliant, tough as nails. I love the guy. He's very funny, and when I worked for him in the NHL office, he was a great boss."

What I have noticed is that newspapers love to run photos that cast Gary Bettman in a dark light. If they can make him look bad, they will. By 2013, he had been commissioner for twenty years. He is *not* a basketball guy—he is now a hockey guy, and he knows and loves the sport. Canadian media and fans are really down on him. I read and hear the ugly things they say about him in letters to the editor or online comments or on talk radio. Yet Gary soldiers through. He gets it much worse than I ever did.

When he was badly booed while presenting the Stanley Cup in Vancouver, I immediately emailed him and apologized for the boorish behaviour of the Vancouver fans. Perhaps some of them were the same ones who rushed out and trashed the city after the game. I also found the way that Gary has been interviewed by Ron MacLean unacceptable (I'm thinking especially of the now infamous June 2010 exchange on *Hockey Night in Canada*, which was both vitriolic and confrontational). I guarantee that none of the NFL or NBA rights holders in the United States would ever treat a league commissioner that way. If CBC-TV loses its Canadian TV rights, that interview—it was an attack, really—might well factor in the league's decision.

If you as an NHL team owner make things difficult for him and the league, Gary Bettman and, indeed, all commissioners, have the power to respond: There are many perks that can be offered your team, or not. Did your team get a national broadcast deal? How many of your team's games will be seen on the CBC? Does your arena get consideration as the venue for the All-Star game or the annual outdoor game? Have the league brass helped, or hindered, another franchise coming into your territory?.

I really like Gary. He was always good to me. He was always approachable, always returned my calls and was always willing to hear my ideas and give me advice. But Gary and I did not always see eye to eye. I was always pushing for more financial transparency. What gives Gary some of his power is the lack of transparency. I was a pit bull on numbers. My whole career was based on marketing, but I got good on finances. I'd ask deputy commissioner Bill Daly, "What are we making as a league?" I never got an answer to that question.

I would say at meetings, "I, as CEO of the Leafs, must provide full financial disclosure to our shareholders. Why doesn't the league do the same?" New owners and GMs and their staff who go to NHL meetings are sometimes struck by the governance model. Like the NBA, the NHL is not a democracy. In the fall of 2012, the league locked out players who were asking for too much money. At one point, players wanted to continue getting 57 per cent of revenue at a time when professional football and baseball players were getting 50 per cent. But because there isn't enough transparency, the players don't trust the NHL's numbers and the fans don't understand how unprofitable the league actually is. In a report late in 2012, *Forbes* magazine listed the values of the thirty teams in the NHL. The magazine thought the Leafs were worth $1 billion, and valued the New York Rangers at $750 million, the Montreal Canadiens at $575 million. The St. Louis Blues, on the other hand, were worth only $130 million.

I question these figures—and the suggestion that the Leafs have operating income in the range of $82 million. It's actually more complicated than that. The Leafs' operating profits number is a little lower than the figure listed in *Forbes*—but again that is operating profits, not net income. I agree with the assertion that at least eighteen teams lose money, and again that is at the operating line. The team losses and the total league losses would be much more at net income (after interest, depreciation, amortization and taxes—all legitimate expenses). What I really don't agree with is trying to compare revenue sharing between the NHL and the NFL. The NFL has a broadcast deal that gives each team about $110 million per year. That money essentially pays for each team's payroll. By comparison, the NHL US broadcast deal is tiny and distributes only $5 million per team. The impact of this amount of media revenue and the difference between operating income and net income are things that most sports writers simply do not understand.

As the lockout continued through the fall of 2012 and into January 2013, I found myself siding with the owners on most issues. For one thing, revenue sharing is not the answer when the entire league is losing money. That would be like moving deck chairs around on the *Titanic*. For another thing, the NHL simply spends too much on its players. And big clubs such as New York and Toronto have spent millions in capital to generate their high revenues. As I write this, the Rangers are spending $1 billion of their own money redoing Madison Square Garden. The NBA also had about eighteen teams losing money, but now with lower player costs they are able to share more money, and almost all teams should be able to make money with this new collective bargaining agreement. I just wish NHL owners wouldn't go on shooting themselves in the foot by writing outrageously fat cheques to star players. This is the hot potato that the NHL commissioner has to handle.

Some fans want to know what Gary Bettman's salary is. I actually don't care what his salary is. I want to know about Phoenix. Why are we as a league keeping that franchise afloat? Should the Toronto Maple Leafs be helping out a chronically losing franchise? What's happening with the New Jersey Devils? Are they in trouble? The problem is that some 100 people attend when every franchise is invited to NHL meetings, and there are always leaks to the media. Maybe that's why Gary is not prepared to be fully transparent.

The NBA offers a useful lesson in the value of transparency. When David Stern came out and told the owners, fans, media and the National Basketball Players Association that the league was losing almost $300 million a year at the net income line, it quantified the financial challenge facing the negotiating parties and helped get a deal that will make the NBA's financial future more secure.

The NHL is a healthy league on the ice, with incredible parity (seven different Stanley Cup winners since 2005), and thanks to an excellent sales and marketing effort by COO John Collins, the revenue picture is solid too. But any talk of more revenue sharing makes sense only if the league collectively makes money.

The other thing Gary Bettman and I disagreed about was the size of the league. A lot of good people are trying to make the Southern US clubs succeed, but I simply don't think that some of them will ever make it. I remember sitting in Gary's office about three years ago talking about contraction. I said we should have only twenty-four clubs, but we agreed to disagree. Gary won't talk about contraction, and to the best of my knowledge it was never fully analyzed—and, if it was, it never came to the board.

I asked Burkie that day in his office, "If a fan were to be allowed into the CBA [collective bargaining agreement] talks—a kind of fly on the wall—what would amaze that fan?"

"That fan," he replied, "would be shocked to discover how mundane some details are. It's a 200-page document. How much are the per diems? Is it one to a hotel room or two to a room? If the team leaves on a plane at 2 p.m., does the player get a half a day or a full day per diem? How long are practices? How long is training camp? Some of these players make $5 to $7 million a year—and they're concerned about things like this?"

So much free food is laid on in the anterooms of dressing rooms, Brian said, that "NHL" actually stands for "Never Hungry League." And if fans were allowed into NHL meetings, Burke added, they might also be surprised by the camaraderie in professional sports. "NHL teams compete on the ice," he says. "In the boardrooms, we share best practices." It's why some people from the New Orleans Saints came to the Air Canada Centre to see how we did things; it's why we sent one of our directors, Erol Uzumeri, to Wrigley Field to see how the Chicago Cubs operated. At MLSE, we plundered the best practices of three leagues.

Brian Burke walks in Toronto's Pride Parades as a way of honouring his son, Brendan, who died tragically in a car accident in February 2010 at the age of twenty-one. Brian bought a horse for the Toronto police force in his son's name, with a little BB flash in one corner of the saddle pad. There will always be an ache there.

I had complete faith in Brian Burke. What I observed was someone who was watching a lot of AHL games; for a guy who came to the East so he could spend more time with his family, he's non-stop hockey. He was so accommodating with the media in Toronto. He really gets the bigger purpose. But the media turned on him. He had to relearn that there's no quid pro quo with the media, and he started to pick his spots better. In February and March 2012, he expressed his anger over a Don Cherry remark about there being too few Ontario players with the Leafs. I wondered if that little circus contributed to the Leafs' downward spiral.

I too had to learn that lesson about talking to reporters and broadcasters. You need to feed the beast, but you have to be careful and not talk too much. It's a fine line.

Burkie still calls me The Boss. "I'm disappointed you're not still here," he told me as I got up to leave his office that day. "You were a great leader, and you led by winning the respect of people here. But you were much softer than me. I have lots of enemies. You have none."

He marvelled that he and I never fought. "But if we ever did," he said, "bet on the Irishman."

* * *

Clearly, I did bet on the Irishman, and clearly I lost the bet.

At noon on January 12, 2013, I was sitting in my condominium in Miami. It was a beautiful Florida day and a warm 27 degrees centigrade. Down below, families were gathered on the beach, the kids playing in the sun. Cries and laughter rose up from the sand. All was good.

But 2,389 kilometres up north in Toronto, things were not so good. At the Air Canada Centre, in a packed Rogers Media Centre (somewhat ironic, don't you think, that Rogers and even Bell's TSN used this event to increase their viewing audiences), the mood was sombre and restless. Everyone was waiting for Brian Burke—who had been fired three days earlier—to say his goodbyes to a gathering of more than fifty media people and almost a dozen cameras. I had heard rumblings that the board was not crazy about Burke, but I strongly believed it would give him forty-eight games in the shortened season of 2013 to prove his worth.

I had been sitting in the condo reading three days earlier, and Colleen was on her computer when she turned to me and said, "Brian has been fired." I quickly sent an email to him that started with the word "crap," or at least one like it.

I watched his farewell press conference on the Sportsnet website. I was sad, very unhappy and even angry. This was not what I had imagined when I introduced Brian in the same room on November 29, 2008, to an equally packed room. I believed Brian would finish out his contract and that a new CEO would extend him for another five years. I also believed that Brian would win a Stanley Cup in Toronto (maybe he still will, but it would have to be for a new expansion club).

Brian looked rested. He held it together pretty well. He was obviously upset, disappointed, angry and still shocked.

Doubtless, the team had not done well under Brian's watch with a 128–135–42 record and no playoff appearances. But I was confident that he was building the foundation for a winning team. As one anonymous GM was reported as saying in a newspaper, the new general manager of the Leafs is going to nicely benefit from Burke's work. Was he fired for his record? Sure, you can make a case for that, but if so, then why wasn't it done after the 2012 season ended? Alternatively, why not make that decision after seeing how the team performed in the abbreviated forty-eight game 2013 season?

Or was it because of his style—the "Burke brand," if you like? I hired Brian because he was admired, connected, fearless, unafraid to speak up and, importantly, a winner. Sure he was bombastic, often profane and a little black and white, but between the two of us we could work that out. Every year in April, all full-time MLSE employees receive a written evaluation of their performance for the past fiscal year. We believed that all employees had the right to read about their strengths and weaknesses. We believed that someone had a chance of correcting his or her weaknesses ("development needs," we called them) only if that person clearly knew what they were. I gave Brian three such evaluations—after the first one he said it was the first written evaluation he had received since law school at Harvard. So if style or behaviour was the problem, in fairness to him, was that clearly spelled out? I like to think that if I were still CEO and I and the board had problems with Brian, I would have collected the board members' thoughts and spelled them out clearly to Brian. Would it have worked? I think so, but I don't know for sure. What I do know is that if we still had to fire Brian, he would not have been both surprised and shocked when it happened.

Brian was accountable. He never wavered from his belief that if MLSE gave him the resources and the moral support he needed and the team still lost—then the fault was his. He also understood that he worked for the Leafs as long as the owners wanted him. It was their money and therefore their call. He got a job that he compared to working for the Vatican or the New York Yankees. He is sad that he lost his job and, short of becoming the next NHL commissioner, he will never have as important a hockey job again.

He was the best GM of any MLSE team when it came to being accessible and helpful with fans, sponsors, suite holders and, for sure, in the community. All MLSE general managers are okay to good at that. He was great. In many sports franchises you hear horror stories about GMs being completely uncooperative. Helping on the business side is also part of the job of today's sports GMs. Running a team is expensive (salaries, benefits, operating costs, scouting), and generating revenue in a tough economy needs all hands on deck if you are going to be successful. Brian visited suites, gave incredible time and personal money to the community and went on a lot of sales calls. At one sales pitch, he passed around his huge diamond-encrusted Stanley Cup ring, telling the prospective sponsor, "Join our team and you will share in the victory when the Leafs win their fourteenth."

He left a strong management team in Dave Nonis, Dave Poulin, Cliff Fletcher and Claude Loiselle. Nonis was obviously shell-shocked. (Later I told him that he should do up his tie when the cameras are on, and he told me that he had loosened it because it was so suffocatingly hot in that room and he couldn't breathe.) As bittersweet as it was, Nonis would have been my choice too. I just hope they give him time to win.

I still think Brian is the best GM—in or out of the NHL. Five years ago I studied more than thirty GM candidates, and I still think Brian is the best one.

Brian had previously agreed to be a speaker at a leadership symposium at the Odette School of Business at the University of Windsor a month hence. After the dust settled, I asked him if he still was okay to do that. He said he would do it for me. Brian is that type of stand-up guy to his friends. I told Brian he had a leadership story to tell the students. I added that, since most students would probably be fired at some point in their careers, his firing from the Maple Leafs was actually a good teachable point of view.

I will miss him as Leaf GM. I will continue to follow the Leafs and root for them, but it won't quite be the same. My heart won't be in it for a long while.

This, by the way, is what Catherine Grey, Brian's assistant (now former assistant) wrote in an email to me after the firing: "I will do everything that I can to help him in any way, shape or form. I will miss him dearly. He was a wonderful boss, but more importantly to me, a great friend. We had an amazing working relationship. I will cherish these past years always. It was an incredible honour for me to have been able to work side by side with the best GM in hockey. He will land on his feet again, and he will shine even brighter."

* * *

Today, with caps on spending, it's difficult to outspend the other twenty-nine teams. During the Quinn/Dryden years, the Leafs did spend in the top five of the league, and this did give them a leg up and was, in part, a reason for our success. The battle for championships is now often an "arms race" off the ice, in which teams look for every advantage by hiring the best (and best paid) coaches and general managers, fitness gurus, psychologists, nutritionists and chefs. Burke and MLSE have done a number of things that I strongly believe will cause the team to be much more successful than they've been in the recent past. This process has already started; witness their entry into the playoffs in the spring of 2013. Not all of these have paid winning dividends yet, but they will.

Moving the Leafs farm team from Newfoundland to Toronto, for example, has finally started to pay dividends and will pay even more handsomely in the long run. Until 2005, the Leafs' AHL team was in St John's. While the arena was top-notch and Newfoundland has tremendous Leaf fans, the distant geography and the absence of any East Coast AHL teams presented real problems for the club. Almost all the team's road trips started with a flight to Toronto and then long bus rides from there, resulting in the players being on the road for days and weeks at a time. There was no time left for player development.

Moving players between the two clubs was always a problem because it often took two to three days to get it done. Having the AHL club right next door and only a streetcar stop away makes player moves instantaneous and salary cap management much more efficient. (The Toronto Blue Jays did something similar in 2012, moving their farm team from faraway Las Vegas to nearby Buffalo. Calling up a player from the minors no longer involves a five-hour flight but a ninety-minute drive. And the same synergy applies between the Buffalo Bisons and the Toronto Blue Jays as between the Toronto Maple Leafs and the Toronto Marlboros. It seemed a good bet that baseball fans in Buffalo would be drawn to Toronto and vice-versa.)

Having the Marlies in Toronto has other significant benefits. The Marlies now get watched by Leaf management all the time, and that same management gets to see other AHL players play all the time. This is deeply motivational for the players; Leaf management, meanwhile, has a much better appreciation of the players they have and how they are developing. Leaf resources such as the goalie coach, the team psychologist, medical and strength-and-conditioning staff are all there to help Marlie players be the best they can be.

Also, having one's AHL club in the same city certainly helps attract foreign or US college free agents. The player can move to Toronto and get a permanent place to play, knowing that when they are called up they don't have to move residences. And the young players sure prefer living in Toronto to Albany, Worchester or Grand Rapids. When Ian Clarke and I struck the Ricoh Coliseum lease deal with the city, the people negotiating for Toronto were worried that we would take advantage of them and out-negotiate them. They need not have worried; we at MLSE were the ones who were taken.

Ricoh was renovated, and the funds for that renovation were borrowed. The Edmonton Oiler AHL team (the Road Runners) had tried to run their franchise there one year but lost their shirts and bailed on the market. Ricoh Coliseum had the potential to be an embarrassing white elephant for the city. Ian and I thought that a team of future Leafs wearing essentially the Leaf jersey would be a slam-dunk success. Fans who could not get to see the Leafs play were certain to come see future Leafs play at affordable prices.

Accordingly, we basically stepped into the shoes of the Oilers and covered the debt financing, which exceeds $4 million a year. On top of that, we signed a twenty-year agreement with no escape clauses. Don't ever do that! To this day, the Marlies cost MLSE almost $7 million a year. As I've said, the Ricoh lease was easily the worst I did in all my time at MLSE. But the city is happy with MLSE, and the Ricoh deal set the stage for healthy subsequent negotiations on BMO Field and the lease at the Master-Card Centre.

Every fiscal year, I had to stand up in front of the MSLE board to explain how much the Marlies were costing Maple Leaf Sports and Entertainment and what we were doing to cut into the losses. In my last fiscal plan in 2011, I had Brian Burke and Dave Nonis outline all the benefits of having our AHL team close by. At the end of their presentation, the board essentially said, "We get it, don't worry about annually justifying the Marlies." A bad deal was done, I heard them say. Just do the best you can to reduce the losses.

AHL clubs probably cost most NHL teams less than $2 million a year. Our belief was that if the Marlie model developed even a few Leaf prospects, the extra $5 million a year was worth it.

Dave Perkins of the *Toronto Star* cites Ricoh as an example of MLSE using taxpayer money, and it is simply not so. I have said publicly many times that if anyone else wants to take over Ricoh to host concerts, family shows or other events, I am sure that the new owners of MLSE would happily take them up on that offer. The good news today is that the $7 million Marlie investment is starting to pay dividends. The team was then being coached by an excellent head coach in Dallas Eakins (he's now head coach with the Edmonton Oilers), who was truly developing young players to be future Leafs. When Brian Burke and Dave Nonis took over the club, they saw possibly five players who could someday play for the Leafs. In January 2013, that number was over fifteen, and several of them made the Leaf roster.

I very much admired Dallas Eakins and what he was doing with the Marlies. A former defenceman with eight NHL teams (including the Leafs), he spent most of his pro hockey career in the AHL and the IHL (International Hockey League). I was not surprised at all that he was courted by several NHL teams before finally signing with the Oilers in June of 2013.

He completely understood that his role was to develop future Leafs. Some previous Marlie coaches were torn between developing young players and using a good team record as a springboard to a job in the NHL. Dallas was crystal clear. He gave the young kids time on the penalty kill, the power play and key faceoffs at the end of close games. He put them in a place to experience the pressure and helped them learn how to perform. He held them accountable. And he made sure that his team played a similar system to the Leafs (approach to penalty killing, power play, exiting the defensive zone) so that when players came up to the big club, their transition would be more seamless.

Prior to his Marlie head coaching job, Dallas was the Leaf director of player development: he visited the Leafs' young draft prospects wherever they played—Canada, US colleges, even Europe. He would spend up to forty-eight hours with the prospect. Talk to his coach. Reinforce what the coach was telling him, watch the kid practise and play in a game, have lunch or dinner with him. And reinforce to him that the Leafs were watching him and, no matter where he was, he was not alone. Dallas got to know that individual, possibly a future Marlie or Leaf; at the same time, all this mentoring made Dallas a better coach.

When I talked to him about his experience in that job, he told me, "Every coach should do that role for a year." Dallas believes that to be a good coach you have to know what makes every player on your roster tick. Each player needs to be motivated differently. His role model is Roger Neilson (he coached for eight NHL teams, including Toronto and Vancouver), and he talked about how solid Roger's communication skills were. Dallas also says that he would never ask his players to do anything that he wouldn't do—including in the weight room and on the exercise bike. His work ethic is like that of any great coach.

Both the Leafs and the Marlies practise at the new MasterCard Centre in the west end of the city, on the site of the old Lions Club arena, built in 1951. The Leafs had practised there for years, but the Lions Club and the city both wanted to upgrade and expand the facility to offer more ice surfaces to the underserved Toronto market. Not since 1981 had a new arena been built in the city. The Lions Club and the city were able to get funding for the arena after the Leafs committed to a long-term lease at a market rate of more than $500,000 per year. The Leafs also helped attract the Hockey Hall of Fame and Hockey Canada as money-paying tenants, and MLSE sold title sponsorship to the building to MasterCard and split the sponsor fees with the city.

That was the good news; the bad news was that construction costs of the facility went significantly over budget and now it has a financing issue. I had tried to talk then mayor David Miller into letting MLSE build the arena for the city, since we had a track record for on-time and on-budget results. He declined.

Finances aside, the MasterCard Centre now ranks as the finest "hockey factory" in the world. The new facility is marvellous, with four NHL-size ice pads (sixty by twenty-five metres, with one capable of being transformed into an Olympic-sized rink measuring sixty by thirty metres). The dressing rooms and workout rooms were all built and paid for by the Leafs. If the city ever wants to get out from financing the arena, it would be wise to try to sell it to MLSE.

Meanwhile, what an excellent place this is to develop both the Leafs and the Marlies. The two clubs have separate dressing and strength-and-conditioning rooms, and they work out on separate ice pads. But the close proximity of the Leaf dressing room and the chance to see the Leafs work out is incredibly inspirational to Marlie players. They all want to cross the hall and be a Leaf. Dallas Eakins told me a great story about telling team captain Ryan Hamilton that he was being called up to play for the Leafs—this was in March 2012. Dallas got him on the phone, told him to "pack his best suit and kiss your wife goodbye. You're getting called up." Apparently, there was silence, and then Hamilton said, "Are you kidding me?" It doesn't get much better than that when you are developing young players.

I liked Dallas's custom of posting in the dressing room before each game which NHL scouts were in the building that night. The players already knew that Leaf management was in the building every night (definitely not so in St John's). So the Marlie advertising line—"Every game is a tryout"—is always true. The player has a chance to impress the Leafs or impress another team that might want to trade for him. In my last season with MLSE, the Marlies went to the Calder Cup finals. Despite many crippling injuries, they played well, and sellout crowds finally showed up at Ricoh.

After their last game, a loss, Dallas told me, "It hurts them all so bad. It makes them naked to the bone." Dallas was teaching these young men how to handle the incredible pressure that comes with each and every playoff game, how hard each and every game is. How special is the journey. And, importantly, he was teaching these future Leafs how to win. Dallas and the Marlies are one reason the Leafs are soon going to be a very good team and will stay a very good team for years to come.

As I write this early in April 2013, Nazem Kadri leads the Leafs in scoring and sits tenth among all NHL goal scorers. But in September 2012, at the Marlies training camp, Dallas Eakins was making headlines in the Toronto newspapers by calling out Kadri for his eating habits and body fat. "Unacceptable" is how he put it. The young man got the message. Every player on the Marlies benefits from the mentoring, the leading and the pushing by Dallas Eakins.

By the end of the season, these former Marlies were with the Leafs: Nazem Kadri, Matt Frattin, Ben Scrivens, Tyler Bozak, Ryan Hamilton, Jake Gardiner, Mike Kostka, Carl Gunnarsson and Mark Fraser. All were coached by Dallas since he joined the team as coach in 2009. And as I write these words, the headline in one Toronto newspaper is to the effect that, despite all the call-ups to the big club, the Dallas Eakins Marlies are still winning.

"We keep calm and carry on," Eakins told the *Toronto Star*.

★ ★ ★

The wisdom of emulating the best practices of others holds true in professional sports just as it does in business.

When Gordon Kirke and I were looking for a GM to replace John Ferguson, Jr., we studied the different management teams in the NHL. The one that stood out for us was Detroit. At the time, they had an incredibly deep team in Jimmy Devellano, Ken Holland, Jim Nill, Steve Yzerman, Mike Babcock and Scotty Bowman. They were the gold standard in our eyes because of all their brains and depth and continuity. Since then, they have lost Bowman and Yzerman, but they are still excellent.

Ferguson was slow to surround himself with an experienced management team and that cost him. From day one, I encouraged Brian Burke to surround himself with a great and experienced team that would make him better. He did just that with Dave Nonis, Dave Poulin, Claude Loiselle, Randy Carlyle and Cliff Fletcher. Even with the departure of Burke, I still think that the Leaf management team is one of the best in the NHL.

And whatever money it takes (within the rules, of course), that budget will be there. During my entire time with MLSE, the board never said no to what Leaf management wanted to spend on players or developing players. The Ontario Teachers' Pension Plan often received a bad rap when it was the majority shareholder of the Leafs: the contention was that it was interested only in making money. And yes, it was interested in profit, but it also understood that having winning teams was very good business. In the Dryden and Quinn years, their budget was virtually unlimited. Under the cap system that now helps control player salaries in the league, the Leafs having the maximum money to spend was never an issue. In fact, in the collective bargaining agreement that ended in September 2012, there was a loophole whereby a GM could dump players into the AHL and get that player's salary off the team's salary cap. Each year he was with the Leafs, Burke asked for that and received a multi-million-dollar addition to his budget that we called "cap plus." The board knew that Burke would spend the money only if it made sense and would help the team win.

* * *

To succeed, the Toronto Maple Leafs need just the right combination and quality of players coached just so by the right coach selected by the right general manager. The Leaf team is the toughest team to coach in the entire National Hockey League. The only other team that comes close is Montreal. The pressure to win is so intense, and every cog in the wheel has to be able to take that pressure.

That's why we came increasingly to rely on Toronto psychologist Dana Sinclair, the team psychologist for both the Raptors and Leafs. She has a PhD in sports psychology from the University of Ottawa and a PhD in psychology from Cambridge University. She is smart, impressive and can hold her own in any debate with team scouts. Her company's list of clients includes seven professional sports franchises—the Boston Red Sox and the Los Angeles

Dodgers among them—as well as Canada's Olympians. When I first started talking about using people such as Dana, I was roasted in the media. This testing is simply one more tool in the hiring process. You do due diligence, you check out references (which can be dubious, since the source of the glowing praise might be operating out of pity or fear of being sued—or maybe it's a competitor hoping you will hire the so-called asset they are quite happy to unload). In the end, hiring can still be a crapshoot.

Dana has two roles with MLSE teams. First, she assesses potential draft choices. In the 2012 drafts, she tested twenty-five NHL prospects for the Leafs and fifteen NBA prospects for the Raptors. She tests them for character, how they respond to pressure, their ability to lead and a great many other traits. Recognizing that a team can't have too many leaders, she also looks for fit. She conducts a risk assessment of the candidates. A "red flag" means she thinks the candidate represents a risk to the club; a "flag" offers a caution to the club; "unremarkable" could mean the prospect lacks maturity and aggression; "satisfactory" suggests a self-motivated, mature and disciplined prospect who can develop; and finally there is "outstanding," a ranking that few prospects attain.

Should a team ever draft a red-flagged prospect? Dana believes it is up to management to decide whether they, their coach and the team dressing room can handle him. If they can't, they have a disaster and have wasted a draft choice. When GMs meet with their management team and scouts, Dana is there to share her findings and defend her conclusions. "Some scouts," she says, "get seduced by the talent" after spending years watching the kid play and developing a certainty in his skills and gifts. That scout can get angry with her.

Dana's job is to give the GM an idea of how much risk comes with the athlete. Can he develop? To what extent? In the beginning, scouts had difficulty accepting Dana's reports, but now that they understand the process she goes through, they are more understanding. Dana doesn't make the ultimate decision on a draft choice. She is simply presenting another piece of data for the club to consider when making its call.

Her second role with the clubs is to help "fix" the player. Young players can have many psychological issues that may be negatively impacting their play or slowing their development. When this happened, Burke would often say to Dana, "Go fix him." She would zero in on one or two things for the player to focus on and understand. Her job is to "move them to action."

I asked her if Toronto was a tougher place for hockey players to play than other places. She doesn't believe that the market is the issue. What matters is the players' ability to handle pressure and their emotions. Dana has been working with the Leafs and Raptors for only a few years. Her input on draft choices is being increasingly listened to, and she is being used to help "fix" players more often. This all bodes well for the teams' future.

* * *

I never got too close to the Leaf players. I had not played much hockey as a kid and had followed the NBA more than the NHL. Also, in the early years of my tenure at MLSE, Dryden and Quinn ran the team; I was focused on the Raptors and getting the business side of things straightened out. I felt welcomed by Leaf players, but it was more of a collective welcome than the individual welcome I had received from the Raptor players.

My favourite Leaf player was easily Mats Sundin, the Leafs' long-time captain. The holder of many Leaf records, he got into the Hall of Fame in his first year of eligibility. A solid, quiet, authentic man, he led by example on and off the ice. With fans he was excellent and always patient, always classy. Mats took undeserved blame for the Leafs not doing better. When we raised his banner (his number 13) at the Air Canada Centre in February 2012, he announced that night that he was teaming up with the University of Toronto and the world-renowned Karolinska Institute in Stockholm to create a $1 million fund of which he will contribute one-third. The money will be used to financially support postdoctoral candidates at the two universities who are studying both maternal health and how early life experiences help determine health, learning ability and overall well-being. I have no fear of Mats not delivering on his promise.

I also had a good, friendly relationship with players Curtis Joseph, Darcy Tucker, Tie Domi and Dion Phaneuf. I often enjoyed talking to Phil Kessel. Phil is a bit of a cynic, but he's smart and extremely interested in the business side of things.

Another big part of the Leaf family are the many ex-Leaf players who make up the largest and most active alumni association in the league. Leaf alumni play an important part in the club's marketing and community initiatives. One of the best former players is the ageless Johnny Bower, nicknamed "The China Wall"—not because he put up a wall-like defence against pucks (though he did that too) but because he was considered ancient even in his playing days. He didn't make the Leafs until he was thirty-four years old and didn't retire until age forty-four. Most pro hockey players get a quick stamp at customs as they cross back and forth between Canada and the United States; Bower, though, was often questioned because border officials wondered how someone his age could possibly be playing in the NHL. When MLSE first formed, Johnny dressed up as Santa Claus for the team and staff party. Johnny is often around the Air Canada Centre, and when he shows up in the stands, he always receives a terrific fan ovation. He may well be the most popular player ever to wear the Leaf uniform, and even at his age (he's in his late eighties) still does thirty to forty fan and community appearances every year.

Past Leaf captain Dave Keon came back to the Leaf fold, albeit briefly, in February 2007 when John Ferguson did a wonderful thing: he reunited almost all of the 1967 Stanley Cup winning Leaf team to mark the fortieth anniversary of the victory. It was a great weekend reunion. Over my entire time at MLSE, Ken Dryden, John Ferguson and many others tried very hard to have the former Leaf captain reconnect with the team. We wanted to raise his banner (number 14) with the other Leaf greats. Not interested. He is apparently still angry with the club over how he was treated by Harold Ballard. But the anger is clearly misdirected, since no one who wronged him all those years ago is around now. When he came to that reunion, he got a one-minute standing ovation, but he made the time-out gesture (palm of the right hand tapping on the fingers of the left hand below). Leaf fans love him and want to see him honoured, but he evidently does not want that. Things remain, as they have for decades, in Keon's camp.

At the dinner on the Friday night of the reunion weekend, former Leaf captain George "The Chief" Armstrong was to formally introduce me to the team. But George is pretty shy about public speaking and when the time came to go up to the podium he was nowhere to be seen.

Former captains Wendel Clark and Darryl Sittler continue being valuable members of the Leaf family. They're always willing to meet fans, sponsors and suite holders. They never miss an event and are very much a part of the Leaf magic.

My best Leaf alumni moment came when I took a team of them down to open a new public arena in Amherstburg, in southwestern Ontario, near our place on Boblo Island. The Leafs were to play the

Amherstburg All-Star team. Before the game I went into the Leaf dressing room to see how they were doing. There were only eleven of them, all over fifty years old, and they were all having a beer. I told them that the team they were going up against had twenty-six players—all under thirty. I also told them that I was tired of being teased about the Leafs losing, so they had to win. They won 15–7, but I suspect they could have won 25–0. They slowed the game right down, and with accurate passes onto the stick of their teammates they had the younger All-Stars running all around the ice hopelessly chasing them. In addition to showing that they had pro hockey skills, they put on an entertaining show—much like the Harlem Globetrotters. Later that night, Bill Derlago, Gary Leeman, Mark Osborne, Bob McGill and Mike Pelyk got together over dinner, and I had a great time listening to stories of their days with the Leafs.

All in all, most of the Leaf players I met were quality guys on and off the ice. They handled their many community events with professionalism. Leafs regularly lead the NHL with community and fan appearances. Almost to a player they all behave very well despite a media and fan base that, while loyal, expects a lot from them—and sometimes behaves horribly. As Brian Burke often said, "The current team is not responsible for the forty-five-year Stanley Cup drought."

The Leafs are arguably Canada's favourite team. Canada's New York Yankees, if you will. The team is always a strong draw on the road in Canadian arenas, with thousands of Leaf jerseys present. I emailed Brian Burke during a Leaf victory in Ottawa, commenting on the way the Ottawa arena sounded and looked like a Leaf home game. I joked that he should have the players go out to centre ice after the game and salute their fans with raised sticks. The two of us laughed about how Eugene Melnyk would have gone ballistic had the Leaf players done that.

Despite lousy on-ice performance for more than half of my time as CEO, the Leafs in all that time were the most profitable team in the NHL. They were also leaders in terms of TV audiences and initiatives such as Leafs TV and many innovative digital platforms. I'm proud of that fact, and of the practice facility we built (the MasterCard Centre for Hockey Excellence). The league regularly uses the facility to test new rules and to tweak the game. And I'm proud of Maple Leaf Square.

After one NHL initiative we hosted, Brian Jennings, the NHL's executive vice-president of marketing, wrote us to say, "The Leafs organization represents the very best in our game and your modern business practices, seamless integration and world-class venues provided the backdrop for other NHL teams to see the endless possibilities. Perhaps above and beyond that are the people of the Toronto Maple Leaf organization, who gave tirelessly of their time to ensure we exceeded our expectations."

The Leafs clearly did not get the job done on my watch. But I strongly believe the vision and pieces are now in place to move forward to a fourteenth Cup. In his book *Leave No Doubt*, Detroit Red Wing coach Mike Babcock writes, "Preparation drives execution, execution leads to success, success gets reinforcement, reinforcement grows confidence, confidence raises expectations, expectations drive excellence, and excellence demands greater preparation. It is a virtuous circle that never stops." I think that circle has now started for the Leafs and will soon deliver excellence.

* * *

Late in April 2013, Maple Leaf Sports and Entertainment announced that Tim Leiweke would join the company as the new president and CEO. This was not the news that Tom Anselmi was hoping to hear, but I have to commend the choice. Leiweke oversaw the Los Angeles Kings and the Los Angeles Galaxy, along with having a stake in the Lakers—the largest sports portfolio in North America.

Tim Leiweke is bigger than life, he's confident, he's gregarious and he loves to grow companies. I like him. He is going to be a handful for everyone who crosses his path.

# CHAPTER 10

# THE TWO Vs: VISION AND VALUES

At one point, I was the biggest farmer in Ontario—growing beans, peas and corn when I was with Pillsbury in the late 1980s and Green Giant was one of our iconic brands. I spent quite a bit of time in our plant in Tecumseh, in southwestern Ontario, site of the Tecumseh Corn Festival, held every year in late August. In that part of the world, corn is king.

I had some fun in that plant. I thought it would be good for morale if I joined the mostly female plant workers who were doing the job of manually pushing the corncobs onto the assembly line. These line operators found it hilarious that they were clicking along at the rate of eighty cobs a minute while I could only manage twenty.

It's quite spectacular to watch a can of corn being produced at dizzying speed, a process that culminates in a taste test. One year—it was my third year running the company, so it would have been 1987—the testers came back with their finding that the Green

Giant cream-style corn was not up to the usual quality standard. There was nothing wrong with the product, it posed no health risk and we could likely sell it. It just wasn't up to snuff. What to do?

The canning of corn has come a long way since the tin can was invented in 1810. The trick to the mass production of canned corn (one, anyway) is speed. Our aim was to get the corn from the moment of mechanical harvesting to a finished and labelled can or frozen bag in just a few hours. That way freshness is preserved. Our plant in Tecumseh then produced millions of cans a year via a process that involves a lot of conveyor belts and chutes and mechanical devices (along with some manual labour) to remove the husks and then the corn kernels before water, salt and sugar are added. The last stage is what we called "the cook."

I was a farmer in a suit, but I shared the same worries as a farmer in coveralls. Frost, for example, can ruin your year. One year an unexpected frost cost the company a million dollars. The growing season has to be staggered; you don't want all the peas, for example, maturing at the same time. The vegetable pack—as we called the canning process—occurs in specific growing and harvesting windows. In the case of corn, that was July through September.

The problem with the subpar cream-style corn was not the corn itself—but the cooking of the corn in that can. Two other sizes of canned corn were fine—the quality-control issue was with eleven million cans (450,000 cases) of, specifically, fourteen-ounce cream-style corn. Both the testers and consumer research identified that it was not quite up to Green Giant quality. I can't remember the exact problem. Was it the spin of the can? The design of the can? In any case, the issue was later resolved. The question now was what to with all this corn, this substandard corn.

At Pillsbury we believed that Green Giant seed was better than anyone else's, that we got the fresh corn from field to package quicker than the competition and that because of this our Green Giant corn retained more nutrients than the other guys' corn. That was what we prided ourselves on, but now we were, as it were, in a pickle.

At one senior management team meeting, we went over the consumer, retail trade and financial implications if we did not sell the product. On the one hand, this product represented a small percentage of all the corn we sold; on the other hand, the implications were significant. That particular product would be off grocery shelves for a year, the cost would be in the $5 million range, we would miss our corporate profit plan and staff might not receive their annual bonuses.

The young brand manager who presented all the pros and cons of the situation was Allan Oberman, the marketing star at Pillsbury whom we made director of preferred supplier when that position was first created. When he had finished his presentation and the senior staff had asked all their questions, I turned to Allan and said, "So, what should we do?" Without hesitating, Allan said, "We have no choice. Our core value states that quality is essential. We can't sell the product."

I knew that the credibility of Pillsbury's vision and values hung in the balance depending on what I decided. I quickly said, "Allan is correct. We can't sell it."

I can't recall exactly what was done with the corn. I know it was dumped (one hopes in an environmentally friendly fashion). And yes, the financial cost of the decision was steep. But we turned the problem into an opportunity. The vice-president of sales, Eric Hellstrom, and I went and told the story to the heads of all our major retail accounts. They understood and applauded our dedication to quality. When we got back into business a year later, they gave us back our shelf space, and our share of market actually went up.

\* \* \*

When I got to Pillsbury in 1985, I was pleased to find that it (like many companies at the time) had just launched its own vision and values statement. I had heard that a consultant had been paid almost a million dollars to create and launch the program. In the company's Canadian headquarters in Toronto, beautifully embossed vision and values plaques had been hung on the wall, and everyone had a very nice vision and values calculator. Good start.

The statement itself was very long (389 words), but the mission statement contained within it was brief: "Our vision is to be the best food company in the world." As previously mentioned, Pillsbury's core values were likewise brief and to the point: "People make the difference." "Quality is essential." And "Excellence must be a way of life." I liked these core values and figured I could work with them.

I asked my senior management team what had been done to reinforce these values since the plaques had gone up. Nothing. I immediately started using the values to drive changes in our approach to the business. We dramatically increased our focus on people (recognition, communications). We upped our effort to improve our already great product quality, and we strove for excellence in everything from customer service to new products. Also, the entire company now knew that vision and values amounted to much more than just plaques on walls, that Pillsbury had guiding principles. Allan Oberman, by the way, went on to become a successful president elsewhere and today heads up a large company in the United States, Teva US Generics. He still believes in, and still puts into practice, the theory of vision and values.

In 1989, Pillsbury was sold to Grand Metropolitan. I wasn't at the meeting in Minneapolis that reviewed the performance of all the international divisions of Pillsbury, but I heard that when it came to consider Pillsbury Canada, Grand Met asked, "What's going on up in Canada? Why are their results so much better than most of the rest of the corporation?" I understand that the

Pillsbury presenter said, "Oh, that's Richard Peddie. He has a cult going on up there."

Pillsbury Canada was the only part of Pillsbury that really championed and religiously practised those 389 words. Most of the other divisions stopped at the plaque and the calculator. At Pillsbury, I learned that if you were going to be successful with vision and values, there could be no time outs. You couldn't just follow the company values when they suited you financially and ignore them when they didn't. That vision, those values had to guide the way every one of your staff thought, talked and worked—every day and in every way. Are strong and ingrained vision and values a little cultish? Maybe, but if the mission is to be the best in what you do and the core values are solid, that seems perfectly fine to me.

\* \* \*

While I was writing this book, I asked Tom Knowlton, my fellow University of Windsor grad who worked with me at Colgate and who was later dean in the Faculty of Business at Ryerson University, for his take on vision and values.

"I think they are hugely important," he told me, "and I hold that opinion more strongly than just about anyone I know. I sit on boards, and I drive them *crazy* by focusing on vision and values. There were only a few organizations I have been involved with that embraced vision and values. One was Kellogg's and one was Wrigley. At Wrigley, I worked with both Bill Wrigley Sr. and Bill Wrigley Jr. We lived by those principles; they were built into our performance reviews. It was worth 25 per cent: how well did you in the past year live vision and values? At Kellogg's, I can remember the top-ten people meeting and going over the principles. Did they need to be tweaked? It was such an invigorating process."

When Tom taught at Ryerson, he talked a lot about vision and values to his students. But the point he stressed is that not only does a company need principles but also it must live them. It angered him that Enron had a written series of values but that they apparently meant nothing. One of Tom's prime examples of a company living by its principles and benefiting in the long run is Johnson & Johnson's recall of Tylenol in 1982. Seven people died after taking the pain medication and it was eventually discovered that someone had tampered with the capsules and inserted poison in some of them. Johnson & Johnson issued a nationwide recall, a move that cost the company $100 million and lost market share (from 35 per cent to 8 per cent). The company's response earned it kudos in the press, and within a year the analgesic had rebounded to become the most popular in the United States. And packaging was improved—a triple seal was designed to stop tampering, and a childproof top was created.

That's how to do it. And this is how not to do it: A few years before I made the decision to dump all that corn and when I was still with Hostess, I toured a StarKist plant in New Brunswick (it carried Hostess potato chips in its cafeteria), where I was less than impressed by the sanitary standards. The place smelled of fish, of course, but my sense was that it felt dirty and probably was. Then on September 17, 1985, the CBC's *The Fifth Estate* broke a story about then fisheries minister John Fraser overruling fish inspectors and allowing tainted tuna to be sold. A million cans of tuna were on the line.

Fraser allowed the sale, then reversed his decision. StarKist in Canada never recovered. In 1991, the company left Canada after its share of the market plummeted from 35 per cent to zero. Some 400 men and women lost their jobs.

* * *

I went through four years at the University of Windsor business school and never heard a word about vision and values. I worked at Colgate-Palmolive and General Foods for fifteen years and never heard about vision and values. Most fiscal years started off with some company theme that was intended to motivate the sales force, manufacturing plants and office people, but it turned out mostly to be a flavour of the month that was soon forgotten.

I became president of Hostess in 1983. I had had a lot of great experiences and had acquired solid functional skills, including finance, marketing, brand strategies and sales. Interestingly, I had not received much leadership training and now I was running a relatively autonomous company a hundred kilometres from head office. I had been reading books to help fill in the leadership and business void in my education.

In 1982, Thomas Peters and Robert H. Waterman Jr. wrote *In Search of Excellence*, then praised as "the greatest business book of all time." I don't know whether that is true because I have since read terrific business books by Noel Tichy, Jim Collins, Jack Welch, Richard Davis and many others, but I do know that this book had the greatest impact on my business beliefs, approach and style.

Peters and Waterman were consultants working for McKinsey—a global management consulting firm—who had studied forty-three American companies to see what distinguished the successful ones from the not-so-successful ones. Today, more than thirty years later, many of those companies identified as successful are still thriving (Four Seasons Hotels and Resorts, Procter & Gamble, IBM, Frito-Lay, the Boeing Company). Peters and Waterman came up with eight basic principles.

Ones such as "a bias for action," "close to the customer" and "productivity through people" resonated with me, and I used them successfully as I led Pillsbury, SkyDome and Maple Leaf Sports and Entertainment over the next three decades. But the one chapter in the book that really got me thinking was the one entitled "Hands on, Value Driven." The authors discovered that successful companies all had something in common: "Every excellent company we studied," they wrote, "is clear on what it stands for and takes the process of value shaping seriously" and "virtually all of the better performing companies we looked at in the first study had a well-defined set of guiding beliefs."

Peters and Waterman went on to outline the beliefs commonly held by most of the successful companies: the importance of being the best, a belief in the importance of people, a belief in superior quality and service, and so on. As a direct result of *In Search of Excellence*, mission statements and corporate values became the number one management tool in North America for almost a decade and still rank in the top ten today. A great majority of Fortune 100 companies still have a mission statement. But having a mission statement and stated core values does not mean they are being followed. Enron had such a statement, and "integrity" was one of its core values. We all know where that got it.

I read the book and was keen to try some of these ideas at Hostess, but at the time I was interviewing to be the president and CEO of Pillsbury. The company was smaller but it had great-quality brands, and I would have autonomy—running my own show in Canada. I took a vacation in southern France, where I sat on the beach and read the book, underlining the interesting points and making notes (this was quite difficult because it was a topless beach, but I soldiered on). I realized that all of my thinking and creativity were focused on what I would do if I joined Pillsbury, not what I would do if I stayed at Hostess. The book and its theories did not cause me to make the decision to go to Pillsbury, but it sure helped.

After four years there, I decided to follow my dream into sports and entertainment by taking on the president and CEO role at SkyDome. I chose a small team of people from across the company and with different levels of authority. I gave them a little presentation on the theory and benefits of vision and values and set them loose to do the preliminary thinking on what the vision and core values should be. They later came back to senior management (who were as green on vision and values as they were) and we modified their recommendations.

McDonald's was the concessionaire at SkyDome, and I admired its core guiding principles: quality, service, cleanliness and value. As I said earlier, we at SkyDome came up with a 160-word statement with a vision of being "the world's greatest entertainment centre" and three core values: quality, service, people. We built it into everything we did—from an in-house training program called SkyDome U to the shows we hosted to the fan service we provided.

Creating SkyDome's vision and values was one of the first things that we focused on and launched. The SkyDome director, who had problems with me focusing so much on vision and values, didn't understand their power. That individual clearly thought that vision and values was a soft concept. I proved to myself with the Green Giant corn issue that it was quite the contrary. I knew that if core values are adhered to religiously, there is no room for the company or the staff to behave in a way that is inconsistent with them. And I knew that this would eventually pay dividends.

As I mentioned, SkyDome went on to have a number of great years after its management articulated our vision to make it the world's greatest entertainment centre. SkyDome, remember, was recognized as the North American Stadium of the Year four years running, we regularly hosted five million guests a year and our operating profits were solid. I was also pleased to see that employee attitude surveys indicated that 100 per cent of our full-time staff understood SkyDome's vision and values and believed in them.

When I joined NetStar, I chose not to champion vision and values. In my assessment, the five presidents who reported to me would not embrace the theory, nor could one vision and values statement possibly apply to the entire company—TSN, RDS (Réseau des sports), Discovery Channel, Dome Productions and LCI Sales. Also, I was not the most senior leader in the company. Gordon Craig was an excellent CEO, but I knew he would not champion company vision and values in the way they would need to be if they were to be successful. So I decided to bide my time and introduce them if and when I became CEO. But then the Raptors came knocking on my door.

When I took over the Raptors, we immediately started working on a vision and values statement for the basketball team and their new arena, the Air Canada Centre. That was interrupted when the Leafs bought the Raptors. But then I did the same thing I had done at SkyDome. I formed a diverse team to do the preliminary thinking on what the vision and core values should be for Maple Leaf Sports and Entertainment. Many of the people who were on that committee are still with the company fourteen years later.

One was Randy Licastro, a unionized carpenter (really, a jack-of-all-trades and a stellar employee). Not only did he contribute to the creation of our vision and values statement but he was, at my urging, one of its presenters when we showed it to all the staff. He'd never done anything like that before and it terrified him. For the next fourteen years I kidded him about making him present again. I never did, of course, but at the company party celebrating my retirement, Randy joined other MLSE staff on stage to give me a retirement tribute book and video.

When Randy and other employees presented to the senior management team, everyone waded in—from Ken Dryden to Glen Grunwald. We came up with three values: "Excite every fan," "Inspire our people" and "Leaders in our community," with a fourth, "Dedicated to our teams," coming later. Three words appeared printed below the statement: "passion, pride, performance." Finally, we agreed on a vision to "create champions." After a few years of limited playoff success, the board was questioning whether MLSE was focused enough on winning. Management thought we were, but if there were any question, then we would have to strengthen our vision and values statement.

We changed our vision simply to "WIN." We believed that "WIN" was much clearer and spoke not only to winning on the ice, the court and the football pitch but also to winning on the business side—with strong financials, new successful businesses, excellent service metrics and so on. "WIN" also applied to individual company business teams or individuals earning recognition inside and outside the company.

Brevity is one of the strengths of the statement, which comprises a mere eighteen words. Over the years, various vice-presidents wanted to add more words to the existing eighteen but I vetoed them every time. When it comes to vision and values, I strongly believe that less is more. The NBA mission statement, for instance, takes 220 words to make some excellent points about the fans, the teams and the players. But I don't think many in the NBA offices ever think about it, nor are the thirty NBA franchises much aware that it exists.

The Ontario Teachers' Pension Plan is one of the largest and most successful pension plans in the world. When he was its CEO, Claude Lamoureux and his team created the plan's vision and values. It's called "Teachers' Way" and it speaks to the mission of "outstanding service and retirement security for our members—today and tomorrow."

Nordstrom is an American fashion retailer. The company was started by John Nordstrom, a Swedish émigré who had come to the United States with $5 in his pocket and not a word of English. He ended up opening a shoe store in Seattle, with a business philosophy rooted in some time-honoured values: exceptional service, selection, quality and value. A third generation of Nordstroms today runs what has become a multi-million-dollar company. In the Nordstrom employee handbook is a simple five-by-eight-inch grey card.

It welcomes the new employee, cites Nordstrom's number one goal of providing outstanding customer service and expresses confidence that the new hire will set high personal and professional goals—and achieve them. The card then sets out "the Nordstrom rules," though really there was only one rule:

"Rule #1. Use best judgment in all situations. There will be no additional rules. Please feel free to ask your department manager, store manager or division manager any questions at any time."

Again, when it comes to vision and values statements, less is more. By adding words, you just ensure that people won't bother with the statement or will forget what's in it. When MLSE talks about inspiring our people, this means that we as a corporation need to develop people strategies to ensure that we communicate, develop and motivate our people. And the bosses have a responsibility, if they want to be great leaders, to work with those reporting directly to them to accomplish the same things. We could have used thirty words or so to better explain what we meant by "Inspire our people," but would it have been any more effective? I think not.

Enron, that famously failed and fraudulent energy company, had listed "integrity" as one of its four values (along with communication, respect and excellence). Its ethics code was sixty-four pages long. One of its executives, Kenneth Lay, had written this in his preface to the code: "Enron's reputation finally depends on its people, on you and me. Let's keep that reputation high."

Exxon is an oil company still synonymous with the disastrous oil spill off the coast of Alaska in 1989. Exxon's vision statement was "to provide our shareholders with a superior return on investment." First of all, I don't for a second believe that references to return on investment or share prices or profits belong in a vision and values statement. Yes, these things are important, but a strong statement of core principles will usually deliver on those financial metrics. Would the company have handled the *Exxon Valdez* oil spill differently if it had been focusing on things such as protecting the environment and ship safety instead of return on investment? I cannot say for certain, but I do know that the company was severely criticized for its tardy response to the crisis and for its failure to admit responsibility. Almost a week went by before Exxon's CEO said anything to the media, and almost three weeks passed before he arrived at the site. Guided by vision and values in such a crisis, you own up and you put your best people and resources on the job immediately. Exxon didn't do that, and its reputation remains tarnished to this day.

Over the course of my career, I was called on to give many speeches. In the early days, the topic was usually marketing or customer service. Later on, I often spoke about leadership. But in the past ten years, no matter the audience or topic, I usually came back to vision and values. I constantly talked about the importance of them because I strongly believe that they are key to the success of one's company and key to one's career.

I tell people who are starting out in their careers or changing jobs to make sure they understand the vision and values of the companies they are looking at. Go to the company's website, do your due diligence, see what's being said about the company and talk to their employees to find out what it's like to work there.

Do you truly want to work for a company that has no clear vision? Do you want to work for a company that doesn't articulate its values? Or even worse, for one with bad values? All companies have values. And only if the company leadership takes the time to think carefully about what they should be and then builds them into everything they do will these values be successful. If the company leadership doesn't take the time to do this, bad values could emerge—an abusive leadership approach, unsafe plants, poor environmental policies.

In 2002, I taught a course called Strategic Leadership at the Odette School of Business at the University of Windsor. A fourth-year optional course for twenty-four students, it ran from September to early December. The first two lectures and the first test I gave were on vision and values. My goal in the course was to put everything the students had learned in business school into context. I wanted to show them that *everything*—leadership, corporate strategies, brand strategy, customer service, financials, legal help and human resources—flowed from vision and values. In researching for the course, I read the opinions of academics and authors who believed that corporate strategies come first in the continuum and that vision and values should flow out of them. I disagree. Strategies need to change with the economy, the competition and shifting technologies. Vision and values dictate corporate culture and have to be rock-solid.

The corporate vision should encapsulate the company's enduring purpose. *What* is the company supposed to be striving for? It has to been seen as something possible and reinforcing—but a stretch at the same time.

The corporate values are *how* the company will deliver on that vision. These are the principles or standards that should guide corporate and individual behaviour and decision making. They are also what ultimately create an organization's culture. Again, they should be rock-solid and not change easily. The strategies and tactics that flow out of them may change—but the values shouldn't. They are, in the company's eyes, the rules of the game.

I became a disciple of the theory of vision and values because I have seen it work. Research shows that a compelling vision helps attract and retain employees. Research by global management consulting firm Hay Group indicates that 74 per cent of employees will stick with an employer because of management's ability to point to clear and compelling vision and values.

Core principles can also make a company more resilient during the inevitable bad times. When I was running MLSE, we suffered through three work stoppages: one entire year in the NHL and two partial years in the NBA. The "Inspire our people" value guided us through these periods. I remember going to the board in the fourth month of the NHL work stoppage and talking about what we should do with our people in terms of layoffs, salary cuts, and so on. The board knew that we had a strong group of motivated sports and entertainment people. I made the case that we needed to retain them so they'd be there when hockey returned. Treating them well, I said, would inspire them to stay and perform strongly during and after the lockout. The board quickly grasped the point and agreed that there would be no layoffs or salary reductions during the lockout.

Is there a right set of vision and values? I don't think so. Some companies need to focus more on customers, some on innovation, some on employees and some on the products or services they sell. Two companies can have radically different values but both can be excellent, visionary companies. I have gravitated to customers, employees, quality and community when choosing corporate values, but I think that the actual value is not as important (assuming it is a good value) as how deeply the company believes and consistently lives its values.

* * *

As I mentioned, when I was there, Maple Leaf Sports and Entertainment was driven by four values, ones that we embraced and, in real terms, practised. (The wording of these values changed somewhat after I left.)

*Excite every fan.* This naturally started with trying to create winning teams. But it also involved ensuring that the food and beverages we served were second to none, that our in game entertainment was some of the best in the NBA and NHL, that our service to our fans was top-notch, that the quality of our TV broadcasts and digital platforms was professional, creative and up-to-date and that our digital video boards for watching replays represented the technology of the day.

*Inspire our people.* This drove our communications, people development, and recognition and compensation strategies.

*Leaders in our community.* The MLSE Team Up Foundation raises more than $2 million each year to invest back into our communities, refurbishing rinks, courts and pitches, enabling the clinics we put on for youth. The examples our players set, the facilities we build with MLSE's own money and the events we attract: all have a positive economic impact on our city and surrounding area.

*Dedicated to our teams.* This drove us to do everything to help make our teams more successful, from replacing the artificial turf at BMO Field with natural grass, to creating world-class training facilities such as the TFC Academy and the MasterCard Centre, to investing a couple of million dollars to dramatically improve ice quality for the Leafs, to the quality and nutritional meals our executive chefs served the players at every practice and before and after games.

The key to a successful vision and values is that it drives everything in the company, from objectives to strategies to board and management decisions. And it's critical that vision and values be consistently and frequently communicated to everyone in the company. If a company gets into vision and values, it has to get in all the way. There is a Japanese proverb: "Vision without action is a daydream. Action without vision is a nightmare."

* * *

In my time at MLSE, the company grew from an enterprise value of around $300 million to $2 billion. What started with the Leafs and Raptors working at cross-purposes became four teams working synergistically together. It went from one old arena to two new arenas plus BMO Field and Maple Leaf Square. And it went from selling off broadcast rights to creating three specialty television networks. Vision and values had a lot to do with that but so did the strategic and disciplined approach we took to creating and running the business. And that too flowed from vision and values.

MLSE does a thorough annual fiscal plan every June that maps out the strategies and tactics for the coming fiscal year. The company has done this since 1998. The whole approach to the business was gathered in a white binder that held a 200-page document, and every year the contents of that binder changed. We never stayed still.

At MLSE, everything was and is connected in a way that was planned and well thought out: the uniforms, the branding, the marketing, the food and beverage division. From top to bottom, the approach to service and, indeed, to every single aspect of the enterprise had to be all of a piece. If your broadcast division was performing brilliantly but your restaurant wait staff were rude, the company could not succeed. What irks me more than anything is bad service, so every oar had to be in the water.

When I first came to the CEO job at Maple Leaf Sports and Entertainment, a new industry model was emerging. What I was bringing to the table was a more sophisticated and strategic approach to marketing and service, one that blended sports and entertainment with high-end food and beverage. I knew that a vision and values strategy could pay huge dividends. All that I had learned in my consumer product days—about customer service, about surrounding yourself with great people, about branding, about market research—was eminently transferable to this new arena.

Every November, MLSE also did a five-year strategic plan. For many years, that plan had the same three objectives:

1. WIN on and off the playing field.
2. Grow MLSE's enterprise value.
3. Be an exceptional place to work.

Once we finished the November plan, we immediately started thinking about what would be in the next one. We viewed each plan as another chance to recommend and launch new and exciting investment ideas. Larry Tanenbaum challenging me personally to be a better CEO deeply motivated me to come up with new ideas to grow the company. Strategic planning can be a "mug's game," with fictitious projects and poorly thought-out financial projections. That wasn't our experience at all. Creating great strategic plans is tough.

The late Peter Drucker, probably the father of modern management and the pre-eminent business philosopher, once described the challenge of strategic plans this way: "Trying to predict the future is like trying to drive down a country road at night with no lights while looking in the rear window." Our strategic plans got the board thinking. The plans sensitized it to what we were thinking, and when we finally, in sales parlance, "asked for the order"—that is, decided to actually proceed with what had been to this point little more than an idea or a trial balloon introduced several years beforehand—it was in agreement and supportive. In my time running MLSE, our owners never took any money out of the company and instead let senior management invest it back into growing the company.

In his book *The Management Mythbuster*, author David Axson argues that "strategic plans are of little use in times of great volatility and uncertainty." But that wasn't our experience at all. Likewise, in his book *The Rise and Fall of Strategic Planning*, Henry Mintzberg contends that "only ten per cent of most companies' actions arise out of their strategic planning." Again, not our experience at MLSE.

On the other hand, a number of items cropped up on these strategic plans and then, after analysis and discussion, they were not pursued. What follows are a few of them and an explanation of why they were dropped.

One idea was to bring an NFL franchise to Toronto. During the recession of 2008, we hired a third party to do a thorough analysis. Assuming a franchise value of slightly less than $1 billion and construction costs of a new stadium of around $600 million, we could not get the financial model to work at all. We then decided to do a financial calculation that would deliver a rate of return of 15 per cent or better and work backwards from there. In other words, what had to happen beforehand to enable that kind of profit? The franchise cost would have to be about $600 million and, instead of a new stadium, the Rogers Centre would have to be redesigned at a cost of $100 million. We thought those two things because an ownership change of the Bills looked inevitable and the recession might push franchise values down. I once thought that Toronto would definitely get an NFL team, but then the NFL did a huge broadcast deal, franchise values climbed back into the $1 billion-plus range and the cost to build a new NFL stadium started exceeding $1 billion. Now I don't see there ever being a chance.

Here's another pipe dream we had for a while. MLSE was interested in buying Sportsnet from Rogers or doing a joint venture with Rogers on the network, but to do that we figured that Sportsnet would want the Blue Jays folded into the deal. So we took a long look at whether we could make the Blue Jays profitable. We thought that we were better than the Jays at selling tickets, sponsorships and suites. But even with more aggressive revenue assumptions, we could not get the numbers to work. We were also concerned that they would always have a much more difficult time making the playoffs without spending millions more on players—which is precisely what they did late in 2012. This was a great move by Rogers, but unless these player moves consistently result in a playoff team and team revenues increase significantly, the team will lose a lot of money and it will be tough for Rogers to justify that spending every year to its shareholders.

Also, SkyDome not being baseball-friendly worried us. The Dome was the last of the multi-use facilities: it's too big for baseball (new baseball stadiums are much smaller) and the playing surface is too hard (natural grass needs light, yet the roof has to be closed most of the time to protect the Dome's electrical parts). Finally, the much older fan base concerned us. So we showed the board our analysis and recommended that we not approach Rogers.

How about a British football club? After our stunning early business success with TFC, we explored purchasing a team in England. Our CFO, Ian Clarke, and I went there and visited a number of Champions League franchises. Unlike North American leagues, there are no such things as salary caps, and most teams over there spend their brains out on players and lose money. This gave us pause. And all the synergistic marketing vehicles that helped MLSE successfully launch TFC would not be available to us in England. The UK press found out that I was there, and soon stories had me personally buying teams such as the Tottenham Hotspur. My wife's mother and father were both born in Ireland, and now the McAnoy clan over there began calling us to see if the rumours were true. I admit, I did go to a Tottenham Hotspur game, but the only employee of theirs I talked to was the young woman who served me lunch. For years after that, whenever a football team was up for sale, Ian or I got a call to see if we were interested. We weren't.

If not British football how about a club in the Canadian

Football League? Twice we looked seriously at buying the Toronto Argonauts. But during my time with MLSE, we had an on-and-off relationship with the Argos. It seemed we were always on the opposite side of every issue, but despite that, Argo owner Howard Sokolowski somehow stayed friendly. Maybe it was because we really did try: as I mentioned earlier, we tried to join the Argos in building a combined stadium at the site of old Varsity Stadium, but we couldn't get that deal to work with the University of Toronto. Then the Argos wanted us to come with them to York University, but our research clearly said that idea would not work for TFC, so we passed. Howard wanted to come into the BMO Field deal at the last minute, but we said no for several reasons, the key one being the pressing deadline of the World Under-20 Men's Football Championship.

Finally, when Howard Sokolowski and David Cynamon were looking to sell their ownership of the team, MLSE considered buying. The price was very affordable, but I still recommended against it for several reasons: to make $1 million a year on the Argos, MLSE would have to spend a lot of time to make the Argos a profitable club. We compared all the work and risk we would have to take on against simply putting on four to six concerts to make the same dollars. I described it as "a long run for a short slide." Also, one of our key corporate objectives was to grow enterprise value. MLSE by this point was already worth well over $1.5 billion. Owning the Argos—with a franchise value of about $10 million—would not have moved our enterprise value dial at all. Finally, I was worried that if MLSE couldn't make the Argos work financially, we'd be stuck with them. Who else was going to buy them when they constantly lost money? And MLSE could never simply shut down one of the most storied franchises in North America.

I presented all those points to the board and concluded that we should say no. Larry Tanenbaum still had a soft spot for the

Argos, and I knew that Howard would phone him directly to try to change his mind. "So Larry," I said, "when Howard phones you next week, what are you going to say to him?" Larry's face grew red and he quietly said, "I will tell him we are not interested." Howard did phone, and Larry did stick to the script.

I must also admit that I loved having four team logos on my business card and on the sign that hangs over the entrance of the Air Canada Centre's underground parking lot. But as much as my ego wanted more teams and a larger company, senior management always tried to make objective and strategic recommendations to the board.

So, one can see from all this that our strategic planning process was good for what we decided to do—and not to do. A blend of both outcomes should be the norm if your strategic planning process is thorough, disciplined and objective.

Our batting average on things such as football, television, condos, music and restaurants was well over 70 per cent. Our plans were real and they worked. How did our vision and values fit with our strategic course? We believed that our values were rock-solid, for now and into the future—and we knew that change was a constant. Our values were lived by our employees and helped sustain their effort. Our strategies were for each year and got our people going on specifics. Our annual and strategic planning process was company-wide and involved many mid-level managers and directors, as well as all the vice-presidents.

In his book *The Leadership Engine*, Noel Tichy observes that winning leaders are always doing two things: looking to the future and developing the leadership abilities of others in the firm. Winning leadership, he says, "is about building an organization that responds to customers' demands today, and is able to do so again tomorrow and the next day . . . For the short term, they [winning leaders] watch the horizon to spot impending changes in the market place so they can develop ideas and structures that will allow the organization to respond efficiently and effectively[;] ... for the longer term, it means that they prepare their organizations to continue to thrive beyond the foreseeable future."

I clearly believe in vision and values. I know a lot of people who think they are just fluff. David Axson, for one, dismisses them as "a long awkward sentence that demonstrates management's inability to think clearly." On the other hand, he goes on to say, "But if you want one[,] keep it simple. If a fifth grader gets it, you are probably okay."

At MLSE, the vision and values statement came down to eighteen words. Pretty simple.

ket place so there can develop ideas and structures that will allow the organization to respond smoothly and effectively [...] for the longer term, it means that they prepare their organizations to [...] time to thrive beyond the foreseeable future."

I clearly believe in a vision and values. I know a lot of people who think they are just fluff. David Axson, for one, dismisses them as "... long, awkward sentence that demonstrates management's inability to think clearly. On the other hand, he goes on to say, "But if you want clear, I keep it simple. If a fifth grader resists, you are probably ok."

At MLSE, the vision and values statement came down to eighteen words. Pretty simple.

# CHAPTER 11

# LEADERSHIP 101

I n 2002, I taught a course on leadership at the University of Windsor for an entire semester, as I mentioned. In the fall of 2012, I launched a series of ninety-minute interactive lectures on that same subject. Each lecture is targeted specifically at the class year. RP (my initials, in case you're wondering) 101 is aimed at first-year students, RP 201 at second-year students and so on. Each lecture builds upon the one before it so that, by the time Odette students graduate four years later, they have been exposed to an increasing level of sophisticated leadership strategy and execution.

Students sometimes ask me, Where did your soaring ambition, your desire to lead, come from?

My brother, Tom, and I were teenagers watching the Boston Marathon one year. We agreed then and there: the first one to run a marathon got $200 from the other—who then had the option of nullifying the debt if he could match the feat a year later. In May 1978, when I was thirty-one years old, I ran one. (That fall, Tom ran the Detroit Marathon with me and nullified the bet.) As I went through my career, I often talked about leading a sports franchise. I could *see* it, just as I could see myself crossing the finish line at the Boston Marathon. I always had a vision to succeed.

Both Tom and I are quietly competitive—with ourselves. Of the two of us, I have the more Type A personality. Tom remembers me setting the record at high school for pull-ups on a raised bar, and he remembers when I worked part-time at Air Canada while going to university and wanting to set a record for sales.

My thinking was this: what gets measured gets done. Take the marathon running, for example. In 1978, I started running seriously (in low-cut Converse basketball shoes—serious running shoes only came along later). I knew that the qualifying time then for the Boston Marathon was under three hours. That spring, I ran a marathon in 3:46. The next one in Detroit, I ran in 3:22. Then I got down to 3:02. Finally, in Toronto in 1980, I ran it in 2:58. Then the qualifying time for Boston was changed to 2:50. I once ran for 444 consecutive days (that kind of regimen would be frowned on by modern fitness gurus, but that shows how committed I was). I was running up to 150 kilometres a week. Finally, in 1983, I ran the Detroit Marathon in 2:46:03 and earned the right to run in Boston. In 1984, I ran the Boston Marathon in 2:46:18.

That's how I was. There was a number, a goal, and I set out to attain it. And the numbers offered the ultimate feedback. I accomplished two things with the Boston Marathon: I realized a dream, and I got rid of an ulcer. Running cleans the blood vessels and clears the mind, and it extended my life. A lot of stories were written about my running, and I became known as "the marathon president." Running put pressure on me and was very much a part of me. And that carried over into the business world.

As for Tom, he ran an Ironman competition at Mont-Tremblant in Quebec in the summer of 2012—at the age of sixty-four. That race comprised a 3.8-kilometre swim, a 180-kilometre bike ride and a 42-kilometre run. His time was nothing special; in fact, race marshals were not long from closing up shop when he finally drifted in. But it's an astonishing feat nonetheless. "I had to learn to run slower," he told me. "And to break the race into chunks."

The Peddies go long and hard. And we're not afraid of work. The difference between good work and excellent work is hard work. Larry Bird, the legendary player with the Boston Celtics, put it this way: "I don't know if I practised more than anybody, but I sure practised enough. I still wonder if somebody—somewhere—was practising more than me."

As for the lofty ambition, I think some credit should go to my father. Dad instilled in all of his children the confidence that we could do anything we put our minds to. "It's not how many times you fall," he would say, "but how many times you get back up."

I also credit some of my professors and fellow students at the University of Windsor. Several of my classmates in the 1960s were older students working for banks, which had offered them scholarships to go back to school. A few of these young men were already parents. They raised the bar.

I remember a classmate saying, "I want to make vice-president by the age of thirty-five."

But in my seminars and lectures, no one was talking about leadership, and in my days at Colgate and General Foods, no one was mentoring me on leadership. I had to learn that on my own. In this chapter, I lay out what I learned.

When I retired from Maple Leaf Sports and Entertainment, I enjoyed my farewell tour—one that was marked, more than anything else, by one theme: leadership. I told my colleagues that if they were planning some sort of parting gift for me, they might consider doing something for the University of Windsor. With my CFO, Ian Clarke, acting as quarterback for the project,

MLSE owners and my colleagues and friends raised a staggering $750,000 for the Richard Peddie Leadership Initiative. The initiative involves three elements: the Centre for Leadership Competency Measurement, the Leader-in-Residence Program, and the Richard Peddie Invitational Speaker Series. I was overwhelmed by the size of that gift and deeply honoured to have such an initiative bear my name. I loved that it recognized my lifelong passion both to create future leaders and to be the best leader I could be. My aim now is to use the initiative to help make the school renowned for creating twenty-first-century leaders. I am also continuing to spend time at the university as a leader-in-residence, passing on the lessons I have learned and have outlined in this book.

* * *

The ability of a CEO to remember employees' names and circumstances matters a great deal. Remembering a name is sometimes the highest honour a leader can pay. Everyone thinks I have a better memory for names than I do. When MLSE was smaller and I had just hired someone, I'd sit down and reread that person's resumé and psychological profile. Even when the company climbed to 700 people, before a meeting I would often check to see who was attending, consult the company's intranet site and look at names and photos. I took the time to do this because in the end it made the staff feel important and recognized.

* * *

Leadership can't help but be entwined with vision and values. For a company to adhere consistently to its values and to realize its vision, it requires strong leadership.

Leadership is not just about being a president or vice-president. Leadership for most actually starts early in life. For me, it was being named captain of the school safety patrol (following in the footsteps of my sister, Carol, who was the first girl captain six years earlier). I was thirteen years old.

During high school, my brother, Tom, was either captain or a natural leader for the high school golf, basketball and football teams. I was mostly a follower. And I have no recollection of formal leadership training while attending the University of Windsor. However, we did have an active and accomplished business school class that stayed close for all four years. Many of my classmates were very good leaders, and I picked up some invaluable skills from them. A decade after graduation, our class started to be referred to as the "famous class of '70." It's true that classmates such as Mike Mueller, Bob Humphrey, Terry Connoy, Neil Donnelly, John Craven and Pat Palmer went on to do very well in their corporate careers, but largely our class's career accomplishments are on a par with that of many other Odette graduating classes.

I am convinced that we got our "successful" reputation because we were very active and simply marketed ourselves well. I did, though, learn a lot about leadership after being elected to executive positions in the Commerce Club, student council and university senate. My next decade or more at Colgate and General Foods was also largely devoid of formal leadership training. Most learning was simply done on the job, making mistakes, copying others. There was no one who really inspired me to be a great leader—or as Ralph Waldo Emerson said, "Our chief want is someone who will inspire us to be what we know we could be."

Years later when I taught at Odette and the annual Elite class at MLSE, I always asked the class, what makes a great leader? Every time, course participants called out things such as "recognizes great work . . . communicates . . . excellent mentor . . . honest . . .

authentic"—all of which I would write in a column on a white-board. Then I would ask, what makes a bad leader? And every time the answers were the complete opposite of what I had just noted as attributes of great leaders: "No recognition . . . lousy communicator . . . no coaching or mentoring at all . . . not trustworthy and not genuine . . ."

Then I would say to the class, "Fantastic. You all know exactly what it takes to be a great leader. You can pass the course right now if you promise to follow only the 'good' column." But, of course, nobody ever left the class because great leadership is difficult.

Dee Hock, the founder of Visa, created something called "The 60-Second PhD in Leadership." Essentially, she advised making two lists, one describing all the things you abhorred in a certain former boss, and the other describing all the winning traits of a different boss—one you absolutely adored. The trick is to *always* emulate the great boss and *never* to act like the terrible boss.

But even great leaders have trouble with consistency. Today, leaders at all levels are being challenged. Business has never been tougher. There are more rules and procedures to follow than ever before and therefore increased accountability. Your actions are more visible, and the bad ones are often played out (negatively) in the media. And the company's shareholders have greater and greater expectations. Leadership is very stressful in the twenty-first century, and it is easy either to not take the time or to forget what it takes to be a great leader. When I worked in the consumer products industry, the CEOs of General Foods, Nestlé and Procter & Gamble typically kept their jobs for ten or more years. Not today. By 2010, the average tenure of a CEO was less than four years. About 70 per cent are victims of mergers and acquisitions, having resigned or been fired.

That I lasted almost fifteen years at MLSE and never got fired once in my career frankly amazes me to this day. Early in my career

I started thinking about becoming one of the better leaders in industry. Since I was not really getting help from the people to whom I reported, I turned to books. Authors such as Tom Peters, Noel Tichy, Jim Collins, John Maxwell and Peter Drucker were my mentors. I absorbed their ideas and tried many of their suggestions, adopting some and discarding others. And I decided that I wanted to be, and needed to be, a student of leadership if I was going to be successful in my career.

Noel Tichy, for example, strongly resonated with me. His take on leadership and what he called the five pillars (values, edge, energy, ideas and teachable points of view) stuck with me, and I found myself interviewing candidates for jobs with that list in my head.

Dana Sinclair, the psychologist used by the Leafs and the Raptors, measures leadership across six variables: cautious to assertive, introverted to extroverted, fast-paced to methodical; independent to detailed; undisciplined to disciplined; and stamina and energy low to stamina and energy high. This is how she described me:

*You tend to be an expeditor with progressive, impatient orientation toward producing results. You are stimulated by changing environments, becoming bored with routines. You tend to keep pressure on subordinates, giving them deadlines to meet and decisive direction. You also tend to respond to pressure situations, reacting rapidly to challenge and competition (in this sense you are restless and hard driving). You are proactive, willing to take risks and use initiative even in unfavourable circumstances. In doing so, you are likely to show irritation if things are not moving at a fast enough pace. You show a desire to make changes for improvement, emphasizing personal initiative and attention to detail while expediting projects to obtain desired results without delay. You are generally*

*able to influence others toward your selected course of action*
*through good communication skills and self-confidence. You*
*create a pressure-type environment and will take action to*
*remove obstacles. You will be demanding and expect a great*
*deal of yourself and from others. You will push subordinates to*
*be responsible and accountable within their abilities.*

I think Dana has me pegged pretty accurately.

She believes that my capacity for leadership was there from the beginning. And that raises the question, are leaders born or can they learn to lead? Tom Knowlton, himself a former business leader and one who taught business students about leadership, has thought a lot about nature versus nurture when it comes to business leaders.

"I lean to nature," he told me. "There are so many leadership styles, but the ability to motivate people to follow you, to set the vision, to hire and surround yourself with the best people and then get out of the way . . . It's hard to teach that." I lean a little more toward nurture than I do nature, though I believe both play a role.

Tom well remembers speaking a number of years ago to seven members of my executive team at Maple Leaf Sports and Entertainment. He talked about the different levels of leadership as defined by author John Maxwell in his book *The Five Levels of Leadership*. The first, the lowest level, was about *position* ("people follow you because they have to"). Next was *permission* ("people follow you because they want to"). Then came *production* ("people follow you because of what you have done for the organization"). The penultimate step was *people development* ("people follow you because of what you have done for them"). Finally, there was *pinnacle* ("people follow you because of who you are and what you represent").

Tom praised me in front of my peers for what I had accomplished, my communication skills and the range of my experience.

But I told him and the class that I didn't think I had attained the fifth level, the pinnacle level—that my ego got in the way. Tom countered that making such an admission, being that honest and that candid, is itself a strength.

Tom and I had something in common. We devour books. At MLSE I became known as someone who read books—business books certainly, but not just business books. At MLSE we had an intranet site where I posted the titles of books I had read and was recommending. Being a great leader is a process, and one way to grow as a leader is to read books and newspapers and magazines.

* * *

I probably decided on my leadership formula when I became president of Pillsbury. Over the next twenty plus years I constantly updated and modified it, but I think the base was established then. Of course, it started with having a vision. I like what Father Theodore Hesburgh, the former president of Notre Dame University, said about the importance of a vision: "The very essence of leadership is to have a vision. It's got to be a vision the leader articulates clearly and forcefully on every occasion. You can't blow an uncertain trumpet." Tom Peters likewise had hooked me on the importance of values. As I outlined in the previous chapter, all my leadership strategies flowed from vision and values.

As president of Pillsbury and SkyDome, I made sure that a lot of my leadership beliefs were translated into aggressive people strategies. But it was at MLSE that my beliefs really came together. When I hired Mardi Walker as vice-president, people, I told her that I had good news and bad news. The good news: I was a president who was mightily interested in human resources. The bad news: as such, I was going to be involved and interested in what strategies she came up with.

I always knew that MLSE could not be as good a brand company as, say, Procter & Gamble or as superb in service as, say, Four Seasons Hotels. But I definitely believed we could be as good as anyone in the people area. One of our core values was "Inspire our people," and the third objective in our annual strategic plan was to be an "exceptional place to work"—so we had the clear formal motivation we needed. The strategic people equation we came up with was this:

Attract + develop + motivate + unleash + retain = an exceptional place to work.

We decided on an umbrella concept called "play to win," which successfully executed the following strategies.

## ATTRACT THE BEST

Attracting people was not difficult. MLSE would get 15,000 to 20,000 job applications every year. Selecting the best was the challenge. Many people had great functional skills but would not "fit" with a high-energy, high-service company that required staff to work long, tiring days. So we tried our best to hire for attitude and then train for skills.

My advice to anyone looking for a job with a certain company is to read all you can about that company before the interview. I interviewed someone at MLSE who was looking for a senior job in our people department. Mardi believed that he was the person for the job, so my talking to him was supposed to be a mere formality—or so we both thought. His credentials were solid and I was impressed. At one point, I asked him what he thought about MLSE's vision and values statement. He didn't know what they were. Silence. His face went blank, then red. We expected all applicants to know our vision and values—especially someone who was expected to train our staff.

"I just lost the job, didn't I?" he said.

"Yes, you did," I replied.

I asked at the end of every interview, "Do you have any questions?" And that candidate had better have a long list of rich questions. The hiring process took a long time, and it typically involved a number of sessions, a dinner, a close examination of references, psychological testing and a presentation by the candidate. On average, it took us sixty-two days to hire someone. Our mantra: Hire slowly, fire quickly.

When people came in for an interview at MLSE, we expected them to know all about us. As one of the most public companies in Canada (with eleven websites), that should not be a problem for anyone. We recognized that hiring the right people was one part art and one part science. Sometimes we hired from our volunteer interns because we believed that interns gave us a chance to test-drive them and for them to test-drive us. Most times, the interested candidates came via our mlse.com website. We would vet hundreds of resumés for each job.

I'm wary of false claims on resumés. So many times I found myself staring at resumés with the same claim: "I launched Irish Spring Soap." Too many jobs over, say, a fifteen-year span is a red flag. Where's the evidence that this candidate is growing? Was he or she getting promoted? Has this individual worked the resumé to mask gaps? My advice to an ambitious twenty-something is to change jobs. But don't do it until you have been promoted at your current company at least once. And whether you stay with your company or leave, don't ever stand still with your leadership learning and growth.

After a culling of resumés, we phone-interviewed a select few candidates, calling in three or four for formal interviews. As we zeroed in on the final two, we conducted Personal Profile Analysis or Caliper testing on each candidate. We did extensive background checks. Each candidate went through multiple interviews. And then the final two had to prepare and deliver a formal presentation on a topic of our choice that usually centred on vision and values. There was always pressure to hire quickly, but we tried to resist this temptation. If MLSE could attract the best, we had to absolutely make sure we hired the best.

## DEVELOP THE BEST

The MLSE "training camp" on the sixth floor of the Air Canada Centre runs all year long. More than 100 learning events are held here each year.

In 2005, I started teaching an annual Elite training course to individuals on staff who had been identified as what we called "high promotables." Most of these men and women were already or about to become directors. The course was modelled on the one I had taught at Odette, and I used the same continuum—starting with vision and values and moving through leadership, strategic planning and so on. This was a good exercise for me as well because it forced me to rethink a lot of things, such as strategy, while keeping my leadership skills fresh and up-to-date.

But all of the classes were modified to be MLSE-centric and in real time. As the company grew and changed, the course changed to suit. The course ran from September to May, and over the years some fifty middle managers and directors were carefully selected; the opportunity was never turned down. Today, there are still thirty-two graduates in the company. Nine graduates have gone on to become vice-presidents, and most of the others have either been promoted or transferred to other areas to broaden their experience. Future vice-presidents will be sure to come from the remaining graduates.

For three hours every three weeks over the course of nine months, these managers and directors were in Elite classes. Their class times and assignments typically represented about 3 per cent more work in addition to their already heavy job responsibilities.

This was a *live* course. By that I mean that when I showed the class an MLSE strategic plan in November, it was not some document from years past; it was exactly the same strategic plan the board was then considering.

In the MLSE Elite course one year, I asked the students to consider a fictitious character I had created. He was our best salesperson, but he'd been selling by lying, exaggerating and pushing some of his costs onto another department. Everyone in the course agreed: this guy had to go.

I told the class that sometimes there are tensions between the sales force and freewheeling marketers, and between the sales people and the financial people. You need incentive plans for those in sales, and you need to manage the jealousy of those who must work with them.

I did most of the teaching but frequently brought in outside speakers from our corporate partners or industry leaders, people such as Paul Alofs, Tom Knowlton, Harry Rosen, John Cassaday, board members of the Ontario Teachers' Pension Plan such as Jim Leech, and author Dr. Richard Davis. Larry Tanenbaum was our commencement speaker each May, and he handed out framed diplomas. The eight students were marked on three assignments. At the end of the course in May, everyone in the class was ranked on how they did (top two, middle three, bottom three). They were all "elite," but to further our meritocracy philosophy, they—and their bosses—learned how they stood vis-à-vis their classmates. Graduation from Elite was an important event at MLSE. It would be a shame if it dies with my retirement, but that looks now to be the case.

Right across the company, every full-time employee is supposed to receive a verbal performance review in November and a formal written review in April. The evaluation covers everything from adherence to and living vision and values to leadership to functional results. In preparing the evaluation, the boss *must* be as candid as possible with the individual, since the evaluation impacts raises, promotions and bonuses—and senior management's view on whether the individual is a high promotable, or not.

The quality of evaluations improved over the years, but try as I might, I could never get the team GMs to do decent evaluations on their staff, which I think was a real shame. The highest score one could get was "Elite." The lowest was "Needs improvement." I always believed that a person had no chance to improve unless his or her boss was clear and candid on what that person needed to work on. If the individual clearly knew what needed improvement and still did not get better, then clearly that weak individual would soon be removed from the company.

Year after year, we tracked the performance of our people. The group we were most interested in were the people evaluated as "Elite." From 2006 to 2011, this group averaged 17 per cent of our workforce. We identified these high promotables for advancement, cross-functional moves and special assignments, and if senior enough, they became candidates for Elite training. The middle group of evaluations (approximately 70 per cent) were marked either "Meets expectations" or "Exceeds expectations." We also viewed these people as key to the company, since many had the potential to go into the Elite group or were the very competent "glue" that kept the company going.

The final 10 per cent or so were marked "Needs improvement," with some of those being marked as "Unacceptable." Every year, our total company turnover was around 10 per cent. I paid special attention to two key aspects of that turnover number. If we wanted to have the best people at MLSE, we constantly had to be raising the performance bar. Therefore, it was important that we were weeding out the underperformers. So I regularly watched to make sure that three to five percentage points of our turnover consisted of people whom we either encouraged to leave or let go. I also carefully watched the turnover among our Elite/high promotables. I worried about any turnover percentage of that group that exceeded three percentage points.

Our approach was similar to what Jack Welch followed at General Electric. We definitely believed in differentiating our people. I want to stress that ours was *not* a ranking system. Microsoft has received a lot of criticism for force-ranking its people. A July 2012 *Vanity Fair* article suggested that "stack ranking" (treating a pre-set percentage of employees as top, middling and inadequate performers) in *every* department has hurt Microsoft's ability to innovate and successfully compete with the likes of Apple. At MLSE, by contrast, one department could have a number of employees marked "Elite" or "Exceeds expectations" and another department none. We simply wanted to identify our best—no matter where they were. I can say that if one department featured a lot of high promotables, it did cause us to question whether that boss marked too easy. Or if another department had consistently low evaluation scores, was that boss possibly a poor leader or one who marked too hard?

Twice a year, the executive management team met to go through an exercise called "corporate engineering." I started this practice when at Pillsbury, and I used it at SkyDome as well. Our executive team reviewed each of the high promotables separately and talked about what their bosses needed to work on with them so they could get even better. We practised succession planning by identifying backstops and by moving some people into broadening roles so that we created strong management bench strength. Our executive leaders also debated and signed off on senior promotions.

## SUPERB COMMUNICATION

The vast majority of corporate problems are caused by poor communication. That's the bad news. The good news is that the vast majority of corporate problems can be corrected by superb communication.

I worked very hard to be an excellent formal and informal communicator, both in writing and speaking. In trying to reach all employees, I was sometimes criticized for over-communicating, but I believed that every communication had to be put in context so the employee could understand its importance and where it fit. Accordingly, our communication tactics were comprehensive. In my last six years as president at MLSE, I did monthly podcasts in which I put the spotlight on one part of the company: from interviewing executive chef Tony Glitz on how he ran the Real Sports Bar & Grill and made the best chicken wings in Toronto to broadcasting from the construction site of Maple Leaf Square to interviewing the full-time staff who kept the ACC so clean. These podcast scripts were written by me and filmed by our broadcast people. No teleprompter was used and little rehearsal was done, as they were purposely kept quite casual. I also used them to introduce new members to the MLSE family and to recognize length-of-service awards. Needless to say, the production of these eight-minute podcasts required a few takes to get them in the can.

After a few years of this, someone decided they would show my bloopers of mispronounced names and the occasional swear word at the annual town hall meeting. These bloopers were always a big hit. Just as working on the line at Green Giant did, the blooper tapes made me look both fallible and human. MLSE was starting to become sizeable—with staff at the ACC, BMO Field, Ricoh Coliseum, Maple Leaf Square and our own broadcast facility, so we created an elaborate and expensive intranet site called All Access that kept employees up-to-date on all activities and happenings.

The site was like a chat room where all our staff were encouraged to discuss topics of their choice. At the end of my podcasts, I often invited everyone to weigh in on a particular topic. Other communication tools were email, voice mail and, of course, department meetings. The big, important communication event of the year was our annual town hall meeting in November. It was held in the ACC bowl, with full stage and lighting.

Our MLSE in-house band, Play to Win (with Tom Anselmi on rhythm guitar), always performed. The staff heard from me, from each of the GMs and from departments that were launching some important corporate initiative. And, finally, we used the town hall meetings to recognize our award winners. This annual event is a big deal, with lots of information on what MLSE was doing, lots of entertainment—including that screening of my bloopers and various skits—and with a motivational component coming from the award presentations. The bill for such an event would normally be close to a quarter of a million dollars, but because MLSE is in the event business, we put it on using our own people and own resources for a fraction of the cost.

My overall communication philosophy was that I wanted our employees to know everything that was going on in the company and the rationale for all our initiatives.

We were a private company, with about fifty media types watching our every move, so confidentiality was a potential issue. Before each town hall meeting, I'd say something like, "Today we are going to share some confidential information with you. We think it is important that you hear this information, and we trust that you will do the right thing with this information." (Only once, to my knowledge, in my time at MLSE did someone break that trust.)

When I retired I received a number of personal notes from staff. One was from Jim Heeley, a unionized worker at ACC. When I first met Jim, he told me that I should not pick up garbage at the ACC because that, he said, was union work. Jim does an excellent job making sure the thousands of square metres of ACC glass are free from fingerprints and marks every day. He sent me a handwritten card, which I have kept because it touched me deeply. "Richard," it read, "thank you for your leadership, your business acumen, financial responsibility and especially for your communicative skill."

## MOTIVATION AND RECOGNITION

Over the course of my career, I met a few people who said that they didn't need recognition. My hard-nosed, excellent vice-president of operations at Hostess, the late Stu Cairns, was one of them. I told him he was full of it. All people want and need recognition, even if they say they don't. I wish I could credit whoever said "The greatest need of every human being is the need for appreciation." Another sage comment from Author Unknown.

But to be effective, recognition has to be specific, personal, timely (catch them in the act) and varied. When I was at Hostess, I created a folded card. On the front were the three Munchies—cartoon characters that were an integral part of our marketing campaign in those days. The inside of the card was blank. I used the cards to write personal notes.

And I developed similar cards for Pillsbury, SkyDome and MLSE (the latter featured the vision and values statement on the back). My sister, Carol, has a gift for penmanship, something I could not learn. But she did teach me to write thank-you notes. I strongly believe that a note written by hand with a fountain pen is as personal and authentic as you can get. I often wrote a couple of notes per day over the last thirty years of my career.

Once when calling on John Lederer, who was then president of Loblaw, he said to me, "I went into the office of Glenn Murphy [one of John's buyers] and I saw a personal note from you displayed prominently on his desk!" John laughed at how effective a personal card could be. Glenn went on to successfully turn around Shoppers Drug Mart, and today he runs the Gap family of retail stores. I wrote notes to employees who had done special things, and I wrote them to friends who were in the news. Usually, the notes were about happy events, but sometimes they expressed support for people going through difficult times. When I retired from MLSE, I wrote more than 200 such personal notes. Now the entire company has access to MLSE blank cards, and many are taking the time to recognize their peers, subordinates, customers and friends. Perhaps in part because so rare, a handwritten card is personal and powerful.

In addition to a personal approach to recognition, MLSE created an excellent corporate recognition plan modelled on sports awards. Every year, Coach of the Year, Rookie of the Year, Most Valuable Player of the Year and All-Star Team awards were presented. Coming up through General Foods and Hostess, I saw some awful corporate awards, poorly thought out, given out haphazardly, often to the wrong people. MLSE has the best corporate awards I have ever had the pleasure of helping to hand out. At the town hall meeting where they are presented, the previous year's winner talks about winning the award the year before and then introduces the new winner. The speech by the presenter and the new recipient are almost always inspiring. The audience of teammates and peers gives the winner a standing ovation. And, as I mentioned earlier, when the recipient cried, I knew we had got it right.

When I worked at General Foods, I hated how most people were treated the same and often managed to the lowest common denominator. Those who got better results, it seemed to me, should be treated differently.

In his book *Winning*, Jack Welch has an excellent chapter on differentiation. "Cruel and Darwinian?" he writes. "Try fair and effective." He goes on to argue that "a company has only so much money and managerial time. Winning leaders invest where the payback is the highest. They cut their losses everywhere else." MLSE was already in the most merit-based industry in the world—professional sports, where winners are few and losers are many. Likewise when deciding to invest in strategic initiatives, we were already comparing the merits of one versus the other, spending the dollars on the initiative that gave us the best return on our investment. In 2006, I really started talking up a meritocracy approach for our business people. I first ran it by an Elite class. No surprise, they supported it 100 per cent. After all, they already viewed themselves as elite.

I next went to my executive management, thinking that I might get some pushback on MLSE being so vocal about it. There wasn't any. So off we went. That was when we started identifying the top 20 per cent, making sure that they got the promotions, bigger raises and bonuses and extra development assignments. Even cross-functional moves were based entirely on merit. At General Foods, a lot of leaders just passed on their underperformers to someone else to deal with. At MLSE, doing that was a career-limiting move.

I recognized that not all our staff would embrace a meritocracy approach. In one employee survey, an employee had written in the suggestion section that "everyone should be treated the same." The survey was completed anonymously, so I didn't know who had written this. Had I known, I would have sat the person down and said, "You're working in the wrong company. Maybe try a heavily unionized workforce, or maybe a government or teaching job." Meritocracy is defined (by *Webster's*, at least) as "a system in which the talented are chosen and moved ahead on the basis of their achievement." But for us, talented and intelligent weren't enough. The individual also had to deliver excellent results in the context of our fans, people, teams and community values.

For instance, if someone excelled in sales but was a horrible team member and lousy leader, that individual was not viewed as having merit. The key to a successful meritocracy approach is a fair and honest measurement system. Ours wasn't perfect, but in many areas we did have measurable metrics such as sales and service results and departmental financial results. Our annual evaluations were another metric, as were our annual surveys of employee attitudes. If a certain department had lower scores than the company average, we started wondering about the boss's leadership effectiveness.

And finally, the executive leadership team used the corporate engineering process to dig deep into the performance of the top people in the company. We practised differentiation, but we called it "earned differentiation"—a way of measuring all the things that one person accomplished in the year and how that person went about accomplishing them. At the end of the year when bonuses and raises were being handed out, the people department could create a chart that showed everyone's evaluation scores, and we compensated accordingly.

I remember one Elite class discussion on meritocracy clearly. I read an article about a Saskatchewan high school that was reconsidering the practice of issuing failing grades to students. They apparently wanted to avoid hurting the students' feelings or prospects. Instead of a failing mark, the student would receive an "incomplete" or "no mark." One of the Elite participants was Randi Jakobsen, director of payroll, who told us a story about once facing the prospect of a serious operation. She said that she had researched the academic qualifications of her surgeons to ensure they were the best in their field. She also said that in future she would make sure that any doctor about to operate on her was not a graduate of that Saskatchewan high school.

I do worry that we may have gone too soft. In some lower-level kids' hockey leagues, all teams—whether first or last—get trophies. Marks in school are much inflated over years ago. It seems that everyone is an honours student today. We even had a few cases at MLSE where the parents of a young employee called the people department to complain about their son's or daughter's poor evaluation or phoned me to complain about the unfair termination of their child.

Performance management, Jack Welch argued forcefully, has been part of everyone's life from first grade. Some make the basketball team or debating society; some don't. This or that college or university accepts this candidate but not that one. "There is differentiation for all of us in our first twenty years," Welch writes. "Why should it stop in the workplace, where most of our working hours are spent?"

When I taught the Elite course, I used the analogy of the gym bag. As a runner, for example, you want the very latest in running gear that wicks away moisture so your sweat doesn't add weight, you want the best shoes you can afford, the latest thinking on drafting—whatever will give you an edge over the competition. The one who wins the race is often the one who wanted it most, who trained the hardest, who wasn't satisfied with a personal best time or even a second-place finish. Meritocracy, which describes, at least in part, my style of leadership, means rewarding that person.

Attract, develop, motivate, unleash and retain were the successful corporate strategies we followed at MLSE in order to be an exceptional place to work. I personally deployed other leadership skills too. I worked very hard, for example, to be authentic. I figured that employees would recognize and want to follow a leader who was authentic. I lead with energy. I was very fit so that I could handle the long hours. I also realized that I could bring a positive emotional energy to meetings. As one employee told me, "If someone came to you with an idea and if you liked it, you would light a fire under that person."

I encouraged ideas. I knew that rich, creative ideas were key to our future. I believed that managers largely manage what has already been created, and leaders create something new. On many weekends I sent out an email to various groups of employees, telling them what I called "my crazy idea of the day." Some were good; some were awful. I was just trying to stimulate their creative juices.

I sometimes used theatrics to effect. I remember debating some of my senior management team at MLSE on the merits of purchasing Gol TV (to televise TFC games and market Major League Soccer). Faced with a lot of resistance, I reminded them how many of them were timid about getting into football in the first place. Still they resisted, so I told them they were being cowards, I swore at them and stormed out of the room. It worked because they all came around, and Gol TV became critical to broadcasting all TFC games that Rogers and TSN would not cover. Brian Burke was born with edge like this; mine came gradually. By the time I was fifty-five, I was cocky and comfortable. I had confidence and experience, and I was okay with pushing and debating.

Above all, I knew that as president and CEO I needed to be a driving force behind the MLSE vision. I had to articulate the right set of corporate and personal values. And I had to continually reflect on those values to make sure they were appropriate to achieving the desired goal of winning. I had to embody the values in my own behaviour—all the time. And I had to actively encourage others to apply these values to their own decisions and actions, as well as aggressively confront and deal with pockets of ignorance and resistance in the company.

*  *  *

In the Elite course at MLSE, we discussed whether leaders were made or born. The participants and I all seemed to agree on one thing: all people have untapped leadership potential and can hone leadership skills if they are prepared to work at it. But to be a great leader takes trial, error and time; it's a learning process.

And no two leaders are alike. In his book *True North*, Harvard Business School professor Bill George—himself a former CEO—interviewed 125 successful leaders and concluded that there is no such thing as an ideal leader. There is no recipe, no list of traits to be checked off. What matters are passion and purpose and life stories.

In the end, I knew that together we at MLSE had created a corporate culture that enthusiastically recognized success. We invested in the development of our people. We trusted them to know everything that was going on in the company and to do the right thing with that information. And we unleashed them to pursue football, groundbreaking food and beverage initiatives, specialty television, and so on, all while embracing a meritocracy approach. This inspired MLSE staff to become one of the finest sports and entertainment teams in the world and, importantly, to stay with the company.

From the size, sophistication and value of the business we created, I knew I had done well as a leader. I also took note of what was said on my retirement.

Debra Watkinson, formerly an MLSE director (she left the firm in 2013), sent me what she called "the RP leadership recipe." Her note read, in part: "You see someone's potential and how they can be all they want to be and more. Maybe no one else noticed, but you do. So you get their attention by noticing. Then you confront them with it. Maybe their biggest fear. Or biggest weakness. Or biggest strength. Or biggest opportunity. Anyway, you make them GET IT. And then you make them grab it. Whatever it is, make them own it and make it theirs. And then they do it well enough that you recognize them for it and tell them why they did it well. And then they know. And are inspired to be what they want to be and more."

Another excellent employee, Wynne James (executive assistant, finance), sent me a much-appreciated handwritten note that read, in part, "Thank you for welcoming me to MLSE with your one-on-one meetings . . . for always treating me as though I was an important member of the team . . . for creating a culture that makes you want to come to work every day . . . for creating a compassionate and caring workplace . . ."

For most of my career I was a student of leadership, knowing that what I knew paled in comparison to what I still needed to learn. John Maxwell, author of *The 21 Irrefutable Laws of Leadership* and many other fine books, best summed up the leadership journey for me: "Leadership doesn't develop in a day, it takes a life time."

# CHAPTER 12

# ON BUILDING A CITY— ONE DREAM, ONE BRICK AT A TIME

In the fall of 2010, forty days before the municipal election, I gave a speech to the Canadian Club of Toronto entitled "My Vision for Toronto." I told the packed crowd at the Royal York Hotel that in the late 1980s, I had a choice between staying in Toronto to further my career or taking my career to the United States. I chose Toronto.

This city has so much to offer—from theatre to art galleries, from restaurants to shopping. I like Toronto's streetcars. I like the bustle, the diversity. Over my forty-plus years in Toronto, I have run thousands of kilometres on its streets and through its parks. In my marathon days, I was running close to 5,000 kilometres a year, and I'd get bored running the same route, so I'd mix it up: Mount Pleasant Cemetery, Wilket Creek, I even liked running up Yonge Street. You can get to know a city by running it.

I have marvelled as the city changed from a homogenous popu-lace to one that today reflects the diversity of the world. Toronto is a great city. Many would say one of the best. But as I travel inter-nationally and read about the developments in many other great cities, I wish for more for Toronto. Much, much more.

I told the audience that day that the citizens of Toronto faced an important decision, one that would affect the fortunes of the city and its citizens for many years to come. The critical decision involved choosing the sixty-fourth mayor of Toronto. The choice of the forty-four councillors, who would hopefully work closely with the new mayor, was equally critical. I hoped that the new mayor and council would move the city forward based on a clear and compelling vision and a few very strong values. I voiced my desire for the voters to elect a great city hall team that would make a positive difference to the future of Toronto. But I also worried out loud that we might elect a mayor and city hall team that would make a negative difference.

I gave the audience a checklist of what I was looking for in a mayor. I wanted a true leader, not a manager. And that leader had to have a crystal-clear vision of the city's future, a view of something possible, something seen in a dream, and it had to be a stretching, guiding statement of intent and commitment. And, as I have stressed throughout this book, that vision statement had to be rock-solid—not change with every annual city budget or change just so someone could get re-elected the next time around.

I had been listening carefully to what the five mayoral can-didates were campaigning on—what they saw as their important strategies and beliefs. I had been hearing a lot about cutting costs and freezing taxes, I said in my speech, but I pointed out that while financial soundness was important, it was not inspiring. It did not get me pumped about Toronto's future. None of the five candi-dates had a real vision, and that worried me greatly.

Was I tilting at windmills by giving such a speech? Maybe. In the days after the speech there was some media coverage, mostly positive. But the candidates' reaction to my challenge was very disappointing. They criticized me, suggesting I didn't know what I was talking about, nor did I understand the challenges of running city hall. There was one really nonsensical response: "I'll listen to Peddie when the Leafs win a Stanley Cup."

After Mayor Rob Ford and forty-four councillors were elected, I wanted them to hear about my thoughts on the importance of having a vision for the city, so I sent all of them a copy of my speech, along with Dr. Richard Davis's excellent book, *The Intangibles of Leadership*. I had hoped to start a conversation, to stir debate. Four councillors sent me a note to thank me, and one came to see me. I doubt that few of the other thirty-nine actually read any of Davis's book. It's a shame, because his take on things such as wisdom, will, social judgment, fortitude and fallibility would have served them all well.

As I write this three years later, it is clear that I had good reason to be worried. Mayor Ford has demonstrated repeatedly that he has no clear vision for the city other than a catchy phrase—"End the gravy train." Without clear vision and values there is nothing to direct what strategies the city should be following. Accordingly, we have seen a dysfunctional council bounce from one tactic to another, with few bold, long-term strategies being created and acted upon. Toronto's leadership is a complete embarrassment.

Low on vision but high in venom. Once again the Japanese proverb rings true: "Action without vision is a nightmare."

Like cities all over the world, Toronto is facing many challenges. Every year the Toronto Community Fund publishes an insightful report on the city entitled *Toronto's Vital Signs*. The 2012 report covers everything from safety, the environment, arts and culture, the gap between rich and poor—ten measures in total. How are we doing in the city? "Not too bad" was the consensus. Construction was way up, and personal bankruptcies were way down. Our cultural industries were strong, and the report proudly noted that Toronto has the largest neighbourhood-based library system in the world (sadly under threat as I write this). Crime was markedly down, and an overwhelming number of citizens surveyed felt the city was generally safe. On the other hand, Toronto ranked as the least equitable metropolitan centre in Canada—the only one to get a C on income distribution. If current trends continue, by 2025 almost 60 per cent of the city's neighbourhoods will have citizens living on low or very low incomes. Youth unemployment was high, and one in three Toronto children was obese. The report identifies many issues, and Toronto has only so many people and financial resources to deal with those issues.

What to do?

* * *

The city needs a vision. In an article in the *Harvard Business Review*, Rosabeth Moss Kanter, who teaches at the Harvard Business School, writes about how really great companies think differently. Great cities do too. Here I quote Kanter, but I have replaced "companies" with "cities." She writes: "In truly great [cities,] society and people are not afterthoughts . . . but core to their purpose. The first step is getting behind a common vision. Top leaders exemplify and communicate the [city's] purpose and values, but everyone owns them, and the values become embedded in tasks, goals, and performance standards."

It's worth pointing out that Toronto is already a highly regarded world city. *The Economist*'s 2012 Livability Ranking tracked 140 global cities on livability indicators such as stability, heath care, culture, the environment and education. Toronto ranked fourth (behind Melbourne in first spot, with Vienna in second; Vancouver, third; and Calgary, fifth). Toronto's ambition should be the top ranking. Standing still is not an option or we will very quickly fall way back in the pack.

Despite Toronto's high ranking, some of our political leaders are still the most critical of the city. During a speech in the fall of 2012 to the Toronto Board of Trade, David Naylor, the president of the University of Toronto, decried such negativism. The Toronto region, he noted, ranks high on many global surveys: number four as an innovation hub; number six in terms of business competitiveness; the third-largest financial centre and fourth-largest health-sciences community in North America. The Toronto area design sector (with 28,000 employees) is the third largest on the continent. The Organisation for Economic Co-operation and Development, said Naylor, credits Toronto with the fourth-highest rate of entrepreneurship among regions in the industrialized world, yet the city ranks fifty-ninth on a list of the world's most expensive cities.

But far from trumpeting these successes, elected officials do the opposite. "It doesn't help," Naylor said, "when your political leaders—the ones who, by definition, are expected to be the biggest boosters—turn out to the biggest busters of city pride . . . with the blackly humorous dramas at city hall, and the endless angst about how we're losing our mojo, Toronto sometimes feels like the Woody Allen of global alpha cities." *Globe and Mail* writer Marcus Gee used the quote in a column entitled "Lose the Self-Pity and Shout Out GTA [Greater Toronto Area] Triumphs, Says U of T President."

\* \* \*

In the summer of 2009, I had lunch with Bruce Kidd, the former Olympic distance runner. We were at the Faculty Club at the University of Toronto. He's a cerebral man who pulls no punches.

"What do you think about Maple Leaf Sports and Entertainment?" I asked him.

"MLSE is not generous enough," he told me. "You're all about money." I didn't disagree. Then I asked him, "Will you chair the board at our community foundation?" He spent a week pondering his decision and in the end said yes—and he's still there, still chair of the Team Up Foundation, the charitable and community-building arm of MLSE.

I like to surround myself with contrary thinkers. When I was CEO of SkyDome, I had Kidd (he's also the warden at Hart House, a student activity centre at the University of Toronto) and Bob White (the former head of the Canadian Auto Workers union) on the board. Both men lean hard to the left, and I'm probably more left leaning than most CEOs, but my political stripes are really small-l liberal; were I living in the United States, I would be seen as a Democrat. No surprise: Kidd, White, I and a great many others on that board tangled.

Kidd, for example, doesn't believe that corporations should be involved in sports. "Hockey belongs to the people," he once told me. His preferred model is community ownership of a team (a model still deployed by the Winnipeg Blue Bombers, the Edmonton Eskimos and the Saskatchewan Roughriders of the Canadian Football League).

Kidd remembers that lunch of ours well. "I knew that the Leafs had always had some sort of philanthropic aspect," he told me recently. "And the Raptors had a foundation. Hockey and basketball players would visit kids in hospital, and the team did give money when asked, but it was all very unfocused. Special projects, recreation, literary festivals, a disease charity, the arts: whenever the owners felt a little guilt, they gave some money. But where was the community impact? That was my criticism at the time."

Kidd's decision about joining the MLSE foundation hinged on whether such a foundation could actually make a difference in the community—or whether the thing was, as he put it, "so controlled, so caught up in branding and marketing." So as he pondered my offer, he did due diligence: he looked closely at how our foundation was run, and he researched what was being done by like foundations in other cities (Los Angeles, San Francisco, Orlando, New York). He found there were some bad ones; the best ones, Kidd found, were semi-autonomous. They can make a difference, and the MLSE foundation, he realized, was semi-autonomous.

"You know," he told me, "you and I don't see eye to eye on a lot of things. But I admire you. You are a quintessentially decent man and the very model of a modern major general." (The last phrase, of course, comes from *The Pirates of Penzance*, the old Gilbert and Sullivan comic opera.) "I remember you saying to me, 'On the community side, the polls say that MLSE is not doing enough. How'd you like to help change that?' And after thinking about it, I agreed to try."

Kidd's overarching concern was that disadvantaged kids in Toronto be a central focus of the foundation. He knew that most hockey rinks are in middle-class neighbourhoods, and he wanted to build football pitches and basketball courts, rinks and playgrounds near community housing. He told me that the need was great and that giving a few million dollars a year to the foundation would not cut it.

To all of that, we said yes and yes and yes.

Today, Kidd is encouraged by what he sees. "The foundation's focus has been sharpened," he says. "We set out to restore publicly available facilities and build new facilities. And we've gone about it using the most up-to-date research on which interventions work and which do not. It's been a lovely partnership. Anything with blue and white on it is always a target in this city, but we've improved it considerably. The foundation is really making a contribution. There has been a 180-degree difference between what was before and what we have now."

Kidd understands the history, he knows that the Leafs have been owned by a corporation since 1926 and he accepts all that—even the fact that MLSE is more focused on the bottom line than anything else. But he tips his hat to Larry Tanenbaum and to me for cleaning up the mess that was Leaf culture at Maple Leaf Gardens: the sex scandal there, Gardens' staff washing Harold Ballard's car and cleaning up after his dog . . . "You cleaned it up," Kidd says, "and you moved it into the twenty-first century. It's professional now, ethical, inclusive of both women and men and ethno-culturally diverse. And it's honest."

In his book *Fixing the Game: Bubbles, Crashes, and What Capitalism Can Learn from the NFL*, Roger Martin (who was then dean at the University of Toronto's Rotman School of Management) outlines the role corporations can play in society: "The people who run these companies have a choice: they can chip away at the bricks of the civil foundation; they can benefit from the existing foundation but not contribute to it; or they can work to add bricks to strengthen the robustness of the foundation."

I am proud to say that MLSE in its entire history has added bricks to strengthen the foundation of Toronto. To be a "leader in our community" is a core value of the company. Its owners, management and employees recognize their obligation to the community.

A 2011 poll revealed that social responsibility is a low priority for most Canadian companies. Only 21 per cent reported having a plan to be socially responsible; 29 per cent said they had no plan but hoped to have one within three to five years. However, an awfully high number—49 per cent—said they had no plan now and no intention to change that. How sad.

Over its fifteen-year existence, MLSE has had such a plan. All the owners during that time (the Ontario Teachers' Pension Plan, the TD Bank, Larry Tanenbaum) were always prepared to give management significant resources to do right in the community. Accordingly, MLSE has been a true city builder. The motto for our foundation is "Changing lives through sports and the power of sports."

In my last year as president, MLSE invested more than $500,000 in four Greater Toronto Area rink refurbishments, provided $120,000 to build Variety Village a new centre court, and refurbished a football pitch in Sorauren Park, on Toronto's west side. Consistent with MLSE's "Inspire our people" value, we encouraged our employees to get involved in the refurbishments—and they did.

Our other community strategy was giving: our four-team, three-sport approach enabled us to fund sustainable programs that give youth access to sports. By the time this book is published, MLSE will have refurbished more than thirty-seven facilities and offered sports development programming to more than one million youth in the city.

And, as I've said, our players have always played a role in the community. Even before Brian Burke announced that community involvement was a must for Leaf and Marlie players, Leaf players consistently led the NHL in community visits and appearances. The Raptors have also been league leaders. Charles Oakley was excellent in this regard, and while we had some on- and off-court problems with Vince Carter, he was pretty good in the community too. Carter's Embassy of Hope Foundation distributed $780,000 to worthwhile community initiatives while he was a Raptor. Team GMs and coaches have largely supported our community initiatives. Brian Burke and Bryan Colangelo were the best at actively encouraging and supporting community engagement, and that makes community organizers' lives a lot easier when they need players to participate in events.

But there were exceptions. One was Raptor coach Kevin O'Neill. When we hired him, I sat down with him to review our vision and values, paying special attention to the value of community. He nodded, said he got it. He then went downstairs and said to our community manager, "Peddie is a good guy, but I think he really believes this shit."

O'Neill did do some community engagement, but he fought it constantly. One of the Raptor traditions is an open house practice to make the fans feel connected to the team. We might put a microphone on certain players or maybe the coach while the practice is under way. O'Neill refused to participate on the grounds that he'd be giving away team strategies. Kevin O'Neill's philosophy was that community relations came down to winning basketball games, plain and simple.

In my last year, every Raptor player and every Leaf player contributed monies totalling $400,000 to purchase tickets so that 2,300 city youth could attend games. Leaf and Raptor players largely have very good images in the community. The Leafs have a slightly stronger image, but that is to be expected in a hockey-mad market. But both get solid marks for their charitable activities and as positive role models.

When Ken Dryden was once asked why being a leader in the community is so important, he replied, "We all have a responsibility to give back. It is the right thing to do." I have heard both Ken Dryden and MLSE executive vice-president and CFO Ian Clarke deliver speeches in which they quoted the Ben Parker character of *Spider-Man* comics fame: "'With great power comes great responsibility." Those of us who are more fortunate have an obligation to help the less fortunate. At MLSE, Ken, Ian, myself: we were all very lucky to be surrounded by colleagues and friends who shared that belief and who acted on it.

I often quote Winston Churchill: "We make a living by what we get, but we make a life by what we give." That was clearly MLSE's approach when I was there. I believe that Maple Leaf Sports and Entertainment can give more to the community of Toronto—a few million dollars more. And that notion is being put forward not just by me. Many of our sponsors insist on some sort of benefit to the community. In the past, MLSE has generated money for its foundation by putting on golf tournaments featuring our athletes or by holding charity dinners at our restaurants; I'm suggesting that MLSE actually dip into its own coffers. When the Ontario Teachers' Pension Plan owned a majority piece of MLSE, it was prohibited by Ontario law from contributing significant dollars to charities. The new Rogers-Bell-Tanenbaum shareholder group is not encumbered by such a rule. Adding corporate dollars to the significant monies already raised by the Team Up Foundation would allow MLSE to be an even more forceful and dynamic city builder.

Bruce Kidd marvels at the opposing tendencies that afflict executives like me. People like me, he says, want to do well and maximize revenue—yet we are also intent on giving back to the city we cherish and call home.

\* \* \*

To improve our cities and communities, companies such as MLSE can use a four-pillar approach. One is more partnerships between the public and private sectors. When MLSE took over Ricoh Coliseum, for example, the City of Toronto was spared a major funding shortfall and gained a new team, the Marlies, to develop future Leafs. That deal saved the city not only a great deal of money but also the embarrassment that would have come from a mostly empty facility.

Another example of a profitable private-public partnership is BMO Field. Built on budget and on time by MLSE and owned by the city, the stadium has generated worldwide attention for its enthusiastic fans and its events such as the World Under-20 Men's Football Championship and both the MLS All-Star Game and Cup finals. MLSE contributed $18 million to the building of the facility and later expanded seating and made the change to natural grass—all on its own corporate dime. Today, the facility generates approximately $400,000 to $500,000 a year for the city.

And the MasterCard Centre in Etobicoke is arguably the finest hockey training centre and practice facility in the world. The centre's four ice pads are used constantly by both children and adults starved for ice time. The place would not have been financed and therefore not constructed if MLSE had not signed a half-million-dollar long-term annual lease—the price it paid so the Leafs and Marlies could use the practice facility.

Finally, a winter bubble was constructed over Lamport Stadium so that the field can be used all year. This earns the city approximately $100,000 in annual incremental revenues.

MLSE believes in public-private partnerships because they work and are good for the city. Some politicians and media are negative about these partnerships, but we proved that if they are approached strategically, well thought out, and fair to both sides, they can definitely work for both parties and can be one of the foundations for Toronto's long-term economic success.

The second pillar is capital investments. Together, the Air Canada Centre and its revitalization, BMO Field and Maple Leaf Square cost almost $1 billion—a major shot in the arm to the construction industry in Toronto and a boon to every hotel and restaurant in the vicinity of the CN Tower. Here's the math: $265 million to construct the ACC; $48 million to expand and upgrade the facility a decade later; $65 million to create BMO Field; $500 million to build Maple Leaf Square, helping to energize an under-used area of Toronto and link the downtown with the waterfront;

$22 million to construct the TFC Academy at Downsview—plus millions of annual dollars over the past fifteen years to keep all these facilities modern.

With the exception of BMO Field, MLSE paid for these capital projects entirely with its own money. Scorecard? MLSE spending: $956 million. Taxpayer spending: $44 million. Plus, MLSE pays $13 million in property taxes every year.

The third pillar is fitness initiatives—a key one, given the rising rates of obesity and diabetes. MLSE's Team Up Foundation has spent millions of dollars to refurbish aging arenas, football pitches and courts in the city.

Finally, major events and corporate sponsorships of such events—football championships, the NHL All-Star game, World Cup hockey—offer a huge source of revenue both to MLSE and the City of Toronto. Some would argue that major events are not part of a city-builder strategy. I disagree. Look at events such as the AutoShow, Pride Week, Caribana and the Toronto International Film Festival. They and others generate excellent domestic and international awareness of the city, attract visitors who spend money, and entertain Torontonians. The film festival alone has an economic impact on the city of well over $100 million a year.

MLSE is constantly hosting major events as well—the 2000 NHL All-Star game, 2004 World Cup of Hockey (Canada won), FIFA Under-20 World Cup, MLS All-Star game in 2008, MLS Championship game in 2010 and the Juno Awards in 2011. The ACC is one of the top concert venues in the world, with up to sixty shows a year. The Maple Leafs hundredth anniversary is coming up in 2017, and MLSE is working hard to host the NHL All-Star game, the NHL draft and a Winter Classic game at BMO Field during that year or the years leading up to 2017.

Big international events are important to Toronto. The Real Madrid game at BMO Field had a worldwide TV audience in the millions. Toronto cannot afford to buy that type of positive international exposure. When MLSE hosts events such as this, it foots almost the entire bill. In the United States, municipal and state governments contribute a lot of the money needed to entice the leagues to host such events in their cities.

* * *

In December 2012, the *Globe and Mail* ran an editorial cartoon depicting a bookstore clerk unpacking a box of newly arrived books, and, in particular, one title—*Toronto 2012—The Year in Politics.* He can't decide where on the shelves it should go: the section on tragedy or the section on farce.

The city deserves better.

# CHAPTER 13

# LESSONS LEARNED

My corporate career spanned almost forty-two years. I worked for eight companies and was president of six of them—for a total of twenty-eight years. All six of those companies were sold while I was president, but I survived every takeover and was never fired. I grew and I changed over the years, and learned—and had to relearn—some things along the way. These lessons served me well, and they may help you too.

## 1. HAVE A DREAM OR VISION

My friend, the legendary Jack Donohue, coached Canada's national basketball team for seventeen years. The New York–born coach enjoyed much success along the way. He always said, "Dream big dreams" (indeed, that was the title of his biography).

When I turned sixty, my wife, Colleen, marked the occasion by installing a bench and planting nearby a Canadian maple in a small park that we could see from our condominium in the Tip Top

Tailors building on Lake Shore Boulevard, close to Lake Ontario. At the base of the tree is a plaque inscribed with Jack Donohue's "Dream big dreams" line.

The point is to dream big and work hard—and you too can realize your ambition. Having a clear driving vision helped me secure the Raptor job, and solid vision statements really helped Pillsbury, SkyDome and Maple Leaf Sports and Entertainment realize major accomplishments during my tenure at each. You may not quite realize your dream, but you are sure to accomplish a lot trying.

## 2. HAVE STRONG CORE VALUES

Your dream represents *what* you wish to achieve—values represent *how* you will realize them. As I always say, values need to be rock-solid and not drift with the times. In this hyper-competitive era, it is easy for a person or company to abandon values in order to gain a financial benefit or achieve a higher position. While abandoning your values may result in short-term gain, doing so also carries great short- and long-term risk.

I consistently used my personal and corporate values to make important decisions in my career. The presence of values helped my companies consistently make the right decisions, and I never once regretted the value-based decisions (I think, for example, of the decision at Pillsbury in 1987 to ditch the substandard corn).

On a few occasions we did not live up to one of our core values. I think of the decision to monitor lineups during the early days of Real Sports Bar & Grill by hiring burly security guards. They were big and menacing and not the welcoming image we wanted for the restaurant. We switched to engaging young women to do the job. I think of the so-called October Revolution at BMO Field when we unwisely jacked up ticket prices after a failed season. I think of the section 108 brouhaha at the Air Canada Centre when we suddenly denied access to the suite area behind that section—access that had been allowed since 1998. We should have anticipated fan unrest. Reducing fees has not calmed all the waters; some fans sitting in that area are still not happy.

Take the time to decide on your personal core values and live them consistently. If you are considering a job at a company, study its values. Are you comfortable with them? Importantly, does the company actually live them? And if you are a senior leader in a company, isn't it time—if you have not done so already—that you firmly and in a very public way stated the company's core values? Build them into everything you do—but don't start the process if you are not going to seriously live them.

"Vision" and "values": These two words have been my mantra for decades; maybe they belong on my tombstone.

## 3. PEOPLE MAKE THE DIFFERENCE

I had started to learn the value of people and the importance of people during my early training at Colgate when I worked in the plant, sales force and market research department. That lesson was further reinforced in my years at General Foods and Hostess, but it was really brought home to me at Pillsbury, where, as I've mentioned, one of the three core company values was "People make the difference." Good people make good differences—mediocre people can do a company great harm. I did not surround myself with the best team at Hostess, but I did at both Pillsbury and MLSE, where great teams helped both companies realize some terrific accomplishments. To create and importantly retain a great team, a company has to attract, develop, motivate and unleash the team so it can be the best it can be.

## 4. EDGE MATTERS

Noel Tichy has some excellent advice on how to be a great leader. One of his five key points is that you have to have edge. Winning leaders, he says, make tough decisions while encouraging and rewarding others who do the same. Even early in my life I had edge, and though it never led to fisticuffs, it did put me in a difficult position once in a while.

As I became a more experienced president, I developed more edge. I used that edge at MLSE, for example, to accomplish many things: to push my senior staff—despite the reluctance of many of them—to get into football and later to buy Gol TV. I used that edge to push through the MLSE board everything from the launch of the successful e11even restaurant to the renewal of Bryan Colangelo's contract. I also used edge to build a superior senior management team at MLSE. I let five business vice-presidents go because of performance issues or because they were not keeping up with the growth and sophistication of the company.

I also pushed for candour in the annual written evaluations of all full-time staff, many times sending the evaluation back to be rewritten. Once I sent back an entire department's evaluations. When I joined Pillsbury, I inherited written evaluations on all my senior staff. They were pablum, and I promised myself then that I would always ensure, as best I could, that all company evaluations were honest and true across the company. When I left MLSE, "edge" was very much in the lexicon of the company. Still, the company has a long way to go in the edge department—from the vice-presidents on down.

## 5. MERITOCRACY WORKS

Reward the people who deliver measurable results—the people in the top 20 per cent of your organization. Too many employers spend too much time trying to improve the bottom 10 per cent, who will never deliver. Former Leaf coach Ron Wilson would bench even the team's stars if they failed to produce, and I was all for that. Failing to demand the best of your veterans and stars lowers the bar for every player on the team. Who gets to start, who gets time on the power play or the last minute of a close game: athletes put a high value on all of that. Sports is the ultimate meritocracy environment.

Much has been written about the value of meritocracy in business and in the field of education. Everyone agrees that better teachers make for better, more accomplished students. But how do you measure teachers? I will leave that to the educational experts, but my advice is: don't give up. On the business side, one can create a meritocracy environment that rewards the high performers and ultimately eliminates the bottom underperformers. In business there are numerous financial yardsticks to measure employee performance—from sales numbers to customer-service scores. But a true meritocracy can exist only when the bosses have edge and candour.

We made progress on this at MLSE, but even as I left, I was reading too many annual reviews that were not candidly assessing performance. As mentioned, at MLSE, we recognized the top performers who demonstrated the most merit with bigger raises, higher bonuses, promotions, cross-functional moves and even special projects. And when selfish individuals go outside their teams to gain higher results for themselves, if their bosses are on top of that behaviour and if they have edge, they can deal with it and the teams will not be compromised by those individuals.

## 6. "THE GROSS IS NOT THE NET"

In consumer products, we absolutely had to know our dollar and percentage margins and could never let them erode. At MLSE, I quickly discovered that key departments did not know their margins or their net results. The sales guys would happily trumpet a big sale, but when I asked about net profit growth, the deal didn't shine quite so brightly.

When I worked at SkyDome, I had a very creative vice-president in David Garrick, who had a plaque on his office wall in which was carved: "The gross is not the net." David was good at his job and I loved the guy, but I don't think he knew what the line meant—despite his claims to the contrary. Realizing I had some teaching to do at MLSE, I asked David for the plaque and started taking it to meetings, propping it up on the chair beside me. Everyone soon started getting the message, and profit margins started growing across the company.

On my retirement, staff created a Richard Peddie bobblehead holding a sign that reads, "The gross is not the net." I acquired some leftover bobbleheads and handed them out to a few people I had mentored. One was David Bussiere, a wonderful marketing professor at the University of Windsor's Odette School of Business. During the summer of 2012, David's new marketing and sales strategies increased applications to the university as a whole by 15 per cent—versus the Ontario average of 6 per cent. David was pretty pumped and rightly so. I took him out for dinner and gave him a bobblehead before explaining that applications to Windsor were the gross and actual students choosing Windsor was the net.

## 7. WHEN IT COMES TO THE MEDIA, LESS IS MORE

The general manager or president of a professional sports team can't get away for long with "No comment." On the other hand, there is no merit in being too quotable too often. What heady stuff it is when you first lead a professional sports franchise and you see your name constantly in print. With so many media covering everything from sports to business to lifestyle to community, someone in my position at Maple Leaf Sports and Entertainment was much in demand. And early on, seeing myself on TSN's "Off the Record" or hearing myself on the radio was pretty cool. Anyone lucky enough to run a Major League professional sports organization should be wary of the adrenalin rush that comes with all that exposure.

Every time I talked, I opened myself up to saying the wrong thing, to being misquoted, to being accused of meddling (because I knew too much) or of being a media hog. Quickly the shine comes off. Only eventually did I learn never to answer a team question even when I knew the answer and to instead defer to the GM. As I mentioned, when I first started dealing with the media, I figured I had some equity in the bank because of how often I responded to their inquiries. But at the peak of the Babcock hiring and firing, I learned that I had *no* friends in the fifth estate. The media are extremely competitive in Toronto, and if making a person look bad helps sell newspapers or increase clicks on a website, then someone like me is fair game.

I learned by the end to dial down.

## 8. OPTIMISTS HAVE MORE SUCCESS THAN PESSIMISTS

I have always believed that optimists have more success than pessimists, and there is research to back the contention. A psychology professor at the University of Pennsylvania, Martin Seligman, found that optimistic individuals are not only happier than pessimistic people but they also enjoy better results as students, athletes, politicians and entrepreneurs.

At MLSE we did a lot of things that were innovative, different and even risky in the sports business. We analyzed our ventures carefully, created solid plans and usually executed superbly. When we were ready to go, we always approached the new initiative with great optimism. And when there were early hiccups, that optimism helped carry us through.

We were optimistic about football despite all the previous failures in Toronto. We were optimistic about selling condominiums at higher-than-market prices at a time when some thought the condo market was about to crash. In 2008, we had a number of suites—expensive suites—unsold in the lower bowl at MLSE. I wanted to eliminate several of them and create a unique high-end club. Research was inconclusive. Suite staff were leery. I was optimistic that I was right and using edge (see above), I decided to go forward. We created the premium Chairman's Suite—sold it out, in fact—and in the process created a new sports best practice.

If, in my fifteen years, I was not optimistic—or even worse, pessimistic—MLSE would never have become a $2 billion company. I could have played it safe and not been so optimistic, but that wouldn't have been me, and I would not have been as successful. I also think that one has to display a positive attitude all the time, and especially if you are leading a team of people. When I went to university, the leader in our business classes was a man named Michael Mueller. When you asked Mike how he was, he always said, "Excellent." Soon the whole class was responding that way. He went on to be second-in-command at Price Waterhouse. To differentiate himself from the rest of the graduating class, Mike now says in response to the how-are-you question, "Most excellent."

## 9. STAY CURRENT

The Greek philosopher Heraclitus (c. 540 BC – c. 480 BC) said, "This river I step in is not the river I stand in." That quote is written on the steel arch over the Queen Street Bridge in Toronto, which spans the Don River. When teaching, I often ask students what the phrase means. Only a few get it. The philosopher was making this point: a river's current is constant, so the water you step into is soon downstream and you are surrounded by different water. It's the same with life, sports and business.

I was aware in my career that the times were always changing and that I would surely be left behind if I didn't stay current. In every company I led, I was always monitoring changes in customer attitudes, technologies and competitor strategies. As I mentioned, in 2002, I taught a fourth-year class at the Odette School on strategic leadership. I used the preparation and teaching of that course to modify, update and improve my own leadership and business skills. I was painfully aware that approaches I had used successfully at Pillsbury in 1989 would not work in 2005.

I am a Luddite when it comes to technology. My wife, Colleen, who is younger than me, is my IT department. She taught me to use my iPhone and iPad, and how to order online.

In my last year of university, I took a computer course that used stacks of punch cards; the running watch I use today is more sophisticated than that computer. But my own lack of tech savvy did not stop me from funding and encouraging MLSE's young leaders as they embraced new digital technologies that are being successfully used today to engage fans of all our teams. For me, standing still was not an option.

## 10. DIVERSIFY YOUR EXPERIENCE

The trajectory of my career may *look* like a well-planned and thought-out approach that led inexorably to the job at Maple Leaf Sports and Entertainment. But it wasn't nearly as well planned as it looks. My dream was to run a basketball team, so I knew I had to learn about human resources, finance, accounting, sales forces, market research, broadcasting and facilities management. I knew I needed a wide range of experience if that basketball dream was ever going to happen.

The point I want to stress here is that a range of experience will serve you well down the line, and that means moving on when the time is right. At MLSE, we strived to retain our best people. Our turnover as a company was just under 10 per cent, with about 4 to 5 per cent of that number constituting forced turnover. What we especially watched was turnover of the top 20 per cent, the "high promotables," as I called them. We worried when that number exceeded 3 per cent. Today, MLSE has a number of superb young leaders who are capable of being vice-presidents someday soon. We kept them engaged and improving through training, promotions and special projects. Promoting from within, however, can be somewhat incestuous—these young people know only one company. I, on the other hand, could draw on a body of work in consumer products, facilities and television that was broader than any of my vice-presidents. On many issues and initiatives, I sometimes missed having vice-presidents with more diverse outside experiences.

If you decide to stay with one company, prove yourself by getting promoted several times but also embrace cross-functional moves. At the same time, don't be afraid to work for other companies in other industries. Just be sure that it's the right company for you, and that your moves are not lateral and come only after you have proven yourself at the company. Whenever I looked at a resumé, I did something I call "forensic CV." I divided the number of years worked by the number of jobs the person had in his or her career to date. If the number was too low (one to three), I worried. If the number was too high (over ten, say), I worried. If the jobs all seemed to be lateral moves, I worried even more. So diversify your experience, but do it strategically, with much thought and preparation. And obey this cardinal rule: Never leave a company without being promoted at least once.

## 11. PAY YOUR TAXES

I don't quibble about the taxes I pay. I'm with Warren Buffett on this. I've been blessed, and I give a lot to charity. A recent study revealed that 70 per cent of Canadians would be willing to pay higher taxes if they knew the money was going to health care and education.

CEO salaries in North America are crazy. The top twenty-five hedge fund managers in the United States make $1 billion a year, some $2 billion; some pay as little as 15 percent in income tax.

Before he resigned in November 2012 to pursue a political career in his native Austria, Frank Stronach of Magna International—the auto parts giant—was making $50 million a year. He was being massively overpaid, and major pension plan investors in Magna–including the Ontario Teachers' Pension Plan–balked in 2010 at a share restructuring plan that swapped his voting control of the company in exchange for $1 billion. Some corporate boards pay members' salaries of $300,000 to $400,000 a year.

How about salaries based on performance?

And can we lose all this fear and trepidation about paying our fair share of taxes? In his keynote speech at the 2012 Democratic convention, the mayor of San Antonio, Texas, Julian Castro, called for a municipal sales tax increase of one-eighth of a cent to finance pre-kindergarten education for thousands of children in low-income families. The *New York Times* referred to this suggestion as "his biggest political gamble." Some US states have passed laws forbidding any tax increase.

The compensation I earned positions me well for the future— unless my investment analysts make a mess of things or we experience a 1930s-like depression. Then again, I have always wanted to try being a bartender, barista or school-crossing guard, so maybe I can do those jobs in my eighties.

I pay a lot of taxes but I don't complain. I grew up in a blue-collar family in Windsor. Today, I am very fortunate, and I believe people like me need to give back. Give back of our time and our money to make the communities we live in quality places for all to live.

## 12. ATHLETES ARE ASSETS

Don't get too close to the players because assets sometimes have to be moved, as I said in Chapter 5. After a player left the Raptors without even bothering to call Larry Tanenbaum (who had been so kind to him), Larry said, "Some of them disappoint you."

## 13. WORST PRACTICES CAN LEAD TO BEST PRACTICES

I remember well at General Foods one of the worst practices: "analysis paralysis." Every new move was second-guessed, and the consequence was that the company never led but followed the lead of others. Lesson learned: I vowed to be more aggressive and to take risks.

Strategic plans at General Foods were a joke. Again, they were analyzed to death, but they were also devoid of great ideas and ironically were never really approved. That's because the strategic planning department—located south of the border—always sent our plans back with more questions. Lesson learned. I would henceforth push to create strategic plans that were full of rich, creative ideas backed by well-thought-out and solid financial projections.

There was leadership training at General Foods, but not nearly enough. Again, lesson learned. I would henceforth build a robust leadership training program in the company to train future leaders.

General Foods managed to the lowest common denominator and worried most about how to improve the bottom 10 per cent of employees. The lesson: to move out the bottom 10 per cent, and to work hard to recognize, develop and retain the top 20 per cent.

General Foods had no vision. Every year a theme based on the latest trend was launched with great fanfare—and was dead a few months later. The effect was to make most employees jaded about any new large corporate initiatives. The lesson: companies need to stay with one vision for a while.

I don't mean to beat up General Foods here. It was the '70s, and maybe lots of companies suffered from these types of problems. I was a president at the age of thirty-five, and this is what I saw: too many silos, too many politically charged offices. The company would not move high promotables to other divisions. Leaders were selfish and kept talented people instead of letting them develop in other areas. In the end, those talented people left. The lesson: total company performance is the important bottom line—and therefore I needed to break down silos.

General Foods discouraged marketing people from calling on customers. The sales force wanted to keep the power by "owning" the relationship with the trade, and it did that by keeping marketing in the dark. At the same time, most marketers were uncomfortable calling on the trade, so they did not fight this exclusion. The lesson: have marketing and other areas of the company get to know the customer. The result is better service. New ideas mean better decision making.

After a few years as a vice-president at General Foods, I was getting impatient. I wanted to be a president. I tried to get transferred to the restaurant division; I even offered to be vice-president of human resources. But again, the company was not progressive in that way and did not believe in cross-functional moves. The lesson: I needed to orchestrate cross-functional moves. I learned to push people out of their comfort zones and to stretch their experience. I would, for example, put a marketing person in charge of a plant.

## 14. NEVER UNDERESTIMATE THE POWER OF BOOKS

I am a voracious reader and have learned a lot by reading. Jim Collins (*Good to Great, Built to Last, How the Mighty Fall*). Jack Welch (*Winning*). Tom Peters and Robert H. Waterman Jr. (*In Search of Excellence*). Noel Tichy (*The Leadership Engine*). William Manchester's three-part series of books on Winston Churchill. Keep reading. I am always championing the reading of books.

## 15. PROMOTE FROM WITHIN

The best people are the ones to promote and fill job vacancies. For a senior position, try not to hire from outside. Reward individuals who are doing a great job. That means surrounding yourself with good people, some of whom will be angling to get your job.

## 16. THE CUSTOMER IS ALWAYS RIGHT—BUT SOMETIMES YOU HAVE TO FIRE THE CUSTOMER

When I was president at Hostess, I was fond of quoting two rules:

1. The customer is always right.
2. If the customer is wrong, reread rule #1.

But after a few years, I started questioning these two rules. What finally changed my mind was a book by Kevin and Jackie Freiberg about the founder of Southwest Airlines, Herb Kelleher. In *Nuts! Southwest Airlines' Crazy Recipe for Business and Personal Success*, they describe how he turned the aviation industry on its head—starting in 1971—by offering cheap fares and no onboard meals (only peanuts) and by hiring people with a sense of humour who didn't mind, say, singing flight announcements. The company built a reputation not only as a safe airline but also as a fun place to work. Kelleher was ranked at one point by *Fortune* magazine as the best CEO in the United States.

In the book, there is a story about Kelleher firing a customer, a woman who was constantly complaining to Southwest Airlines about how it conducted its business. Many of her complaints were about services that the airline had quite consciously decided not to provide. Southwest is the only North American airline that has been profitable every year since 9/11. Most other airlines have not been profitable and have sought bankruptcy protection or merged with another airline.

Eventually, Herb wrote the woman a short note that began, "Mrs. Smith, we will miss you . . ."

At MLSE, we always tried to make things right with our fans.

The version of All Out Recovery we used at SkyDome (discussed in Chapter 5) is much more comprehensive and faster at MLSE today. At the same time, we have to treat fans in an even manner. We can't let squeaky wheels always get better deals because they will definitely keep squeaking and what you do for one fan always gets out. There are no secrets in the fish bowl that is pro sports, even on the fan side.

Today at MLSE, if a fan is being abusive or unreasonable and this behaviour shows no sign of abating, that customer will be fired. This is not done easily or quickly, but it does sometimes happen. We worked hard to be an exceptional place to work. Part of that was training our people well, empowering them to do the right thing and also having their backs. They needed to know they did not have to put up with abuse from unreasonable fans.

## 17. A CEO HIRES STRANGERS AND FIRES FRIENDS

When you hire an employee, you are often hiring a stranger. You may have done significant due diligence on the individual's education, career and character, but this person is still essentially a stranger to you and the company. After the person has worked for you for a while, you get to know him or her. You meet the employee's families and friends. Maybe play a round of golf or share a few beers while watching sports in a bar. And this individual may become a friend. But sometimes the hiring doesn't work out—his or her performance isn't what it should be, or maybe the company is cutting back. And you have to let this friend go—never pleasant, but often necessary.

## 18. BE CONFIDENT

With strategic thinking, innovation and superb execution, know that you can hit home runs. The Air Canada Centre's $12 million, 1,000-seat Real Sports Bar & Grill—with the largest sports screen on the continent—opened in 2010 and was named the best sports bar in North America by ESPN Mobile within three months of launching. Just days before the Grey Cup game in Toronto in late November 2012, the *Globe and Mail's* food critic, Chris Nuttall-Smith, offered a guide to those wanting to take in the game at a downtown bar or restaurant. This is what he had to say: "Real Sports might just be the greatest sports bar in North America. From its nachos, salads and Cajun lime salt riblets to the 67-oz rib eye called 'The Hail Mary,' the food is way better than you might expect from sports bars, and the beer list goes long and wide. But it's the 200-odd TVs that make the place—the largest being the two-storey, 39-foot screen at the front of the room. There are even televisions at every urinal, in fact."

Such bold and expensive enterprises are not for the timid and the faint of heart.

## 19. DON'T BE AFRAID TO INTIMIDATE

Intimidating comes with the position. I learned from Bob White the power and value of theatrics. When I stormed out of the Gol TV discussion, I was deploying that tactic.

## 20. KNOW YOUR ENEMY

Anyone who competed with Maple Leaf Sports and Entertainment for the sports entertainment dollar was my enemy. Just as between Coke and Pepsi, every dollar that went to the Jays or the Argos was a dollar I wanted. In everything I do, I am there to win. It hurts to lose. That's one reason I retired. I got tired of going to the games and losing. But business? I *loved* business. Fixing broken businesses, creating new ones and developing people was almost always fun.

## 21. ALWAYS SAY THANKS

Whether it's the server at Starbucks or the person who holds the door for you, always say thank you. So many people forget to do that or have never learned how. Recognition may well be the greatest human need. Over my career, I learned the power of thanks. When one of my staff, or an entire department, did a great job, I was quick with praise—specific timely praise. Many times the appreciation was only through a handwritten note, but other times it was through the use of my personal Raptor, Leaf or concert tickets. Many times the individual being recognized thanked me in return. My response always was "No need to thank me; you earned it."

So always, always say thanks. It's polite and powerful.

## 22. EXPERIENCE AND LEARNING ARE OFTEN TRANSFERABLE

One thing I quickly realized as I moved between industries is that the lessons and disciplines I learned in one industry can often be applied to another, completely different industry. For instance, vision and values worked very well for four of the six companies I led, and with time, I am convinced, would have worked for all of them. The marketing and sales disciplines I learned from working in consumer products easily applied to sports and entertainment. My broadcast experience at NetStar ultimately had a huge and positive impact on MLSE's enterprise value. And my basic leadership pillars of communication, recognition and development spanned my entire corporate career. Jack Welch called emulating best practices "legitimate plagiarism." Wherever I was employed, I always reflected back on what had worked for me previously and then thought about whether it might work for the new company I was with. I was also very mindful of the mistakes I had made, taking comfort from the saying, "Mistakes give you experience, and experience gives you wisdom."

Most of you will never get the chance to run a professional sports team, a television network, a stadium or an arena. But I strongly believe that the experiences and anecdotes I have shared in this book can be applied wherever a group of people come together to lead and run a business—no matter what that business might be. Gary Bettman is more than an ex–basketball guy, and I like to think I'm more than an ex–soap salesman.

* * *

As 2012 wound down, Colleen and I made our plans for Christmas and New Year's. One weekend in December we were off to our place on Boblo Island and a four-kilometre charity run in which every runner was to wear a Santa costume. New Year's Eve celebrations would include a four-mile fun run in New York's Central Park—along with 5,000 other runners. While the ball was dropping at Times Square and the fireworks burst overhead, the revellers revelling at midnight, the Peddies were off to the races. We each wore a runner's watch to record our times. What gets measured gets done.

What will I do in retirement? Mine will be an active retirement. I'll sit on a few boards, get fitter, play a little golf, travel, take up the piano. I'll give it a try. And I'm thinking seriously of launching a café in the little town of Amherstburg, at the mouth of the Detroit River.

I would certainly enjoy the commute to work. From our place on Boblo Island to the open-air, fifteen-car ferry is about 500 metres, and the ferry takes you right to town in four minutes. I've had a good long ride, one that lasted forty-one years, and I do appreciate a short one.

# POSTSCRIPT

When *Dream Job* was first published, I went on an extensive book tour. People kept asking me the same two questions over and over. First: Why did I write a book—was it something I had always wanted to do? That was a bucket-list type of question, I guess. Second: Did I plan on writing another one?

My answer to the first question was always a little vague. Like many people, I liked to muse about writing a book someday. I was never sure if I could write or whether my book would be any good, but my agent, Michael Levine, made me really consider the idea. He said, "You can't out-Collins Collins" (Jim Collins, the bestselling author of such books as *Good to Great*). He said that I should instead write about my lifelong dream, and how I had made it come true. I took his advice to heart. But I made him promise that if he thought the book wasn't any good, then he would tell me to pull the plug. The fact that you are reading it now tells you how our agreement turned out.

My answer to the second question was always quicker and definitive. Comparing myself to players on the University of Kentucky's basketball team, I told everyone that I was "one and done." You see, writing a book is damn tough. It's a lot of work, and when it's finished, the author competes in an industry that is very challenging and very competitive. Today I worry about the state of the Canadian publishing industry—specifically the future of writers, independent book retailers and even publishers themselves. Authors and companies are chasing fewer and fewer dollars. So will I write another book? My answer continues to be "no."

Nevertheless, a number of personal benefits came out of *Dream Job*. I must admit that I liked getting complimented on it, being asked to autograph it and even seeing it for sale in airport bookstores.

As well, the book gave me the motivation to get involved in politics. During my career I have always tried to be a corporate city builder. In the chapter "On Building a City—One Dream, One Brick at a Time" I talked about the need for everyone to get involved and add bricks to the civil foundation. I also wrote that I wanted to be active in the 2014 Toronto municipal election. So to prepare myself I read a great deal. Along with reading books like *Walkable City* by Jeff Speck, *Human Transit* by Jarrett Walker and *Walking Home* by Ken Greenberg, I also searched out best practices from cities all over the world, such as New York, London, Paris and even Portland, Oregon. I soon realized that some people would think the ideas I now believed in were too left-leaning, but I became confident that they were just progressive. Bullish ideas on the need to adopt best practices from around the world could make Toronto the world's most liveable city. I also started to think about who I would actively support, and then picked someone that surprised most of my friends—Olivia Chow. I chose Olivia after much due diligence, and after reading her bestselling book *My Journey*, I got very involved in writing her platform, raising money for her campaign and introducing her to many of my business contacts. By the time you read this book, you will know whether I backed the right candidate. I sure hope so!

But most importantly, writing this book gave me the chance to tell my leadership story on many university campuses and present it to a number of community and business groups. On some occasions, the audience may have just expected to hear funny and insightful stories about the Leafs and Raptors, and may have been disappointed when I instead focused on the importance of having a personal or corporate dream and realizing that dream through rock-solid core values. And while my lessons-learned messages weren't for everyone, I know from the questions and numerous emails and tweets I received that my story definitely resonated with many. The people I most enjoyed getting through to were young students. Today's graduates face a much tougher job market than I faced when coming out of the University of Windsor years ago. So I tried to inspire them to have a dream and gave them constructive advice on how to make it happen, along with the caveat that even if they didn't realize their dream, they would achieve much from trying. The career game plan I offer to young people is as follows: Have a dream. Be sure to write it down. Have strong core personal values. Get your ticket punched. Invest in your journey. And always be mindful of John Maxwell's quote "Leadership doesn't happen in a day. It takes a lifetime."

Thanks for reading *Dream Job*. I really hope that this book and my talks help a number of people to realize their dreams.

Still actively retired,
Richard Peddie

P.S. I still haven't opened that Amherstburg coffee shop yet.

# ACKNOWLEDGMENTS

This book is a collaboration between a ghost writer (that would be me, Lawrence Scanlan) and the man at the centre of the memoir (that would be Richard Peddie). Some readers might be curious to know how that process worked.

It went like this. For each chapter, Richard wrote a block of notes or copy, which formed the basis of face-to-face interviews—sometimes at the Air Canada Centre, sometimes at a friend's office on Bay Street, sometimes at my place in Kingston, Ontario, or at Richard's place in Toronto. The point I want to make is that, for the most part, the words—and certainly the thoughts—are all Richard's. The two us of were working on a patchwork quilt; the squares came from Richard and my task was to arrange them and connect them in what we hoped was a pleasing pattern.

Each time I take on a project like this, I am parachuted into some new and unfamiliar world. I have been a Toronto Maple Leaf fan all my life, but my focus had always been on the players. Now

I was seeing things through the eyes of the man several rungs up: the CEO who hired the GM who drafted the players and hired the coach ... the buck stopped with Richard Peddie, and my task was to help him tell his story.

Richard and I first met over lunch in a private room behind the Real Sports Bar & Grill at the ACC. Writer and subject had to meet face to face to get a sense of whether the collaboration could work. What struck me was how *unstriking* he is. I saw a smooth, smart and confident man, and as we later walked briskly through the ACC, he greeted and was greeted by the security staff, the cleaning staff, the restaurant staff. Everyone seemed to know him, and everyone seemed to like him. I guess I thought he would be more imposing, edgier, tougher, taller. The guy drives a Porsche but has a Volkswagen manner, and the longer I spent with him, the more I realized that this common-man touch of his is both strategic and genuine.

His roots are Windsor blue collar, but he moves easily among the rich and famous and is himself rich and famous. He straddles two worlds. Naturally, he has his contradictions: a man known for fancy clothes and exotic cars is also a naturalist who loves to garden. He's a man who creates, and thrives on, buzz and adrenalin, yet one of his favourite places on earth is the back porch of a country home on Boblo Island, where he and his wife, Colleen, can watch the birds fly by or the freighters course up and down the Detroit River. The location reveals a hint of his sentimental side: the island was once an amusement park he had frequented as a child when the sight of freighters was one of his favourite things.

Barb Weinberg was Peddie's executive assistant ("his right and left hand," as someone once called her) for five and a half years. She replaced Alda Byers, who had been Richard's executive assistant since 1985, when he was the CEO at Pillsbury. But on July 17, 2006, at the age of forty-nine, Alda suffered a devastating brain-stem stroke. The end result was locked-in syndrome: she can only blink her eyes to communicate. The rest of her body is paralyzed. The eight-person Board of Directors at MLSE, including Richard, made sure that her medical plan was extended to cover her considerable expenses, and he still visits her every few months.

Barb Weinberg is the soul of discretion, but she is also a straight talker. "He's not the most warm and fuzzy guy in the world," she said. "It's his upbringing. He showed me more affection and warmth and compassion toward the end. He's 'on' all the time. Everything is business, business, business. He'd never sit back and relax. We were at the Rogers Centre the other night [the stadium drew almost 48,000 fans—a record home crowd for the Toronto Football Club—because David Beckham and the Los Angeles Galaxy were in town for a CONCACAF, or Confederation of North, Central American and Caribbean Association Football, Champions' League quarter-final. TFC's home turf, BMO Field, seats less than half that number and was unavailable because of cold weather]. Richard is supposed to be retired but he's still asking, 'What's the gate?' I wanted to say, 'Oh my God! Shaddup!' That's how he's wired."

I told Ms. Weinberg that the book I was helping Richard write would be that much better if she could muster some fair criticisms of her old boss. "What," I asked, "was the hard part about working for this man for almost six years?"

"There were no hard parts," she said. "Before coming here, I worked on the staff of former Toronto mayor Art Eggleton. He was amazing. You could not put anything by him. Richard was like that too. He's confident and direct. He knows his stuff. Everyone here—90 per cent, 100 per cent—admired and respected him. Always there was respect."

*Forbes* magazine once called Richard Peddie "a bum" to the fans and "a wizard" on enterprise value creation. One journalist called him a "maverick," a title he doesn't mind one bit. He is, by his own account, stubborn, aggressive and outspoken—but he won admirers by being creative and positive, and by demanding the best from everyone around him.

On the day I interviewed Weinberg, Bryan Colangelo and Brian Burke popped into the meeting room on the fifteenth floor where Richard Peddie and I had dug in for the day. They hauled him out to the room next door, presenting him with a brand-new set of golf clubs. "If you need some quotes," Burke told me as he left, "I'm happy to talk to you. I love this guy."

This seemed to be loyalty above and beyond what one might expect. One MLSE staffer talked about how "militantly supportive, even protective" they were of their old boss.

Roy Mlakar, former president and CEO of the Ottawa Senators, was among those who contributed accolades to a handsome hard-bound book (an MLSE in-house production called *Celebrating Richard Peddie*) that was presented at his retirement party. What Mlakar remembers is that when Richard rose to speak at an NHL Board of Governors meeting, "You could hear a pin drop." That was the measure of the respect he commanded.

Chris Hebb, then a senior vice-president in MLSE's broadcast division, likewise contributed to *Celebrating Richard Peddie*. This, in part, is what he wrote of his former boss's tenure:

> It has not been a career of simply managing what exists, but rather a cavalcade of new ideas, risky ventures, ownership apprehension and somehow getting normally even-keeled and buttoned-down executives to go along with what he often referred to as another "crazy-ass idea."
>
> For Richard Peddie to reach back into his history with this book and bring forward the fruits of a career in packaged goods, broadcasting, facility management and sports is a

*thing of "beauty." By beautiful I mean the marvelous way he would prepare us all for a Board Meeting, like a prize fighter dancing with a sparring partner. There was beauty in the way he could run a meeting and consistently come out of the room with actionable decisions. There was beauty in how he would cut off whoever was speaking, once he understood what point they were making and nobody ever felt put down. There was beauty in his facility for distilling a complex set of circumstances and magically making the path look simple. . . .There was beauty in his ability to force confrontation and draw a point of view out of everyone, while still maintaining a collegial atmosphere around the management table. There was even beauty in the fear he would inspire when someone didn't "know their numbers," and that made all of us more accountable and better leaders. . . . He is the purest businessman I have ever seen and there is beauty in purity.*

One aspect of the Richard Peddie story, though, had always puzzled me. Why would a man who loves history express no interest in his own family history? I kept asking that question and was never satisfied with the answer. Finally, at a lunch at Bensimon Byrne (the ad agency where Colleen Peddie works), I came back to that question, and this time both husband and wife weighed in. Richard, for the first time, talked about how abandoned his mother felt when his father died. No one from either side of the family offered help. Maybe, he wondered, that's why exploring his genealogy holds no interest for him.

Colleen had a different take. "Richard does not look back," she told me. "He's always looking forward."

—Lawrence Scanlan

\* \* \*

Just as it takes a lifetime to become a leader, it takes a lifetime to create the opportunity to work with so many good people and develop so many great friends. My leadership lessons started well before my corporate career and then ramped up during my forty-one-year tour of six companies. This book is dedicated to all the people in my life who helped me realize both corporate and personal success, who helped me recover when I made mistakes, and who contributed to my many lessons learned and relearned.

So many thanks . . .

To my parents June and Lee Peddie, who gave be a solid foundation based on excellent personal values—ones that helped shape every one of my life decisions.

To my brother, Tom Peddie, who is my very best friend. Every day I value and learn from his experiences and wisdom on everything from business to sports to nature. To my sister, Carol, who taught me basic etiquette skills early in my life and who is still one of my biggest fans.

To the University of Windsor, where my basketball dream started. To my business professors, who made sure I received an excellent education, one that jumpstarted my career. And to the class of '70 for pushing me, for inspiring me and, to this day, for being some of my best friends.

To Trudy Eagan, who helped me through my many learning years in consumer products and the stressful years at SkyDome and the start of the Raptors.

To the thousands of great employees with whom I worked at six different places—from Colgate to Maple Leaf Sports and Entertainment. In almost all cases, we broke new ground, achieved wonderful things and had fun doing it.

To Alda Byers, my executive assistant of almost twenty years.

Alda was a solid professional who made sure that I was always prepared for every business day. I just wish we could have worked together longer.

To all the consumers and fans who supported my career by purchasing products such as Colgate toothpaste or Pillsbury crescent rolls, by watching TSN, or by rooting for the Leafs, Raptors, TFC and Marlies.

To my many bosses—especially those at the Ontario Teachers' Pension Plan, TD Bank, Dale Lastman, and especially Larry Tanenbaum. And to all who encouraged me and gave my business teams the resources we needed so we could do so many amazing things.

To my literary agent, Michael Levine. Dale Lastman had suggested that I talk to Michael about my crazy idea to write a book. After describing to Michael my concept, I was thrilled that arguably Canada's best literary agent would want to represent me.

To my editor at HarperCollins, Jim Gifford, for having the patience to work with a rookie author and for suggesting only "light edits." I forgive Jim for encouraging me to run as the mayor of Toronto, and I thank his entire team at HarperCollins for their keen attention to detail.

To my literary partner in this project, Lawrence Scanlan. When Michael Levine saw my early work, he knew I needed an experienced pro to help me get my story out. Larry and I were complete strangers to each other and we came from very different backgrounds, but ours has been a fabulous partnership. The book's title, Dream Job, was Larry's idea, and the book would not have been nearly as good without his help.

And to my wife, Colleen. At our wedding, I told all our gathered friends and family that Colleen and I were completely different people. She is an accounting wiz, I am a marketing weenie; I am analogue, she is digital. And we won't even talk about the significant age gap between us. Colleen is a wonderful partner who always gives me great advice and support. And, as evidenced by the story of her willingness to fight a threatening TFC fan, she always has my back.

I didn't just have a dream job. I had a dream career. And all of you listed here contributed to it.

Thank you.

—Richard Peddie

# INDEX

Bergeron, Patrice, 176
Bettman, Gary, 112, 149–50, 152, 173, 180,
    182, 183, 185–86, 188, 290
Bing, Dave, 108
Bird, Larry, 235
Bitove, John, Jr., 111, 112, 113, 114, 116
Bitove, John, Sr., 74
BMO Field, 145, 147, 271
    construction, 81, 154, 155–56, 270
    financing and ownership, 154, 195,
        269–70
    natural grass pitch, 157
BMO Financial Group, 154
Boblo Island, 290
Boeing, 215
*Book of Basketball, The* (Simmons), 126
Bosh, Chris, 16, 17, 132
Boston Marathon, 233, 234
Boston Red Sox, 201
Bower, Johnny, 204
Bowman, Scotty, 22, 200
Boyes, Brad, 176
Boys and Girls Clubs, 132
Bozak, Tyler, 200
Brace, Rick, 105
Bregman, Michael, 78
Bryant, Kobe, 108, 126, 142
Buffalo Bills, 227
Buffalo Bisons, 194
Buffett, Warren, 282
*Built to Last* (Collins), 285
Burgess, Thornton, 32
Burke, Brendan, 189
Burke, Brian, 171, 255
    as GM of Anaheim Ducks, 181
    as GM of Toronto Maple Leafs, 7–8, 10,
        20, 180, 181, 182, 183, 184–85, 188,
        189–90, 191–94, 196, 201, 206, 267
    as GM of Vancouver Canucks, 177, 180, 181
Bussiere, David, 278
Byers, Alda, 121


Cairns, Stu, 51, 250
Calder Cup, 199
Calderon, Jose, 131
Camby, Marcus, 133
Campbell, Colin, 11
Campbell, Gregory, 11
Canadian Club, 259
Canadian Football League (CFL), 157, 264

Canadian National Exhibition, 154
Canadian Soccer Association (CSA), 148,
    149, 156, 162
Canadian Soccer League, 156
Candy, John, 75
Carlyle, Randy, 84, 85, 200
Carter, Butch, 133
Carter, Jeff, 176
Carter, Vince, 11, 23, 25, 123, 126–27,
    128–30, 133, 267
Casey, Dwane, 3, 137
Cassaday, John, 53, 62, 98, 245
Castro, Julian, 283
CBC, 103, 127, 129, 168, 185, 214
CEOs
    average tenure of, 238
    salaries of, 282–283
CFL (Canadian Football League), 157, 264
Chamberlain, Wilt, 108
*Cheers*, 78
Cherry, Don, 189
Chicago Bulls, 126
Chicago Cubs, 189
Chicago Fire, 145
Childs, Chris, 129
Christie, Doug, 124
Churchill, Winston, 48–49, 269, 285
Cirque du Soleil, 66
Clancy, King, 50, 166
Clark, Paul, 54, 68
Clark, Wendel, 169, 205
Clarke, Ian, 123, 174, 175, 195, 196, 228,
    235, 268
Cleveland Cavaliers, 131
Coca-Cola, 63
Cohl, Michael, 68, 69
Colangelo, Bryan, 113, 131, 132, 136, 140,
    142, 267, 276, 294
Colangelo, Jerry, 113
Colgate, 5, 39, 40–43, 44–45, 108
Collins, Jim, 215, 239, 285
Collins, John, 188
Colonial Tool, 30
CONCACAF (Confederation of North,
    Central American and Caribbean Asso-
    ciation Football), 159
Concert Productions International, 68
Connoy, Terry, 237
Continental Basketball Association, 121
Coriat, David, 117
Corus Entertainment, 53, 98, 100